D1739599

Untranslating Machines

Jacques Lezra is Professor and Chair in the Department of Hispanic Studies at the University of California—Riverside. He received the PhD in Comparative Literature from Yale University, and taught at Yale, the University of Wisconsin-Madison and NYU before joining the faculty at UC-Riverside. His most recent book is *Contra todos los fueros de la muerte: El suceso cervantino* (2016). Other books are *On the Nature of Marx's Things: Translation as Necrophilology* (Fordham, 2018); *Wild Materialism: The Ethic of Terror and the Modern Republic* (2010; Spanish translation 2012; Chinese translation 2013); *Unspeakable Subjects: The Genealogy of the Event in Early Modern Europe* (1997); and (with Liza Blake, eds.) *Lucretius and Modernity*. Lezra has edited collections on the work of Althusser, Balibar and Macherey, and on Spanish republicanism, and published articles on Shakespeare, contemporary and early modern translation theories and practices, Freud, Althusser, Woolf, animality studies, the New Materialism, and other topics. He is the co-translator into Spanish of Paul de Man's *Blindness and Insight*. With Emily Apter and Michael Wood, he is the co-editor of *Dictionary of Untranslatables* (2014), the English translation of *Vocabulaire européen des philosophies*. Paul North and he edit the Fordham University Press book series IDIOM.

New Critical Humanities

Series Editors: Birgit Kaiser, Associate Professor of Comparative Literature, Utrecht University

Timothy O'Leary, Professor of Philosophy, University of Hong Kong

Kathrin Thiele, Associate Professor of Gender Studies and Critical Theory, Utrecht University

This series has a twofold aim: to apply the best humanities methodologies in the study of a wide range of issues that are of global, transnational significance and, at the same time, to develop a self-reflective critique and transformation of those methodologies themselves. The books in this series will contribute to a re-imagination of critique itself: its powers, its strengths and its possible effects.

Untranslating Machines: A Genealogy for the Ends of Global Thought
Jacques Lezra

Untranslating Machines

A Genealogy for the Ends of Global Thought

Jacques Lezra

ROWMAN &
LITTLEFIELD
——————INTERNATIONAL
London • New York

Published by Rowman & Littlefield International Ltd
Unit A, Whitacre Mews, 26–34 Stannary Street, London SE11 4AB
www.rowmaninternational.com

Rowman & Littlefield International Ltd. is an affiliate of Rowman & Littlefield

4501 Forbes Boulevard, Suite 200, Lanham, Maryland 20706, USA
With additional offices in Boulder, New York, Toronto (Canada), and Plymouth (UK)
www.rowman.com

Copyright © 2017 Jacques Lezra

All rights reserved. No part of this book may be reproduced in any form or by any
electronic or mechanical means, including information storage and retrieval systems,
without written permission from the publisher, except by a reviewer who may quote
passages in a review.

British Library Cataloguing-in-Publication Data
A catalogue record for this book is available from the British Library

ISBN HB 978-1-7866-0508-5

Library of Congress Cataloging-in-Publication Data Is Available
ISBN 978-1-78660-508-5 (cloth : alk. paper)
ISBN 978-1-78660-509-2 (electronic)

♾™ The paper used in this publication meets the minimum requirements of
American National Standard for Information Sciences – Permanence of Paper
for Printed Library Materials, ANSI/NISO Z39.48–1992.

Printed in the United States of America

Contents

Acknowledgements

I grew up between places and their languages. Madrid, Tangier, West Virginia, Caracas; English, Spanish, French, Arabic, Hebrew, *Jaquetía* – so translation has always been with me. I first banged my head into it as an academic matter, though, when I set out to translate Paul de Man's *Blindness and Insight* into Spanish with my friend and teacher Hugo Rodríguez Vecchini. His Spanish was from San Juan; mine from Castille. It took us any number of nights of debate and conversation to get it done. Hugo's been gone for twenty years, but every page in this book is addressed to him, signed in his hand too and works at making those conversations last still, as if writing about translation and its sombre and joyous ends could bring back the moving worlds of agreement and disagreement we were discovering.

Three or so years ago, Emily Apter said to me, 'Why don't you publish a book on untranslatability?' In many ways this book originated in that question, and for it I thank her.

Some parts of the chapters in *Untranslating Machines* have been previously published, though I've revised them to varying degrees for publication here and translated one into English. I'm grateful for the permission to return to this material and for the opportunity to draw these essays into the common shape and argument you will find in the book. The essays are 'Soberanía o traducción: las decisiones de Sancho', in *El lugar de la literatura en el siglo XXI*, eds. Juan Pablo Hormazábal, Josefina Rodríguez and Nicolás Vicente (Valparaíso: Ediciones Universitarias de Valparaíso, 2016); 'On Contingency in Translation', in *Early Modern Cultures of Translation*, eds. Karen Newman and Jane Tylus (Philadelphia: University of Pennsylvania Press, 2015); 'This Untranslatability Which Is Not One', *Paragraph* 38:2 (2015); 'The Animal in Translation', *Postmodern Culture* 24:1, September 2013 (March 2015); 'Translation', in *Political Concepts:*

A Critical Lexicon (New School for Social Research) and the full version in Hebrew translation, at *Mafte'akh* (University of Tel Aviv), tr. Liron Mor; and 'Nationum Origo', in *Nation, Language and the Ethics of Translation*, eds. Sandra Bermann and Michael Wood (Princeton: Princeton University Press, 2005).

Introduction: This Untranslatability-Which-Is-Not-One

Comparison in place of real communality and generality.

To compare money with blood – the term circulation gave occasion for this – is about as correct as Menenius Agrippa's comparison between the patricians and the stomach. To compare money with language is not less erroneous. Language does not transform ideas, so that the peculiarity of ideas is dissolved and their social character runs alongside them as a separate entity, like prices alongside commodities. Ideas do not exist separately from language. Ideas which have first to be translated out of their mother tongue into a foreign language in order to circulate, in order to become exchangeable, offer a somewhat better analogy; but the analogy then lies not in language, but in the foreignness of language. [Ideen, die aus ihrer Muttersprache erst in eine fremde Sprache übersetzt werden müssen, um zu kursieren, um austauschbar zu werden, bieten schon mehr Analogie; die Analogie liegt dann aber nicht in der Sprache, sondern in ihrer Fremdheit.]

The exchangeability of all products, activities and relations with a third, *objective* entity which can be re-exchanged for everything *without distinction* – that is, the development of exchange values (and of money relations) is identical with universal venality, corruption. (Marx, *Grundrisse*, Notebook 1: 'The Chapter on Money')[1]

Globalization has taken our tongues from us.[2] We want otherwise; we want something other than this 'we' we fashion and that's fashioned for us. We turn from the venal, flat prospect of capital's market of markets towards its folds and scars, its nicks and crags; here we find instead autochthony, linguistic nationalisms, fundamentalisms, the politics of identity, barter economies and untranslatability. We've turned in vain; these ontological commitments don't do the job. They are always and already absorbed into

1

the global market of markets, as tokens or values to be compared, traded and translated.

My goal is to describe a position of resistance to, even rebellion against, the globalization of culture that does not stand on, commit us or lead to fundamentalism. For now, I'm giving it a paradoxical name: an untranslatability-which-is-not-one. The notion is paradoxical in some of the ways in which Luce Irigaray's famous title is – *Ce sexe qui n'en est pas un*, translated into English as *This Sex Which Is Not One*: not a *sex*; not a *single* sex; not a phallically single sexual organ but lipped, more-than-one-thing ones. Envision, Irigaray asks, forms of expression not subject to the principle of non-contradiction: this sex I'm pointing to, this thing, 'ce sexe', can both be 'a sex' and 'not a sex'; an 'untranslatability' may also be 'not an untranslatability'; and so on. Establish, Marx says, forms of relation among distinct entities whose residual difference, *Unterschied*, survives translation into a 'third, objective entity,' call it 'money' or a common, global language: these third, objective languages may be, for instance, commercial English, 'globish,' or formal languages or codes. Now protest against the unlikeliness of both – of the injunction to envision statements not subject to principles of coherence or non-contradiction and of the call to establish forms of relation, community and generality that escape the venal reach of exchange value. We may still marshal the defective and indecisive concept of untranslatability against principles of equivalence, comparison and analogy and against practices of translation coloured historically by a 'globe' that trade has served to define since the earliest modernity. We'll be disfiguring translation and translatability. We'll look across disciplinary borders – from literary studies to political philosophy and economy; from continental to analytic philosophies; philology; history – without *translating* entirely what one field offers into another's lexicon. What sorts of defective institutions will support this transversal practice and serve to produce and guard what Marx calls, in the Utopian key, 'real communality and generality' (*wirklichen Gemeinschaftlichkeit und Allgemeinheit*)? What sorts of political institutions, academic ones, disciplinary institutions and comparative fields?

My approach in *Untranslating Machines* will be genealogical, and I'll tell my stories mediately – no unambiguous principle of translation between earlier and more recent periods will be found; neither will a general principle of *untranslatability*, of the sort liable to make the past a foreign country. I'll focus instead on the *defective* shape of these principles. Consider. The principle of global translatability is (among other things, but definitely today) a mercantile one, so my story partly concerns, and begins at, the moment when mercantile economies come to be explicitly articulated with imperial projects and with state and nation forms: the moment of early European modernity. Spain and Britain are the twin and tense foci for the elliptical articulation of mercantilism, imperial projects imaginary and practical, and the emergent nation form in the period: the figure of translation in and between their literary and philosophical culture proves determining to the long genealogy of global thought. The principle of global translatability is then shaped in inter-European, but also in colonial encounters, when established metropolitan tongues must find their way into and out of American, African and other languages (some notional, some imaginary *as* languages: the 'language' shared by primates and a figure of the uncouth like Sancho Panza) – and do so on the shoulders of the emergent universalism of markets and religious doctrine. Finally, global translatability is a thought, and a principle, divided on a crucial matter: the translatability or untranslatability of the language and authority (the relation between the two being anything but given) of the sovereign. Translation is then a defective philosophical operator and an incoherent ideological, social, political and economic practice. It is both a primary resource *and* an internal limit for the consolidation of 'modern' state forms; for the conception of sovereignty that attaches to these forms; and for the identity that human animals would express in local, as well as universal languages. This last point – the broadest – deserves underscoring. A principle of global translatability runs up against limits – God's language; the muteness of intractable things; non-human articulation. Just where, in a symbolic landscape that includes angelic speech, Edenic and primal languages, machines that mimic human thought, Mandevillean and fantastical beasts and the natives of America, just where, by whom, to what ends and with what consequences are those limits drawn? Policed – by whom or by what institutions, and how? What counts as *human* is set for European modernity in the torn arcs of an ellipse with a third, a fourth, many more eccentric foci – the colony; the cannibal; the animal. The untranslatable language of a 'hitherto untouched people' that W. V. Quine imagines his famous field linguist seeking to translate. The focal point we find in stone, the unresponsive figure of providence. The point that does not speak back; the mouth whose words are untranslatable. The contingency and incoherence that this cloud of extimate foci introduces into or discloses within the arc of modernity are irreducible: translation is always inhabited by untranslatability. The genealogy of European enlightened modernity is tied inseparably to the erasure of that insight.

THOUGHT AT THE END OF THE GLOBE? A UNIVERSITY BEYOND THE MARKET OF MARKETS

This is how philosopher Barbara Cassin has posed the problem. 'I cannot – nor do I want to – speak of "the untranslatable" in the singular', she writes,

since, to my ear, the untranslatable in the singular refers us to . . . that which literary translators *par excellence* must face: the Untranslatable with a capitalized

'U,' the signifier as such, sonorities, rhythms, languages as they are heard and as they are spoken, as they exist. But what's fitting for us, philosophers, is a plural form: to translate untranslatables.[3]

What are these *plural* 'untranslatables'? But first, what do we mean by *translation* and *translatability* today? What are the institutions that support the practice and the concept? Let's turn our attention to the academic-disciplinary university machine in the age of its global translatability, and in particular to the relation between translation and the figure on which that academic-disciplinary university machine stands: the figure of humanistic, unconditioned thought. Here are two theses:

> The humanities remind us where we have been and help us envision where we are going. . . . Together [with the Social Sciences] they help us understand what it means to be human and connect us with our global community.[4]

And this description of a recently formed network of Universities:

> Global University Systems (GUS) is an international network of higher-education institutions, brought together by a shared passion for accessible, industry-relevant qualifications.[5]

In the age of its global reproducibility, the University becomes a conforming, converting, *translating* machine – industrial, 'industry-relevant'.[6] 'Global reproducibility' means the systematic drive to produce systems of study, protocols, curricula, International Baccalaureate, certificate programmes, master's degrees, exchange programmes, systems of flows between institutions of higher learning, international research collaboratives – a differentiated, rhizomatic industry of industry-relevant forms of legitimation and recognition, helping to unify the global information economy, forms of legitimation translatable universally and universally consumable. The age of the global reproducibility of the University is the age in which the conception of 'universality' tied to the ancient humanistic notion of the 'University' has become primarily expressible in the lexicon of 'shared passion for accessible, industry-relevant qualifications', that is, in the lexicon of (economic and technological) 'globality'.

To propose that 'translation' should, under a renewed definition of the term and coupled to an untranslatability-that-is-not-one, stand at the heart of another university and another sense of the humanities is not to assume a reactionary position. I am not looking, having disfigured 'translation' on the nails of 'untranslatability', to restore an 'auratic' experience of the University, of the humanities or of the human animal in the age of global capitalism. I won't be urging a return to the pristine and enlightened days of humanist universalism – days which were not 'pristine', 'universal', 'Enlightened' or particularly 'humanistic', since they turned on and sought to preserve principles of national, racial, economic and religious exclusion. To the contrary. A disfigured 'translation' allows us to envision a *version* of 'universalism' and the 'university', a *version* of translation and translatability and a *version* of humanism and of the humanities. On the account of these that this book offers, at times explicitly and always, I hope, by example, performatively, a form of democratic political association becomes possible, even under and always against the conditions of unrestrained, global neo-liberal depredation we live today. It is 'translation's' *violence* – which is conceptually of an order quite different from the sorts of violence that did indeed characterize the old myth of humanist universalism – that I'd like to enrol for thought, against and within the 'Global' university, against global university systems, as the mark of the ends of global thought more generally.

I say that 'translation' is a master term for understanding the humanities and globalism today, and those of my readers who are familiar with national and academic politics in the United States will hear the ring of broad worries regarding the funding and defunding of language-teaching programmes through the No Child Left Behind Act that U.S. president George Bush promoted, and which became law in 2001. Others will hear, I'm sure, the ring of American and European anxiety regarding industrial and cultural competitiveness, expressed as a matter of access to the languages of commerce and cultural legitimacy. The resurgence of narrowly nationalist sentiment in the United States leading to, and disastrously on evidence after, the 2016 election of Donald Trump has made manifest that these anxieties are no less urgent today in the Anglophone world than they were some years ago, before China's economy began its fast deflation, before Europe's economic and political union foundered in Brexit or on the stones of Greece and before the engine of Brazil's development lost its fuel. When the primacy of global English was in doubt, 'translation' among the languages of commerce was of paramount concern: 'Globish' is the expression of structural anxiety and not only a technical means to produce a market of markets. In the wake of terrible acts of violence in Beirut and in Paris, with the memory of police killings in the city of Ferguson and of fundamentalist terrorism in San Bernardino fresh in our minds, with the repression in Palestine clearly before us, perhaps we will hear in the word 'humanities' a compensatory, or maybe a stubbornly posed, claim or question: are rights, for example, the right to a safe existence, translatable across cultures, languages, races, religions – in the name, or under the aegis, of a purportedly universal standard which is also a universal translating machine: 'Human' rights?

But let's narrow our focus. 'Translation', I say, is a master term for understanding the state of the humanities and of global thought today. I intend the state of the humanities in the academy in the age of its global neo-liberalization. Of course, I am grossly overstating. Whether guided or not by the goal of 'help[ing] us understand what it means to be human and connect us with our global community' (as the American Academy of Arts and Sciences report that I cited in my epigraph puts it), the academy in the United States has always had an intimate relation with the production and reproduction of class privilege. The emergence of the student-debt economy over the past generation, however, dramatically alters the University's role in reducing social and economic inequities – to say nothing of 'understanding what it means to be human and connecting us with our global community'. Focused just on the American academy, you hear in my coupling of 'humanities' and 'translation' echoes of arcane debates regarding the differences between world literature, comparative literature and literature taught in translation.[7] The question how humanists make the case for the value of their disciplines to others – legislators, the great public, friends, administrators, all speaking the sadly familiar languages of productivity, outcome assessment, efficiency and so on – is a matter, it is understood, of translation. Those things that the humanities take to be their concerns, their objects of study, protocols, ends, all need translating into the technical-commercial language ascendant in the era of austerity, economic competitiveness and systematic and ideologically driven defunding of non-STEM (Science, Technology, Engineering, Mathematics) disciplines.

'Translation' is a term nested *within* the humanities (within the practice of the humanities and also within its old, incoherent concept) and serves as a gatekeeper *for* the humanities. 'Translation' so understood serves to draw the borders for and to determine the ends of the globe today: it is the figure of global thought, as it is the figure for the global market.

As to the first, the function of 'translation' within the humanistic disciplines, we're divided. Yes, absent some universal standard (the 'human' as universal bearer of sense and value, as bearer of 'universalism'), the question is open whether a work, a Degas nude, say, or a concept like political autonomy, will be understood and valued, to what degree, how and to what end, in different moments and societies. Recall the Terentian doctrine that what is 'human' about the human animal is its universality: *nil a me alienum puto*, the human is human inasmuch as it contains multitudes, inasmuch as it is the summation or the *end* of all beings, even (Pico's stronger claim, running in the contrary direction) inasmuch as it can *be* any being: I am not untranslatable into anything. Every form of life can be translated into the human and the human animal can, *qua* human, assume the characteristics of any other, translate himself or herself into the quality of any other thing. Inasmuch as my *end* is not given, but lies in my potential translatability into any being, whether animal, angelic or divine or in the potential translatability of any being into me – in this sense it is that I am human.

But, on the other hand, we'll want to say something like this. Yes, the quality of general translatability ('nothing is alien to me, I contain multitudes', the shibboleths of humanist universalism) that makes me human cannot reciprocally, mutually, be translated back into every form of life. I share with other human animals, and with them alone, that undisseverable, primary quality: but what I attend to when I affect to study what we call a humanistic discipline is just what resists translation about the object. It's what makes that Degas sketch different from a universally understandable term, or a term in a formal language, or a mechanically reproduced or reproducible drawing, that I'll be attending to: the *auratic*, the untranslatable. I'll be inclined to say that I affect to call disciplines humanistic when, and only when, their object of study is, to a degree that I am devoted to demonstrating, *untranslatable* into other disciplinary frames and into other systems of value. Non-reproducible, because non-mechanical, non-machinic. This is of course too strongly stated in this form, since it isn't automatically true that all machinic objects, all mechanically produced objects, are *ipso facto* valuable across disciplinary frames and markets. Only when the machine is *universal* is this true: a universal translating machine or a machine for producing general equivalencies against which the value and sense of every machinic object can be assessed: tendentially, the machine of immaterial labor. A global university, say.

And now to the second and third sides of my frame, the sides that understand 'translation' to serve as a gatekeeper for the 'humanities' and to provide the ends of global thought. Here too we're divided. The end of the humanistic disciplines, the neo-liberal economic model teaches us, is to convey cultural value across linguistic, historical and geographical borders. At the same time, whatever it is that is thus conveyed or translated moves across borders in the way that other products, other commodities, do as well, and is to be understood and valued by analogy to such products. (A cultural commodity is the translation of an economic commodity.) The humanities are thus instruments of globalization, ancillary to the great value-producing machine of global capitalism, a set of devices and practices for producing and assessing the value of cultural commodities traded on global and local markets and the product of (one part of) the global economic system. I set the borders and the value of the humanities, and of the objects that the humanistic disciplines produce and affect to study, according to these three, not-quite-coherent ways of understanding the humanities as translating machines and translatable objects or commodities.

What results from the double status and the double value of 'translation'? The term is at work *within* thought and within the humanistic disciplines and also at work *outside* disciplinary thought, in the world, in the globe, as a principal device for designating and defining them, for drawing the edges and ends of their concept, for determining its use, for providing the index by means of which the value of the objects designated as 'humanistic' are assessed and for drawing the edges between the disciplines of thought and the globe and world that they think. A peculiarly unstable, even violently unstable, term. Also, however, and in that same degree, an intellectually productive one, since the way in which the two ends of 'translation' defeat, limit and weaken one another will allow us to understand with some clarity what we mean by 'value', by the 'humanities', by the 'globe' and by their relation.

We'll call bare 'translation,' the gatekeeper internal and external to the humanities and to the human animal that makes the globe its own by means and as an expression of the 'humanities,' by a new name: 'Machine translation' (MT).

First let's wrest the term from its old humanist home: just the domain of linguistic transformation, where we move, word for word or sense for sense, from one natural language to another. Translation, for *zoon logon echon*, will disclose whatever is not accidental (historical, contingent, ephemeral, glottal, merely regional, merely an aspect of this or that human's articulated speech, accentual) about our relation to the word.[8] We maintain, generally, that this linguistic sense of translation is the philosophically densest and most compelling one, and also that it is (perhaps for that reason) the historical ground on which later declensions of 'translation' stand, the literal term to future metaphorical usages, translations of 'translation' into other improper or metaphorical domains. There's ample historical precedent for this translation of translation, of course – the term and the practices it designates move around promiscuously in different cultures and at different times, designating transformations of wildly varying sorts, material as well as symbolic. A quick example, taken from Spain: Juan de Junta, an editor in Salamanca in the mid-sixteenth century, publishes eight translations between 1544 and 1549 – from Italian, Latin. What we call 'translation', he calls not only 'traducir', but also 'trasladar', 'sacar', 'volver' and 'romançar'. The earlier word 'trujama-near', from the Arabic, nestles in the vocabulary of the conquest of America; Covarrubias's 1611 *Tesoro de la lengua castellana o española* refers to 'verter', *to pour*. 'Transportar' is not uncommon. A small controversy haunts even *traducere*, the most common humanist term for translation: is it first used by Bruni, as Italian scholars maintain, or by Alonso de Cartagena, as some Spanish scholars suggest? A matter of claiming historical precedence for different schools and histories of translation – a matter of national pride.[9]

Focus for now on just one translation of translation, for a quick sense of the stakes of the term's iterations today: into the domain of politics. (A further translation, into the domain of political economy, is no doubt at work as well.) In the 1652 *Philosophicall rudiments concerning government and society*, the unauthorized translation of Hobbes's 1642 *De Cive*, Hobbes (or rather his translator) devotes the opening articles of the chapter 'Of the Law of Nature Concerning Contracts' to the proposition that 'certain [natural] rights ought to be transferr'd, or relinquished: for if every one should retain his right to all things', Hobbes continues,

> It must necessarily follow, that some by right might invade; and others, by the same right, might defend themselves against them, (for every man, by naturall necessity, endeavours to defend his Body, and the things which he judgeth necessary towards the protection of his Body) therefore War would follow. He therefore acts against the reason of Peace, (i.e.) against the Law of Nature, whosoever he be, that doth not part with his Right to all things.[10]

The argument's steps are well enough known; their eventual outcome is *Leviathan*'s chapters 'Of the Natural Condition of Mankind' and 'Of the First and Second Natural Laws, and of Contracts'. There, Hobbes will multiply the terms he uses to describe the already-unstable process of 'transferr[ing], or relinquish[ing]' that he describes in the *Philosophical Rudiments*. Some rights are 'transferable' or 'assignable' (others are not). With slight variations in sense, never quite arranged in parallel, the conveyance of a natural right to another is described as 'Renouncing' or 'transferring', 'abandoning' or 'granting away', 'alienating', 'lay[ing] down', 'despoyl[ing] oneself of'; as 'tradition', 'delivery' and as 'translation'. Here is *Leviathan*: 'There is difference, between transferring of Right to the Thing; and transferring, or tradition, that is, delivery of the Thing it selfe. For the Thing may be delivered together with the Translation of the Right; as in buying and selling with ready mony; or exchange of goods, or lands: and it may be delivered some time after'.[11] The rather scattered semantic field that Hobbes intends to cover in the years from 1642 to 1652 is most tightly bordered in the Latin of the 1642 *De Cive*, where the principal terms Hobbes uses for this 'conveyance' are *transfere* and, especially, *translatio*, in the crucial phrase *translatio iuris*.[12] (It is notable that the translator of the *Philosophicall rudiments* avoids using the English 'to translate' and that the *Elemens Philosophiques du bon Citoyen*, the influential 1651 French translation of *De Cive*, by Samuel Sorbière, nowhere uses 'traduction'. Sorbière's terms are 'transport' and, importantly, 'transaction', this latter with the weak nominal sense that we generally grant it in English, but also with a stronger, verbal, reciprocal sense that the Latin seems to invest in *translatio* – an action occurring on both sides of the donation, the side of the transferor and the side of the transferee, as it were.[13]) For *translatio* smuggles in an important, indeed a definitive, conceptual specification. Transference, assignation, alienation, tradition, granting away – all these tend towards the rather blank 'despoyl[ing] oneself of' the transferred right. *Translatio*, however, is strongly reciprocal: what passes from me to another passes inasmuch as the other understands and agrees to receive what

I translate. We understand and agree in a shared tongue – a tongue disclosed to us and to others by this donation. We act, I who translate my right to you, you who recognize it and agree to accept it, in a language we share, despite the incidental differences our natural languages, our particular relation to this right or that, our relative power and scope, might have. We transfer rights to another by *translation*; the arrangement that eventually results in our transferring to the sovereign our rights to (or our desire for) self-protection (what Hobbes calls 'a Common-wealth by Institution') depends on the reciprocal recognition of, and the translatability of our conceptions of 'right', of 'donation', of 'contract' into, a common language, however hieratic we may deem it. And this reciprocal recognition appears definitive, for Hobbes, of the *human* animal – in a state of nature, and as this animal enters into society.

I say that it appears definitive. The dispersal and contradiction of the semantic field that 'translation' covers, and the term's various futures (in translations authorized and not, recognized by Hobbes and not), work symptomatically to disclose the instability of this recognition. Here in Hobbes (and with even greater clarity in Machiavelli), reading the 'translation' of 'human' rights to sovereign instances and representatives from the vantage of these sometimes violently antagonistic terms and from the futures into which 'translation's' divided semantic field appears to be translated, we knock into something other than the reasonable, contractarian system of mutual recognitions that appear to define the *human* animal in translation. Everything is staked on the possibility of translating the dispersed and contradictory semantic field that 'translation' covers into a systematic and coherent vehicle for the production of subjectivities – subjectivities recognizable among themselves, associated on the minimal ground of that recognition, capable of carrying out transactions of an economic, social and linguistic sort upon that basis. But the term's irreconcilable senses and functions attest not to the systematicity and coherence of the term's senses but to the machinic violence required to imagine that systematicity and to its fictitious, even *compensatory* quality. Something disturbing but inescapable stands forth in the earliest uses to which 'translation' is put then – in the early modern definitions we have seen, for instance, or in the ways that Hobbes or Machiavelli will construe the granting of 'human' rights to sovereign instances and representatives under the aegis of a defective concept of 'translation'. From the vantage of these sometimes violently antagonistic terms and from the futures into which 'translation's' divided semantic field appears to be translated, we knock into something other than the reasonable, contractarian system of mutual recognitions that appear to define the *human* animal in translation. This hard, anti-humanist core renders systematic and properly conceptual the senses of 'translation'. Machinic, it captures translation's incompatible functions and semantic registers and translates them into a regulated and perspicuous field:

a system for assigning economic and other values. It makes the transference of rights to others (humans, animals, institutions, positions) and the *recognition* of others as bearers of rights stand upon fictions. We call this hard, anti-humanist core at the heart of the University by the name of 'machine translation'.

Let's entertain a paradoxical thought. We have license to do so. The 'machinic university' helps imagine norms, but it is not a doxology – hence the paradoxical quality, or the defectiveness, of the concepts it produces. Yes, for technical and strategic reasons, it makes sense to turn the humanities towards the figure of translation, and to grant 'translation' its patient and appealing sovereignty internally and externally, to give it pride of place in negotiating the economic and cultural future of the University and to develop it as gatekeeper and definitive term for the humanistic University and most broadly for global thought in the age of the neo-liberal University. But this technical and strategic appeal to the human in translation should not keep us from understanding what *may* be the University's genuinely revolutionary task in the age of the global reproducibility of the University commodity, in the age of the conceptualization of the University as a system for producing industry-relevant information, in the age of the effective transformation of the University into a machine for the production of what Maurizio Lazzarato calls 'the endebted man'. That task is to help guard and produce the violence of translation, which is to say, to disfigure translation on the edges of the axiom of an untranslatability-that-is-not-one. On the condition that they serve this disfiguring function, the disciplines of the 'humanities' allow us to imagine, think through and set in place formal, ephemeral and reversible regimes of democratic association. It is in this machine inside the machine of the globally reproducible cultural commodity form, in this machinic, anti-humanist core and on the basis of non-recognition, of the incoherence of the principle of translation, of an untranslatability-which-is-not-one, that democratic regimes can and should be imagined, that is, *produced*, today.

UNTRANSLATABILITY: MACHINE

Here's a little scene. The magnificent blue dome of the British Library's Round Reading Room; we picture Marx at work on the *Grundrisse*, debating with Ricardo's texts, mooching as usual on Jenny's work and inheritance to live, rather miserably. It is late summer or early fall of 1857. He is trying to understand how to replace 'the unimaginative fantasies of eighteenth-century romances à la *Robinson Crusoe*', fantasies in which *homo faber* is imagined as 'the solitary and isolated hunter or fisherman,' and which 'serve . . .

Adam Smith and Ricardo as a starting point'. In place of these 'fantasies', Marx proposes a 'point of departure' located in 'individuals producing in a society, and hence the socially determined production of individuals' [Der vorliegende Gegenstand zunächst die materielle Produktion. In Gesellschaft produzierende Individuen – daher gesellschaftlich bestimmte produktion der Individuen ist natürlich der Ausgangspunkt].[14]

This is the key step Marx takes in order to redescribe the primitive scene of production, which is also the primitive scene of the production of the dis-cipline of political economy. The 'starting point' given by the 'unimaginative fictions' of bourgeois economics corresponds, in the idiom of political econ-omy, to an equally fantastical scene – one in which, mythologically, 'produc-tion is simultaneously consumption as well'.[15] Since Marx wrote those words (if they are indeed his words), the universalization of markets – the plural is important – has occurred under the loose understanding that the conversation *among* markets is protected by, coded in, referred to and dependent upon a global credit-debt market that stands at a distance from particular currencies, times, exchanges or interests. Both production *and* consumption, as well as their relation of identity and simultaneity, pass through the neutral translating machine of global credit-debt.

My mythology is Manichean, my identities two-termed, partly to fit Marx's own simultaneist mythology: production is *simultaneously* consump-tion; credit is simultaneously debt; whatever-market, particular markets, are in the aggregate the market system; the market system of credit-debt global capital is a translating machine. Markets – systems of production and con-sumption and systems of distribution, exchange and value-creation – work under particular conditions to particular ends, but they work in relation to an abstract and *total* market, a market system, towards which all exchanges tend, and upon which they all depend in the last instance, a market system which guarantees their 'simultaneity' and their convertibility into one another, a vast and universal translating machine filled, as it were, by whatever particulars pertain to each exchange, to each local market.

Say we suspect that this mythological 'simultaneity' obscures some imbalance, impasse, mismeasure or incongruity in the step from whatever-market to the market system. We will suspect that the translating machine or market system turns around something like what Ernesto Laclau calls, in *Contingency, Hegemony, Solidarity*, a 'void', an 'empty place' to be 'filled only by the particular'.[16] What is this 'empty place'?

Academic discourse regarding the global trade system has leapt to answer this question out of exhaustion. Historically, disciplinarily, the languages of classical political economy, of the humanities broadly and of cultural criti-cism more restrictedly, show themselves today to be inadequate to the task of describing, much less of providing ways of understanding, capital in its global, credit-debt and information-commodity form. The specific cause of this discursive exhaustion, which determines the particular form that 'fills', to use Laclau's metaphor, that void at the heart of the translating machine or market system, is more interesting than its philosophically trivial cognate, the crepuscular game of catch-up that concepts universally play with regard to states of affairs.

Let's call what causes this discursive exhaustion, and what also unbalances the translating machine or market system, an axiom of untranslatability *which is not one*.[17] What would it look like? For one thing, it is not an axiom in the classical sense nor does it have a numerical unity. And yet, as I'll try to show in what follows, a less or other than unitary, less or other than quantifiable, less or other than *simultaneous* axiom of untranslatability that may help us to understand how the universality claimed for capital, and for translation, and for the products, objects, texts and commodities in transit over the circuits of the global market system and the global translatability-untranslatability system, produces what Laclau calls a 'series of crucial defects in the structuration/destructuration of social relations' (58). These terrible 'defects' are 'crucial' not only inasmuch as they provide a means of understanding the limits of credit-debt capital but also inasmuch as they furnish grounds, weak but flexible and determinative, for ethical relations based in untranslatabilities.

Take, for instance, the famous phrase from Marx's 'Introduction to the Critique of Political Economy' that I previously cite, in translation: 'Production is simultaneously consumption as well'. We understand this as a point of departure, even a principle, of political economy (as it seems to be in Spinoza or in Hegel, in the shape of the proposition *Determinatio est negatio*), to which Marx will apply strong solvents in the pages that follow – showing how this 'simultaneity' falls out of phase when the unstable costs of distribution and of labour are taken into account. Classical political economy, axiomatically, tends to produce (in addition to, and simultaneously with, producing concepts regarding the production and consumption of commodities) an abstract time in which production and consumption are indeed 'simultaneous'. We might, with every justification, say that this mythological axiom of identity is also a proposition regarding translation: the original statement (for instance, Marx's original statement regarding the relation between production and consumption, or indeed his more famously translated, and translatable, proposition that 'workers of the world . . . have nothing to lose but [their] chains') *is* 'simultaneously' its translation, *is* simultaneously destined to be consumed, without remainder, in another language or indeed in the same language but under altered circumstances of reception. The mythic horizon of this scene: any phrase is *both* uttered or inscribed, here and now, in the language and moment and under the circumstances of its production *and* translated, into whatever-other language, into the moment and under the circumstances of its reception and interpretation, simultaneously, with no loss moment to moment or ecology to ecology. Marx writes under the great blue dome of the British library, for a readership for which that indexical setting is already lacking: he writes *from* whatever-place, on the condition that the signature of that place fall into secrecy, on the condition that it should always/already have passed into the general potter's field where the translating machine or market system buries whatever-markets and places.

We might then entertain this thought. In the age of credit capital, studies of culture undertaken within the network of institutions devoted to systematizing the culture and ideology of credit-debt capital (the modern University being one such: the potter's field of whatever-place, of the index) register their crepuscular ecology, the ambient loss of the mythological identity between their phrases and the state of affairs they seek to translate, as a loss of *credibility* and of *credit*. Think of the clamour regarding the costs of University education in the United States; think of the controversial efforts to link student debt to declining standards of living; think of the Obama administration's proposal to 'measure college performance through a new ratings system so students and families have the information to select schools that provide the best value'.[18] As concerns the way different disciplines appeal to and help to naturalize the universality of the global credit-debt market system, the 'empty place' that Laclau describes emerges within the strong analogy that forms the conceptual basis of the global credit-debt market system, an analogy tying the sorts of equivalences and convertibilities required by the importing and exporting of goods across markets to the phenomenon of linguistic *translation*. A universal principle of exchangeability moves the market of markets that abstractly holds together the circuits of global capitalism; a universal principle of translatability obtains between particular languages, or even more atomically, between idioms or idiolects and languages, and then among languages.

The analogy between these two principles, the principle of global exchangeability and of universal translatability-untranslatability, forms a sort of hinge, and it operates not only with respect to the circuits in which objects, commodities and texts of different sorts are exchanged, imported and exported – economic circuits, cultural circuits – but also with respect to the conceptualization of the objects in motion in those circuits. Traditional commodities become information commodities that serve *simultaneously* as the descriptive means for seizing global capital; as the normative way of promoting it; and as a global commodity retailed in business schools, global University networks, and digital classrooms around the world. A widget, should such a thing actually exist, is not *just* a widget, but is also an *example* of a commodity produced so as to accrue value when it is imported across markets. This surplus exemplarity adds imaginary value to the object, and this added value then provides further grounds for the legitimacy of the global market's system of value production.[19] A word in one language will find an equivalent when it is imported into another – this has always been true – but the conceptualization of a word as destined for another language, as valuable because translatable, as always already imported or importable, has shifted alongside the procedures for value creation installed by the global economy. Our belief, the credit we place, in a word's having value in another language, has changed along with the consolidation and systematization of the global credit-debt system and vice versa.

An untranslatability which *is one* is entailed. *This* untranslatability is related to universal translatability as particular indices are to universals in conventional dialectical schemes. *This* untranslatability in no way troubles the analogy between the principle of global exchangeability under credit-debt capital and the principle of universal translatability. *This* untranslatability is another name for what is at hand concretely; it is the domain of culture, of idiom; it passes into, is translated into, the global market system with no seeming loss, indeed with gains accruing, as cultural surplus value, to that new second-order commodity, 'untranslatability' or particularity. If it contradicts the (political-economic) principle of translatability, it is only to affirm it at a different level: this untranslatability which is one, we might say, is translatability's determinate negation. The determinate principle of universal *untranslatability* holds together the imaginary shape of global culture and brings unity and coherence to the cultural market system. Bollywood is not the same as Hollywood; a film produced here will not find an audience there: but culture, to the extent that it becomes the location for untranslatability, and untranslatability, to the extent that it becomes synonymous with cultural particularity, *add value universally*. They serve as the comparative index guaranteeing that the principle of universal translatability operates. A work of art, call it Picasso's 'Guernica' or that Degas sketch I have been handling or what have you, is universal to the extent, if and only if, it is 'filled' by particulars: that potentiality to be filled by particulars exists *simultaneously* with the work; it is inseparable from it; it constitutes the work.

We believe we know what 'translation' means, and hence what it means to say that something, an expression or a term, is translatable. We've seen that the mythological axiom, 'production is simultaneously consumption as well', is part of a clutch of identity propositions forming a system (though not a sequence) linking political economy with the cultural institutions that produce the ideological form, the cultural ground, on which phrases regarding the circumstances of political economy stand. The couplet translatability-untranslatability, so long as both terms are understood traditionally, so long as it is understood that they are at work *simultaneously*, produces the *simultaneity* of that system of identity propositions.

All this might be said to follow from the mythological axiom, 'Production is simultaneously consumption as well'. But Marx is not concerned with 'simultaneity' in *A Contribution to the Critique of Political Economy*: 'simultaneity' is introduced by his translator to render Marx's *unmittelbar*, 'immediate': 'Die Produktion ist unmittelbar auch Konsumtion', Marx writes. This and other stresses on *Mittel* and *mittelbar* in these opening pages suggest that he is lining himself up with the first moments in Hegel's philosophical trajectory so as to show, still with Hegel, that the mythology of the 'immediate' holds within it the traces of other abstractions, generalities, other times, other senses and matters that take identity propositions outside of themselves – whether what appears immediate is the certainty afforded by the senses; the axiomatic equivalence of production and consumption in political economy; or the mythological identity of the phrase produced and its translation. So Ryazanskaya's English word 'simultaneous', inasmuch as it is a mistranslation of Marx's German (and a tendentious, anti-philosophical one at that), is the signature, as it were, of the whatever-labour and of the whatever-distribution cost of translation at work *in* Marx's text, in advance of its translation and thus out of its time in German. But to that degree, too, the translator's signature performs, for Marx's text, and in advance of the text's specific and open treatment, the steps his argument will take in the pages that follow – the demonstration that the mythological identity between production and consumption is neither simultaneous nor immediate, but always and already destabilized and rendered out of phase by intervening, mediating costs.

Is the translator who, by mistranslating, renders the thrust of the argument more accurately than a philosophically faithful translation could have hoped to, still guilty of a *mistranslation*? Or should we say instead (the idiom is Lacanian) that she translates where she does not *think* she translates? Would we then be saying that the word *unmittelbar*, 'immediate', 'simultaneous', is *untranslatable* or that it is only *accidentally* translatable, unintentionally so? At any rate what we call 'translation' is not *one*, when it is, *simultaneously*, mistaken and correct, invisible and visible, simultaneous and out of phase, an identity and a performance. Would 'translatability' and 'untranslatability' still form the determinate mythological couple we would require, for our analogical hinge to bring into a system the political economy of the credit-debt market system?

Let's take another tack into the folk understanding of the term 'translatability' and bring it back into contact with the notion of 'untranslatability' in a different, more explicit context. This is how Derrida's *Monolingualism of the Other* approaches the terms, in Patrick Mensah's translation.

> Not that I am cultivating the untranslatable. Nothing is untranslatable, however
> little time is given to the expenditure or expansion of a competent discourse

that measures itself against the power of the original. But the 'untranslatable' remains – should remain, as my law tells me – the poetic economy of the idiom, the one that is important to me, for I would die even more quickly without it, and which is important to me, myself to myself, where a given formal 'quantity' always fails to restore the singular event of the original, that is, to let it be forgotten once recorded, to carry away its number, the prosodic shadow of its quantum. . . . In a sense, nothing is untranslatable; but *in another sense*, everything is untranslatable; translation is another name for the impossible. In another sense of the word 'translation,' of course, and from one sense to the other – it is easy for me always to hold firm between these two hyperboles which are fundamentally the same, and always translate each other.[20]

Now Derrida:

Non que je cultive l'intraduisible. Rien n'est intraduisible pour peu qu'on se donne le temps de la dépense ou l'expansion d'un discours compétent qui se mesure à la puissance de l'original. Mais 'intraduisible' demeure – doit rester, me dit ma loi – l'économie poétique de l'idiome, celui qui m'importe, car je mourrais encore plus vite sans lui, et qui m'importe, moi-même à moi-même, là où une 'quantité' formelle donnée échoue toujours à restituer l'événement singulier de l'original, c'est-à-dire à le faire oublier, une fois enregistré, à emporter son nombre, l'ombre prosodique de son quantum. . . . Rien n'est intraduisible en un sens, mais en un autre sens tout est intraduisible, la traduction est un autre nom de l'impossible. En un autre sens du mot 'traduction', bien sûr, et d'un sens à l'autre il m'est facile de tenir toujours ferme entre ces deux hyperboles qui sont au fond la même et se traduisent encore l'une l'autre.[21]

Finally, this is Derrida's excellent Spanish translator, Horacio Pons:

No es que cultive lo intraducible. Nada lo es, por poco que uno se tome el tiempo del gasto o la expansión de un discurso competente que rivalice con la potencia del original. Pero 'intraducible' se mantiene – debe seguir siendo, me dice mi ley – la economía poética del idioma, el que me importa, pues moriría aún más rápido sin él, y que me importa, a mí mismo en mí mismo, allí donde una cantidad 'formal' dada fracasa siempre en restituir el acontecimiento singular del original, es decir, hacerlo olvidar una vez registrado, arrebatar su número, la sombra prosódica de su *quantum*. . . . En un sentido, nada es intraducible, pero *en otro sentido* todo lo es, la traducción es otro nombre de lo imposible. En otro sentido de la palabra 'traducción,' por supuesto, y de un sentido al otro me es fácil mantenerme siempre firme entre esas dos hipérboles que en el fondo son la misma y se traducen además una a la otra.[22]

One sense of the term 'translatable', then, is signalled by Derrida's use of the hyperbole, a figure common to geometry and rhetoric. Here, if we are to take the figure seriously, and if we are to hold fast, first, to the geometrical sense of the term, 'to translate' means to map one point or quantum onto another according to an algorithm: translation is understood as mechanics, as a mathematical function, as measure or common measure. This sort of 'translation' pertains to natural languages if they can be imagined to be mapped onto a smooth mathematical, or mathematizable, or quantifiable space. Both word-for-word translation and sense-for-sense translation, those archaic Cain-and-Abel brothers of the translational Pantheon, can be imagined according to this sort of mathematical, functional paradigm.

But what happens when we 'translate' this sort of functional translation from the domain of quanta to the domain of rhetoric, even of philosophical rhetoric, where hyperbole has a quite different sort of standing? Here nothing like a smooth, mathematizable space prevails, outside of the fantasy of certain neo-Platonist philosophers. Here, on the rhetorico-poetic side of hyperbole, 'translatability' is the name that Derrida gives, hyperbolically, to a failure. On this side, 'translation' happens when, as Derrida says, in Mensah's translation, 'a given formal "quantity" . . . *fails* to restore the singular event of the original, that is to let it be forgotten once recorded, to carry away its number, the prosodic shadow of its quantum' (my emphasis).

So then if 'translation' and 'translatability' are not settled concepts, or rather, if indeed 'translation' and 'translatability' can have more than one concept, one pertaining to the mathematical side of the hyperbole, the other to the rhetorical side, and entail at least two ways of measuring or recording their success, what then is 'untranslatability'? What is untranslatability with/within/without this wonderfully opaque paragraph in which Derrida describes and enacts it?

Not *one thing*. We would want to distinguish two primary understandings of untranslatability.

First, untranslatability as it pertains to mistranslations: one dimension of the concept, if it is one, of 'untranslatability' becomes clear when we edge the term up against the quite different, but related, notion of mistranslation. These may be errors or misprisions; they may be of interest or not; but they are correctable. When Mensah translates Derrida's 'Rien n'est intraduisible pour peu qu'on se donne le temps de la dépense ou l'expansion d'un discours compétent qui se mesure à la puissance de l'original' with 'nothing is untranslatable, however little time is given to the expenditure or expansion of a competent discourse that measures itself against the power of the original', he makes two mistakes. 'Rien n'est intraduisible', Derrida writes, 'pour peu qu'on se donne le temps de la dépense ou l'expansion d'un discours compétent qui se mesure à la puissance de l'original'. Here the issue is not the absence or presence of a syntactical surplus value, but the effect of a counter sense. 'Nothing is untranslatable', Mensah writes, 'however little time is given to the expenditure or expansion of a competent discourse'. The English *should* be, 'Nothing is untranslatable, so long as one takes the time to spend, or to expand, a competent discourse that measures itself against the power of the original'. Pons gets it right ('Nada lo es, por poco que uno se tome el tiempo del gasto'), but Mensah confuses two idiomatic expressions and makes the phrase unintelligible. It's correctable; it's a philosophically trivial, though practically crucial, happenstance. (In this way it is exactly contrary to Ryazanskaya's use of the English word 'simultaneous' in place of Marx's *unmittelbar* – a mistranslation that is practically trivial, but of great consequence philosophically, and which is, in an important sense, *uncorrectable*.)

We may also, as forms of untranslatability attached to or defined against correctable mistranslations, be thinking of under- or over-translations. These are not exactly mistakes but speak rather to a problem in the economy of a particular translation, a problem precisely in the 'time [we have] to spend, or to expand, a competent discourse measuring itself (up) to the power of the original' – as when a word in the original, having two meanings, is unpacked in one direction rather than another. Take, for example, Derrida's phrase, 'En un autre sens du mot "traduction," bien sûr, et d'un sens à l'autre il m'est facile de tenir toujours ferme entre ces deux hyperboles qui sont au fond la même et se traduisent encore l'une l'autre'. Focus for now on the word *encore*, whose double sense in French, something like *yet/more*, is conveniently split into Mensah's English 'Always', and Pons's Spanish 'Además', which means 'even more', 'yet again', 'furthermore'. Now consider, perhaps with greater argumentative consequences, the important French expression *se mesure à*, in Derrida's line describing the infinite possibility of translation if one has 'un discours compétent *qui se mesure à* la puissance de l'original'. Here the French plays amphibologically on 'measuring', understanding it both as an impersonal and as a reflexive act, 'measuring something', and 'measuring oneself up to something', this thing or this expression 'can be measured to' and can 'measure itself up to' that other, that original – a crucial ambiguity that *Castilian Spanish* could capture (the Castilian would then be 'que se mida con la potencia del original') but which Pons's version does not (he chooses instead 'que rivalice con la potencia del original', which captures one sense of 'se mesure à' but not the reflexive sense, and hence could be called an undertranslation of the French). English, though, *cannot* capture the syntactical surplus value of the French amphibology without unfolding the sentence, making it much longer than Derrida's, and thus losing the translation's commensurability with the original, its con-measurability – that is, without producing a sort of economic imbalance, an inflation, with regard to the original.

But we may have in mind, in the second place, what we might call cases of genuine untranslatability: uncorrectable mistakes. Here again we may find it hard to produce just *one* determining example or definition of untranslatability. Recall how Ryazanskaya replaces *unmittelbar* by 'simultaneously'. This mistranslation shows, eventually, something about the term *unmittelbar* that was not yet available in Marx's text but becomes so in the course of his argument, and which is thus only translatable, then, at that moment of the *Introduction to the Critique of Political Economy*, as a failure or as a mistake: *there*, just there, *unmittelbar* is always only mistranslatable, since 'immediate', even 'im-mediate', fails to disclose the lightly traced signature of the translator in the work, of the translator's destabilizing labour and distribution-costs and 'simultaneously' fails to capture the deeply etched echo of Hegel's idiom on which Marx's ironies are built.

A good definition of an 'untranslatable' phrase in this context: what there is *there* that will always only be mistranslated; that, *there*, which we will always fail at translating; *that, there*, which, being mistranslated, cannot be corrected.

'Untranslatability' here is keyed to the argumentative syntax of the original, if not to the phenomenology of its readings: mistranslating *unmittelbar* as 'simultaneously' shows Ryazanskaya's readers, those who have Marx's German with them, that the mythology of immediacy unrolled in the opening pages of the *Introduction to the Critique of Political Economy*, as an axiom in classical political economy, is already as it were out of date. It is not even simultaneous with itself.

We are not dealing with a correctable error, a mistranslation in that first (however interesting) sense, or with a heightened or exacerbated case of over- or under-translation. What is at issue is no longer a principle of measure and economy; presumably, the expression or argument could not be rendered semantically by increasing or decreasing the extension of the translation, or the time it would take to make the translation. Let's return to the hyperbolic phrases from *Monolingualism of the Other* that we've been reading for a further tack into this untranslatability-which-is-not-one. Bearing in mind that Derrida has just been speaking, rather hyperbolically, of 'measuring' the 'power' of the original, and that we should therefore be wary of drawing a too sharp, almost Kantian distinction where Derrida appears not to do so, what does this *dynamic*, as opposed perhaps to a *mathematical*, failure of translation look like?

Perhaps like this. Discussing what he calls poetic economy, Derrida leans on a rather poetic image: '"Intraduisible" demeure . . . l'économie poétique de l'idiome, celui qui m'importe, car je mourrais encore plus vite sans lui, et qui m'importe, moi-même à moi-même'. Here is Mensah: 'The poetic economy of the idiom, the one that is important to me, for I would die even more quickly without it, and which is important to me, myself to myself, where a given formal "quantity" always fails to restore the singular event of the original, that is, to let it be forgotten once recorded, to carry away its number, the prosodic shadow of its quantum'. This is Pons: 'Pero "intraducible" se mantiene . . . la economía poética del idioma, el que me importa, pues moriría aún más rápido sin él, y que me importa, a mí mismo en mí mismo, allí donde una cantidad "formal" dada fracasa, en restituir el acontecimiento singular del original'.

Note how much hangs on the difference between an 'idiom' and a 'language' – an 'idiom' or an 'idiomatic expression' being that tendency towards the one, the singular, the idiolectal at nest within the general, the place where 'une "quantité" formelle donnée échoue toujours à restituer l'événement singulier de l'original'. Derrida is hanging the 'restitution of the singular event of the original' idiom on a three-way aural-semantic pun between the French *importer*, 'to matter to someone; this is important to me'; *importer*, 'to import something or to transfer something in, to transfer oneself from oneself to oneself' (we're in the world of markets, of import-export economies: stress on the poetical *economy* of the idiom) and *emporter*, 'to carry away, take out, remove'. What Derrida calls the 'poetical economy of the idiom' is at work bringing 'moi-même' to *and away from* 'moi-même', importing (*importer*) but also estranging (*emporter*), adding importance by taking away and importing at once. Stress this time on the *poetical*, since, we presume, a *pragmatic* 'economy of the idiom', if such a thing were possible, would tend away, precisely, from the *idiom*, and towards the *language* I share with others, the necessarily public language of transactions, business, markets and so on. Pons renders this complicated movement in Castilian as 'me importa, a mí mismo en mí mismo', roughly 'it's important to me' or 'it imports me', 'myself in myself' or even 'it matters-imports to my inmost-being in my inmost-being, *mi mismo*' (echoing faintly the Spanish philosopher's José Ortega y Gasset's use of 'mismidad' to translate, roughly, Heidegger's *Dasein*), making clear that the movement 'imports . . . myself' *into* 'myself', but tangling this with the preponderant sense of the Castilian preposition 'en', as 'dentro' or 'dentro de', which in this case would mean preferentially 'within', as if the *idiom*, the *idios*, 'imported' 'myself' *into* 'myself' only *within* 'myself' (*mi mismo*, my sameness).

Recall that another name for the complex movement of import-export estrangement of the idiom, of myself to myself within myself and from without myself, is indeed *translation*. The 'poetical economy of the idiom' does not translate or act in the way that the subject of a sentence is said to act upon the predicate, or in the way that someone who measures something, call it the 'power' of an original language, might act. But the 'poetical economy of the idiom' is not, for all this, merely or simply mine, unique, idiolectal. It is not poetical or simply and merely rhetorical, an accidental aspect of the expression of a semantically transportable 'quantum' that could be 'imported' or 'exported' from one person or language to another, evading the undecidable

link of *importer* to *emporter* that Derrida's French makes available poeti-
cally, perhaps in order to persuade or move his readers, that is, to rhetorical
effect. The simultaneous-deferred, mediate-immediate reducibility *and* irreducibility of natural languages and of the moments of articulation of expressions in natural languages to *quanta* or to semantic content is the condition
on which there is *relation*, including the relations of analogy and equivalence:
of oneself to another (I am like you, we share an interest in this or that social
or political or economic outcome), of one natural language to another (this
word in English means what this one in French means), of one hyperbole to
another, geometrical to rhetorical, of 'moi-même' to/from 'moi-même'.

From a disciplinary perspective, Derrida's claim seems to be that thinking
this irreducibility is the condition on which there are properly philosophical
concepts and terms: this is the proper *work* of philosophy. But let's adopt
instead the perspective of the critique of the subsisting analogy between the
structure of general equivalence and the field of linguistic translating – *our*
perspective. From *this* perspective, Derrida's phrase concerning the impossible but occurring translation between the hyperbolic claims that nothing is
untranslatable and that everything is untranslatable, *Derrida's phrase* provides us with a profound description of the sources of what Laclau describes
as the 'crucial defects in the structuration/destructuration of social relations'
under global, credit capitalism. For the work of translating the general equivalences that obtain in the market of markets is work that becomes a *quantum*,
but always, both simultaneously and not, *something else*, something that scans
differently and which cannot be made to measure up to its quantity, which
is *untranslatable* from the hyperbolic form of rhetorical presentation to the
hyperbolic form of mathematical representation. This untranslatability-which-
is-not-one, which is not one inasmuch as it cannot measure up to the *quantum*,
marks the spot where the University and the speculative disciplines at its core
exceed or lose their credit and cease to produce value in and concerning the
identities, the objects and circuits, at work in the market of markets, including – crucially – that object we call the 'globe'. The 'crucial defect . . . in the
structuration/destructuration of . . . relations' emerges just here, where the
principles of analogy, equivalence, exchange and abstraction, that is to say,
where the general principles of translatability and untranslatability-which-is-
not-one, become the *work of thought* inasmuch as those general principles
fail to form a coherent system that could, in principle, become the conceptual
principle grounding a market of markets in global capitalism. And Derrida's
most powerful suggestion is that this thinking, because it concerns what is
impossible in translation, is not only the proper *work* of philosophy; it occurs
not only in the guarded disciplinary groves of the University or the formal
institutions destined to encourage and to protect speculative thought. Translation and the accompanying untranslatability-which-is-not-one are, to return to

Marx's words, a 'point of departure' located in 'individuals producing in a society, and hence the socially determined production of individuals'. Translation and its accompanying untranslatability-which-is-not-one are as they were *first political economy*. They are proper to the ethico-political work we do, I myself and you yourself, at the moment when we encounter one another, when each of us measures up to what is immeasurable for us in the other and in the other's idiom, when we speak out of measure so as to measure out, each to the other, phrases we take to be ours, phrases bearing our names and bearing what matters most to us, *ce qui nous importe/emporte*, Derrida's phrases, even my own to you today.

Can we be more specific about the nature of this 'work': about the conditions under which it takes place; about who – or what – performs this work; what it produces; how it is consumed? Although I have found my way to an ethico-political register, I opened remarking on the 'exhaustion' that characterizes academic discourse regarding the global trade system. The languages of political economy and of cultural criticism turn out to be inadequate to understanding capital in its global, credit-debt and information-commodity form: these, then, are exhausted. Very well. The higher-order language of translation does the trick today for the human animal produced by the global market. By 'higher-order' we mean that the language in which we describe or set the use, value, practices and techniques, limits, history, theory and philosophy of translation among natural languages takes the relations among languages as its object: it *translates* more than one natural language, more than one system of objects corresponding to it and a syntax concerning the relation among the natural languages and their systems of objects, to expressions concerning them of an encompassing order of generality. Translation is a general equivalent for the age of global capital. As for what it is that opens the void at the heart of this translating machine and of the market value system whose concept it provides – it is not just a *case* of untranslatability, in however strong a sense we mean it. It is a sort of thought instead – the product of a different kind of machine than we imagine University disciplines to be, carried out by a different sort of thing than we animals imagine ourselves to be. An untranslating machine.[23]

Chapter 1

Two Dogmas of Translation

'How am I able to obey a rule?' – if this is not a question about causes [*nach der Ursachen*], then it is about the justification for my following the rule in the way I do. If I have exhausted the justifications I have reached bedrock, and my spade is turned [*so bin ich nun auf dem harten Felsen angelangt, und mein Spaten biegt sich zurück*]. Then I am inclined to say: 'This is simply what I do'.

(Remember that we sometimes demand definitions for the sake not of their content, but of their form. Our requirement is an architectural one; the definition a kind of ornamental coping that supports nothing.) (Wittgenstein, *Philosophical Investigations* I. 217)

When I was a child in Madrid, my friends and I took our literary pleasures where we could find them, and we found them very often in translation.[1] René Goscinny's and Albert Uderzo's great 'Astérix et Obélix' series came to us in Castilian furnished with occasional footnotes: 'Juego de palabras intraducible', it would say at the bottom of the page: 'untranslatable word-game' or 'untranslatable pun', referring to a word spoken by a Gaul, Roman, Belgian and so on. At the time, we understood these footnotes to be deliberate characterizations of the Spanish words we had before us, rather than of a French original – and I suspect, in fact, that it never crossed our mind that there might *be* a French original, no doubt because the notorious national rivalry between Spain and France made the possibility unthinkable. For us, it was the *Spanish* that was 'intraducible', the language *into which* the comic could not be translated remaining unspecified; it struck us as particularly hilarious that the Spanish words footnoted for us were commonplace and should thus be utterly obvious in their translation, an indictment of that other, misty language as much as it was proof of Castilian's nuance and particularity. Years later, when I read the works in French and in English, I realized to my shock that these footnotes were not deliberate *parabases* but marks of melancholia or exasperation, a sort of throwing-up-of-the hands left diacritically by a name-less translator who was unable if not unwilling to render into Spanish the French *jeux de mots*.[2] 'Juego de palabras intraducible', he or she wrote when the going got sticky, closing off to Spanish readers of the books the avenue of the linguistically unfaithful but culturally correlative pun – something on the order of turning the name of Obélix's minute dog 'Idéfix' into 'Dogmatix', as the brilliant English rendering does, rather than conveying it, as did the tired Spaniard I imagine, merely as 'Idefix'.[3]

One does not go unscarred through experiences like this. A host of retro-spective reorderings, retranslations and recathectings of primal relations can ensue when the ideas one formed in childhood about this or that important expression become unfixed – with often perilous consequences for one's professional or psychic health. And my choice of topic, translation's 'indeci-sive muse', must surely count as one of the long psychic after-effects of this early shock, the discovery that my fixed, dogmatic ideas about the translat-ability or untranslatability of names like 'Idéfix' or of referential expressions like 'Juego de palabras intraducible' were not merely marks of linguistic ignorance and chauvinism but incorrect to boot. Imagine again my notional, exasperated Spanish translator. The confession of a term's untranslatability speaks to his or her exhaustion, or to a literalistic turn of mind bound to conflict with the subtle extravagance of Goscinny's script (one could reason-ably argue, for instance, that 'Idefix' is not a bad, but rather a particularly *good* translation of 'Idéfix', which like all proper names is untranslatable *as a description* of what it names) – unless, of course, the hilarity that these footnotes and bad *juegos de palabras* provoked among one group of pre-adolescents itself served as a sly correlative for the humour of Uderzo's and Goscinny's *jeux de mots*.[4] On this improbably Straussian reading the marks of the translator's seeming failure themselves *succeeded* in conveying some of the 'untranslatable' wit of the original, as unfaithfully but just as companion-ably as the more conventionally successful Englishing does. Improbable – but how would one know? On what grounds would one make such a decision? What might be at stake in deciding one way or another whether the imagined, unimaginative Spanish translator did or did not mask an acute, dialectically inclined linguistic druid?

Something more, surely, than the comparative linguistic innocence of one young group of Spanish readers. Say one wanted to argue that the Spanish translation of Goscinny's and Uderzo's *bandes dessinées* was poor (because flatfooted or unimaginative, and hence inadequate to the original) or that it was in a way too good (characters' proper names were left rigidly untrans-lated, as if their *descriptive* function in the original had been shorn at the border), but that it did a certain *ideological* work (the work of soliciting adolescent assent that Spanish was indeed 'different', in being untranslatable) with pernicious consequences (to promote Spanish exceptionalism at a time when Spain's exceptionality with respect to Europe was largely *political*, was to bolster that 'exceptional' political model). A reader self-involved enough to examine the source and possible consequence of his literary pleasures *might* well find himself or herself making this sort of observation; any *translator* contemplating different ways of rendering this or that *juego de palabras*, or indeed contemplating any translation whatsoever, might just as well. In both cases, the mechanisms, habits, discursive contexts or rules that we, readers and translators, employ when we make judgements concerning the *effect* or the *felicity* of a translation take into account the historical circumstances of a translation's production and reception: we need *history* to tell us whether this or that translation 'works', and how, and to what ends, to help us to *evaluate* it. Clio watches over the translator's task and it is to that muse that the translator's interpreters turn as well.

And yet this banal observation is beset with problems. Consider. Goscinny's and Uderzo's little Gaulish village, under siege by Roman forces, is devised and first published in the shadow of sieges that France felt much more proximately indeed – the Battle of Algiers, whose double siege – the French population in its quarter, the FLN and its supporters largely confined to the casbah and older parts of the city – so firmly gripped the French imaginary in the years from 1954 to 1960; and the terrible siege of the French expeditionary forces in the valley of Dien Bien Phu, in the course of 1954, which led to France's withdrawal from Indochina. Consider, too, that the besieged but invincible Gauls may well have expressed a compensatory French nostalgia for the movable stockades of 'resisteurs' who fought against Vichy and against German, rather than Roman, occupation – with considerably less success than their cartoon counterparts. (René Goscinny's family were Polish Jews. Born in France, he lived through the war in Buenos Aires and the United States; all his European relatives died in the camps.) Note also that Goscinny's and Uderzo's Spanish translator worked still, in 1970, under the careful eyes of the last of Europe's fascisms, a regime for which the figure of the *siege* served quite different purposes: recall most notably the official and widespread assimilation of the Roman siege of the Spanish town of Numantia, in the second century BCE, to various Republican sieges of Nationalist fortifications during the 1936–1939 Spanish Civil War and, from the Republican side, the similar characterization of the sieges of Madrid and Barcelona by Franco's forces and of the entire exiled population as a 'Numancia errante', in the marvellously evocative words of the socialist leader Luis Araquistáin. To succeed in making Franco's Spanish truly 'different' from republican French (or from any other language) – to make the languages mutually *untranslatable* – and to make a new generation of Spanish readers *enjoy* their difference was to raise *and level* Pyrenees of the mind between Spain and Europe, between the little village or fortified *alcázar* of Spanish *falangismo* and a liberalizing continent intent on invading Spain every August. 'Spain is different', ran the campaign that the Spanish Ministerio de Información y Turismo opened in 1963, marketing Spanish tourism in the exceptionalist tropes used since the eighteenth century to marginalize the Peninsula: *Spanish*, this wily translator seems to have been showing us, is *different* as well. How might a translation negotiate this peculiar set of overdeterminations? What shape might we expect judgments concerning its effects or felicities to take? What work might we expect the claim of 'untranslatability' to do, at the time and under the circumstances?

Other, less clearly 'historical' determinations are at work as well. For our judgements concerning the effect or the felicity of a translation *also* depend upon assertoric statements like 'Idefix and Dogmatix are translations of Idéfix' or 'Idéfix, Idefix and Dogmatix refer to the same thing', statements which are true rigidly and independently of historical circumstance. We would not be able to say that 'Idefix' is a translation of 'Idéfix', good, bad or indifferent; and with this or that consequence; without knowing that 'Idéfix' and 'Idefix' refer to the same thing. How this circumstance came about, whether it may change, what might be the different descriptive charges of the names 'Idéfix' and 'Dogmatix' – these questions are of another order entirely. The notion that a translation should be 'faithful to the original' founders just here: 'faithfulness' is a predicate with two aspects, a concept with two domains, unfaithful in a way to either one. It is drawn, on the one hand, from a structural or grammatical account of reference, which admits, that indeed requires the possibility of synonymy: assertoric statements like 'Idefix and Dogmatix are translations of Idéfix' can be rephrased as 'Idefix is synonymous with Idéfix and Dogmatix is synonymous with Idéfix'. It is also drawn, on the other hand, from a practical, historical account of reference, one which will always understand synonymy to arise as a matter of happenstance. Here on this side we say: 'Idefix and Dogmatix are translations of Idéfix *now*, under these circumstances, for these reasons, with these consequences: it could have been otherwise, it may not last; what one name *describes* about its referent coincides now and to some extent, but not necessarily completely, with what the other describes about its referent'. Each side of this couple is wobbly on its own. For instance, the distinction between a proper name and a description is not always, and perhaps never *a priori*, a clear one: 'Idéfix' and 'Dogmatix' look like proper names that work also as descriptions, but 'Idefix', the Castilian version of both, only works *remotely* (if at all) as a description, the Spanish version of *idée fixe* being something like 'idea fija', two terms that don't readily yield a portmanteau. And the second, practico-historical way of approaching a translation's 'faithfulness' proves as unfaithful on its own to its founding terms and rules as it proves when wed to the structural account of reference that its assertoric shape suggests. For when we judge the felicity and effects of a translation, do we not also need to know, as it were, a history of the translation (and the work's) *effects* yet to come? How might these be reckoned? What temporal and imaginative 'translation' is required of us in order to inscribe upon the translation that we are evaluating the history of its effects to come?

These scattershot questions, addressed to the form that 'decisions' take when we make judgements about translation, flow from the incompatible registers in which the determining notion of a translation's 'faithfulness' operates. Each of these registers furnishes us, too, with answers to the questions that their mutual interference provokes: answers to translation's indecisions, on the one side, reflecting a roughly 'Idealist' approach to linguistic usage and, on the other, answers reflecting a roughly 'materialist' approach to linguistic usage – the two dogmas of my subtitle. My goal in casting Quinean doubts on this tired distinction is not, however, a sceptical one. Rather, I want to argue that grounds for establishing judgements concerning translation today find a compelling weakness in both the surprise of their emergence (they are not determined) and in the dividedness of their conceptual domain (the notion of faithfulness, the notion that the translated word is similar to a proper name – though this name isn't solidly either a designator or a description). The examples I have chosen – taken from the work of Jorge Luis Borges and of Ludwig Wittgenstein – are drawn from terrible years: the period between 1937 and 1940, when both writers observed from abroad the rise, consolidation and aggressions of European fascism, one from Dublin and Cambridge, the other from the basement of the Biblioteca Municipal Miguel Cané in Buenos Aires. Neither could know the outcome of the historical 'darkness' into which they looked, from different sides of the ocean. For both, an ethical disposition towards that great darkness – *der Finsternis dieser Zeit*, as Wittgenstein wrote some years later – passed through the problem and the question of translation. Between them – in a dialogue one can only wish had actually taken place, in public, and well attended, somewhere between Buenos Aires and Cambridge – there develops a determining account of the need for articulating the field of ethics – where responses to the crisis of their times could be evaluated – with the problem of translation.[5]

UNCERTAIN TRANSLATION

A felicitous translation, we might first agree, wearing provisionally an Idealist cap, should be a form of *transport*, as the characteristic humanist etymology would stress: 'del verbo latino *traduco, -is,* por llevar de un lugar a otro alguna cosa', writes Sebastián de Covarrubias in a 1611 definition of 'traduzir': 'from the Latin word *traduco,- is,* meaning to take something from one place to another'.[6] The *thing* remains untouched; topology, rather than interpretation, is at issue; of the translator or the displacement 'from one place to another', no trace remains upon the *thing* or anywhere else. As to what this 'thing' or 'alguna cosa' might *be*, it plainly need not be a *thing* at all – at least not in any ordinary sense of the term 'thing' (after all, a word's 'sense' has no material consistency). And of course this 'thing' need not be an 'idea' either, or not at any rate the sort of 'idea' whose numinous form we associate with the various avatars of Platonism, any more than the 'place' or 'lugar' to which this 'thing' is moved need be a *physical* space – though both 'thing' and 'place' must minimally be coherent and perspicuously regulated entities. The topology of Idealist translation need not remain quite so plodding – indeed, it cannot. The minimal principle of coherence and perspicuity applies *a fortiori* to the rules according to which the 'transport' from linguistic 'place' to 'place' occurs, rules whose 'place' within each language designates the totality of 'places' and 'things' of another (of every other) language. Because *another* language (because every other language) also has a place for the rules of its 'transport' or translation into *another* language (into every other language), the place occupied by the rules of translation in this or that natural language includes hypothetically both every other language and *in and through these others* the 'primitive' language as well.

As I have described it, the Idealist argument for the minimal coherence and perspicuous regulation of the field of language comes closest to the atomic position most commonly ascribed to Russell – even the paradoxical topology smacks of what will become Russell's theory of types. Wittgenstein, who comes to be among Russell's sharpest critics, maintains these principles well through the *Tractatus* and perhaps up to the *Philosophical Investigations.* Though never, it should be said, without certain qualms – especially when it comes to translating to *natural* language principles derived from *formal* ones. 'If I know the meaning of an English and a synonymous German word', he writes in the 'fours' of the *Tractatus*, then 'it is impossible for me not to know that they are synonymous, it is impossible for me not to be able to translate them into one another' (4.243) – and this 'impossibility', *unmöglichkeit,* chimes clearly with the companion stress on necessity and continuity typical of the earliest work.[7] But is Wittgenstein right? For me to know (or judge) that two words I know, one English, the other German, are synonymous, I must judge that what I call (in English) 'synonymy' is *synonymous* with the notion in German – indeed, is something other than synonymous: is identical between the two languages and requires no translation. And in which language will I make *that* judgement? For it is as it were 'in' a language and as an utterance that such judgements are made and such 'knowledges' are registered – and not, as it might seem, by recourse to a separate realm, for instance the realm of a prelinguistic 'intent'. The matter clearly troubles Wittgenstein, who here as elsewhere doubles his adjectives ('impossible . . . impossible') where his argument makes an empirical point apodictically – as if his emphasis were in fact compensatory. He is clearer on the matter at one point in the *Brown Book*'s analysis of *intention*. Wittgenstein is now drafting the *Investigations* and, here, worries the knotty and recurring temptation to view the *intent* of an utterance as a mental state or a mental act corresponding to that utterance. To illustrate, Wittgenstein remarks, in an idiom sharply reminiscent of the earlier example in the *Tractatus*, that if one wanted 'to explain to a Frenchman who doesn't understand English what it was I believed', then it would be useless to say, 'Il croit "It will rain"', even accompanied by a set of 'experiences' that one could transmit to the Frenchman.

> For 'knowing what I believe' just doesn't mean: feeling what I do while I say it; just as knowing what I intend with this move in our game of chess doesn't mean knowing my exact state of mind while I'm making the move. . . . We should say that we had told the Frenchman what I believed if we translated my words for him into French. And it *might* be that thereby we told him nothing – even indirectly – about what happened 'in me' when I uttered my belief. Rather, we pointed out to him a sentence which in his language holds a similar position to my sentence in the English language.[8]

This principle of positional 'similarity' requires the mapping, not of one word or expression onto another with which it is synonymous, but of the totality of one natural or formal language onto another (how would one know what 'position' this or that expression occupies in French or in English, if one did not as it were cast an eye over the two, comparing and mapping them against each other and against themselves?). Wittgenstein is no longer committed to providing a particularly *precise* map (one can say that an expression occupies a position 'roughly there' in the landscape of another language). The stronger claim is that this mapping is not a mental act and in no way concerns the psychological or intentional state of affairs of users of the languages (or rather: if it does concern these, it only does so accidentally, as Wittgenstein's stress on the word 'might' suggests). Note then that if a *tractarian* stress on logical 'necessity' has slipped from the page, its place has been taken by an as-yet-unexamined, supplementary function: the linguistic function of *ostension*, which allows us to *point out* to the Frenchman something about the 'similar position' that a phrase occupies in his language. 'Translation' on this description is a properly *anonymous* procedure, *internal* to the 'world' of propositions, modelled conceptually as well as practically on a topological construction of natural and formal language as extensive, coherent and perspicuously regulated. In *practice*, translation is a properly *ascetic* discipline that entails 'our' disappearance (i.e., translation entails minimally the disappearance of any consideration of the translator as an intentional agent) and the corresponding appearance (in the *Tractatus*) of 'our' schematic double, the almost anthropomorphically lionized notion of *necessity* and (in the *Brown Book*) of 'our' second, gestural, double, the function of ostension in (one) language that allows it to point to something about (another) language. On this complex description, then, the translator's responsibility consists in this: that he or she become the anonymous bearer of knowledge concerning linguistic synonymy, or of intralinguistic ostensive practices that allow the mapping of one natural or formal language upon another. For those who seek to judge the felicity and the effect of a work of translation, the vacuous *generality* of the translator's two doubles furnishes the needed standard.[9]

Now consider the second sort of answer to the question, 'How does one judge the felicity, or the effect, of a translation, or of the claim to untranslatability?', the sort of answer I've ranged on the side of *materialist* approaches to linguistic usage. A felicitous translation, one might say in this context, is one in which the conditioning circumstances of the translation – mechanical, ideological, psychological, economic, 'ethnocentric' circumstances, as Venuti rightly insists – are thematized, presented for reading and interpretation within the translation, as extraneous but determining aspects of the 'new', translated work.[10] These aspects of a translation make apparent the *hic et nunc* of the *work* of translation: they obtain where topology gives way to interpretation and they bear necessarily the *proper name* of the translator. Recall that, under 'tradución', Covarrubias qualifies the definition he gave of translation under the word 'traduzir', allowing that translations must be performed 'with delicacy [*primor*] and prudence [*prudencia*], translating in some places [*en algunas partes*], not according to the letter, but according to the sense'. 'Sense', 'el sentido', enters through the doors opened by 'algunas partes', and by the highly subjective notions of 'primor' and 'prudencia' – and on its back a hermeneutical and a historical, rather than a primarily topological model of translation. In this case, the translator's responsibility no longer lies in preserving the 'thing' that he or she transports or in bearing out the necessary consequences of a synonymy that he or she mutely carries or in 'pointing out' the 'similar place' held by sentences in different natural or formal languages. Rather, the translator is responsible for *establishing* what 'thing' is to be transported, for *marking* upon it the decisions that go into establishing what 'alguna cosa' *is*, for *embedding* upon it the trace of the work of transport and translation, for *inscribing* upon the translated work both that work's effect upon the linguistic and cultural *place* to which it is brought and the effect of its translation upon its 'originating' linguistic and cultural context. No *single* account of the 'position' of an expression in cultural or linguistic fields is available (these fields are characterized by their discontinuity, their incoherence, the hiddenness of the rules determining their borders and uses). No *single* judgement concerning the felicity or the effect of a work of translation is now imaginable. Single account and single judgement both founder upon the rigid historical specificity, the rock of *hic et nunc* that I've metaphorically called the translator's proper name, on which an entirely different class of voiced accounts and overdetermined judgements is then built.

Let me give you an example.

A story takes shape. It is set among more-or-less familiar place names – Buenos Aires, New York, 'Lucerne or London', Memphis, the city of Adrogué, Baton Rouge, Salto Oriental, Ouro Preto and, of course, Tlön, Uqbar, Tsai Jaldún and the disconcertingly fuzzy constellation of place and proper names, the 'fundamentally vague' lexicon that one finds in Borges's puzzling fable, 'Tlön, Uqbar, *Orbis Tertius* '. 'Tlön, Uqbar, *Orbis Tertius*' was first published in the journal *Sur* in 1940,[11] and it describes, in what we learn is a fictional article that the narrator, Borges, claims to have published in a 1940 *Anthology of Fantastical Literature*, the discovery of an encyclopaedia entry referring to an imaginary world. This world comes complete with proper languages, a provocatively Berkleyan epistemology, rudimentary exchange economies, geography and a metaphysics to boot. A notional postscript is appended to that first, supposed article. This seeming postscript, written, we are told, some seven years *after* the 'publication' of the *Anthology of Fantastical Literature* and seven years *after* the issue of *Sur* in which it and the 'original', 'false' or fantastical essay jointly appear, reveals that the fantastical joke-world that the narrator Borges described prankishly in 1940 has mysteriously become actual, perhaps in part on account of the publication of the article in the *Anthology of Fantastical Literature*. The 'real' fiction of Tlön has proven utterly and 'almost immediately' compelling, increasingly enchanting the populations of Europe and the Americas. And now at the close of the story – in the fiction of the story, the date is 1947, some ten years after the discovery of the first material objects from Tlön and seven years after *Sur* published 'Tlön, Uqbar, *Orbis Tertius*' – Borges's narrator melancholically considers the 'yielding' or 'breaking' – *el ceder* – of the world and then ends his tale with these softly apocalyptic lines:

> Entonces desaparecerán del planeta el inglés y el francés y el mero español. El mundo será Tlön. Yo no hago caso, yo sigo revisando en los quietos días del hotel de Adrogué una indecisa traducción quevediana (que no pienso dar a la imprenta) del *Urne Burial* de Browne.

> [Then English and French and mere Spanish will disappear from the globe. The world will be Tlön. I pay no attention to all this and go on revising, in the still

days at the Adrogué hotel, an uncertain Quevedian translation (which I do not intend to publish) of Browne's *Urne Burial*.]

The 'quiet' or 'still' atmosphere of the Adrogué hotel also clings to the position that the narrator takes with regard to the momentous historical changes that he seems in part to have produced: he trades in 'paying attention', *hacer caso*, for visions and revisions of a translation he never intends to publish, an 'indecisive' or 'undecided', 'quevedian' translation of a seventeenth-century melancholic's work.[12] In this story, 'attending to historical circumstance', paying attention to the march of history towards one or another totalitarian 'symmetry', itself seems either useless (in which case Stoic withdrawal is a not unreasonable attitude) or worse, destined to produce disabling, insidious symmetries as well. *Not* to pay attention reads at once as a means of escape from the world of history and battle and as a quiet form of resistance. We are invited, too, to ponder the parenthetical phrase 'no pienso dar a la imprenta', translated variously as 'which I do not intend to publish' or 'which I do not intend to see published' or 'though I never intend to publish'. Surely what is at stake is something more than the narrator's sense of the futility of publishing an arcane work in a 'merely' existent language destined to be erased very soon with the advent of Tlönite languages. Isn't it more likely, we are left to wonder, that the narrator doesn't intend to publish his translation because he fears repeating the unforeseen, catastrophic effects of the publication of the first 'article', the putatively published piece from the 1940 *Anthology of Fantastical Literature*? *That* article, despite being on its face 'fantastical', resulted in nothing less than the Tlönization of the world. What might not an indecisive, quevedian translation of Browne's *Urne-Buriall* produce? Published works – uttered words, printed words, translated words – are like the odd objects whose fictitious discovery that 'first' article narrates, and then in its postscript actually *becomes* – mysterious, strangely heavy and oddly inscribed objects from the world of Tlön, objects which appear and disappear or go through periodic appearances, to the point of becoming 'longer', 'coarser' or even, after concerted numbers of iterations, identical with the original. Once a work reaches the public domain, the consequences are unforeseeable and often tragic. The narrator's decision (if it is one) not to publish his translation seems in any event consistent and commonsensical: this or that decision (for instance, the decision to see a work published or not) can be measured or mapped against consequences plausibly foreseen or reasonably imagined, in the context of a past that is perspicuously available for comparison. For Borges's narrator, *ethical* space, one might say, is imagined as in Kantian ethics to be coherent, uniform and extensive and decisions in that space are imagined to occur necessarily *sub specie aeternitatis*.[13] If the consequences of publication can reasonably be imagined to be disastrous, then it is far better to perish, and to let one or another work perish untranslated, than it is to publish.

And yet the work that Borges's retiring narrator is slowly translating itself has very little patience, so to speak, with this posture. Browne's *Urne-Buriall* opens on a scene that 'Tlön, Uqbar, *Orbis Tertius*' captures and transforms – the accidental discovery in England of Roman bones, strangely transported or translated. From this accident, Browne weaves a striking parody of the humanist reliance upon classical *auctoritas* (I think here of Du Bellay, Ronsard and others inspired by the 'antiquities' of Rome), as well as an equally biting satire of belief in the miraculous power of saintly relics. In antiquity, he writes, 'When the Funerall pyre was out, and the last valediction over, men took a lasting adieu of their interred Friends, little expecting the curiosity of future ages should comment upon their ashes, and having no old experience of the duration of their Reliques, held no opinion of such after-considerations'. Browne continues:

> But who knows the fate of his bones, or how often he is to be buried? Who hath the Oracle of his ashes, or whether they are to be scattered? . . . That the bones of *Theseus* should be seen again in *Athens,* was not beyond conjecture, and hopeful expectation; but that these should arise so opportunely to serve your self, was an hit of fate and honour beyond prediction.[14]

Say then that we suggest that Borges's decision (or his expressed intention) *not* to publish his translation of the *Urne-Buriall* represents the modern counterpart of this ancient, naïve belief that interred bodies lastingly stay buried. And yet consider: the very existence of the supposed 1947 postscript to the seeming encyclopaedia entry indicates that at least *one* work by the narrator 'Borges' has found its way into press. It is consistent with the tongue-in-cheeky 'after-considerations' that occasion Browne's work – the 'unpredictable' 'wandering' of bones, relics and antiquities – to consider this provocative thought: that the story itself, 'Tlön, Uqbar, *Orbis Tertius*', *is* the 'indecisa traducción quevediana' of Browne's *Urne-Buriall* that the narrator Borges did not intend to see published (but which appears anyway, like a bone or a wandering relic). On this reading, the 'Postscript' is just one 'after-consideration' or periodic iteration of the original, a 'revision' still redolent of the 'still days at the Adrogué hotel' when it was composed and revised, again and again – and both are versions, relics of Browne. In *this* case, then, 'Borges's' Stoicism in the face of the assault of symmetries, or the 'quiet' resistance of the writer who does not attend to the world, *que no hace caso*, turn out to be compensatory fantasies designed to reinscribe the translator's project *within* the classical ethics of deliberative and intentional decision that their very appearance (in a wandering work) has begun to dismantle. For if a written work, an encyclopaedia entry for instance, can 'travel' in translation beyond the horizon and beyond what its author intends for it, acquiring a public shape to which the author did not destine it, to arise 'beyond prediction',

'opportunely' as in Browne or disastrously as in Borges's story, then judgements concerning that work's felicity, its consequences and effects can no
longer be imagined and evaluated according to perspicuously available rules.
No 'after-consideration' will provide what Browne calls the 'oracle of one's
ashes', a perspicuous glance at the *effect* of a work or of its translation, in
the context of the circumstances of its production (the guilty quietism of the
Adrogué hotel, the war in Europe).

And yet, Borges suggests, judgements concerning the *felicity* of translations can legitimately take place only within that impossible horizon.

But surely this only obtains, one might object, if we hang our reading of the
story on the thin reed of Browne's proper name, and allow the opening and
the occasion of his *Urne-Buriall* to work itself backward (or forward) onto
the project of translating it, if we allow the seeming decision on the part of
Borges's narrator (and, we add, of Borges the writer) to translate the *Urne-
Buriall* to bear on the *type* of translation the narrator might hypothetically
produce and on the story's general reflection upon the problem of translation
broadly. In reality, one might well argue, this sort of formalistic, metonymous
move, *from* a characterization of the text translated *to* a characterization of
the procedure of translating, is only accidentally legitimate. One 'decides' to
translate this or that text for any number of reasons, for economic reasons,
historical ones or then again quite serendipitously.

True – and yet Borges's narrator supplies a strong warrant for moving from
the matter of the translation to the procedure of translating in his mysterious
use of the term 'quevediano', which immediately translates a proper name
into the characterization or a description of a style of writing – or, to return
to the language of Wittgenstein's *Tractatus*, which translates a *Personen-
name* into *Eigenschaftswort*.[15] Deciding (if it is a decision) to pass from a
proper name to a related modifier or to a related description amounts not just
to translating between utterly 'different symbols' (as the early Wittgenstein
might have it) but also to selecting, from a range of descriptions to which the
proper name might correspond, those that qualify as descriptive predicates in
one or another situation (not all will). That the displacement from 'Quevedo'
to 'quevediano' occurs under the umbrella of the key word 'indeciso', *undecided, uncertain, indecisive*, then allows us to characterize this technique of
substitution or translation (of a proper name by its modifier form or by its
descriptive function) as basic to Borges's critique of classes of *decisions* that
lead to what the story calls 'simetría[s] con apariencia de orden', 'symmetries with the appearance of order' like dialectical materialism, Nazism, anti-
Semitism. In contrast to these decisions, Borges's 'quevedian', 'indecisive'
translation not only furnishes an asymmetrical, anti-ideological means for
understanding the relation between *aesthetic* and *ethical* judgements, but it is
also itself a fundamentally *political* form of resistance.

Certainly, my imaginary dialogue continues, but in this case you have exempted at least *one* decision, and perhaps an entire class of decisions, from the story's indecisions or uncertainties – you left as it were untranslated (or perhaps indeed as untranslatable), or else you translated 'decisively', *symmetrically*, 'with an appearance of order' and necessity; you translated as a 'decision' the movement *from* the proper name to the modifier form, from 'Quevedo' to '*quevediano*'. Neither Borges's story nor the Browne text that his narrator is translating (a translation that may or may not be coextensive with the story itself) does any such thing. Recall the *Urne-Buriall*'s droll remarks concerning the 'opportune' rising of lost bones 'to serve your self, an hit of fate and honour beyond prediction'; remember the irreducibly *undecidable* question whether the text of 'Tlön, Uqbar, *Orbis Tertius*' is or is not the same as the 'indecisa traducción quevediana' of Browne. It is in this regard that Borges (and Browne) presents in the Lucretian sense a 'materialist' counterpart to the *tractarian* account of the perspicuity of translation and ethical judgement's *space*. Translation 'occurs' *or* may always have occurred already. And translation is (or is not) 'given to press' *accidentally* rather (say) than 'necessarily'. And as we cannot decide, on the evidence of Borges's story, whether what we are reading is 'his story' or his 'quevedian' version of Browne – hence whether 'Borges' narrates as himself or as a character from the *Urne-Buriall* – then it is no longer plausible to think that Borges's story yields anything like a *uniform* or continuous ethical space, whether he is a character who translates a work that remains outside the story or a translator who figures within his own translation, whose 'indecisive, quevedian' conceit is to tell the story of the *Urne-Buriall* as though it concerned a character named 'Borges' who 'discovers', not (spurious) Roman antiquities that are passed off as real, but the (false) traces of another world that becomes real. And if this is so, then 'Tlön, Uqbar, *Orbis Tertius*' bears, establishes and narrates Borges's own circumstances, as well as those gathered in the character of 'Borges' the narrator, and those that attend the publication of Browne's *Urne-Buriall* in the first place, and it establishes these circumstances as the criteria on which we base judgements concerning the felicity of Borges's 'translations' (and of Borges's ethico-political positions) but only inasmuch as 'Tlön, Uqbar, *Orbis Tertius*' withdraws 'bearing', 'narrating' and, in particular, 'establishing' from the regulated, perspicuous field of 'human' decisions, of the autonomous ethics of the 'possible', of intentional translation.

I am not satisfied to swing on the twin horns of this old, recast distinction between the perspicuous idealism of some approaches to translation and the Lucretian accident or swerving of approaches that seek materialist ways of considering translation's effects. That the unctuously smooth, uniform, extensive and perspicuous space of judgements concerning translation should prove folded, pocked and irregular or that the historical circumstance of one or another act of translation should find itself 'undecidably' or 'indecisively' turned three (or more) ways – neither of these circumstances means that judgements concerning the felicity and the effect of translation, and hence judgements concerning the *ethics* of translation, do not legitimately and consequentially occur. For instance, I might say that translating Borges's word 'indecisa' into English as 'uncertain' (as James Irby does) fails to capture the notion of 'decision' that the Spanish embeds and so deeply troubles, that it thus fails to enter the ethico-political register on which the story importantly unfolds, that it thus reinforces the view that Borges sharply separated aesthetic labour from any sort of *engagement* in the world of historical circumstance and that as a result the translation is both inadequate to the *historical* urgency that invests the story's circumstances and guilty of obscuring a particular angle of critique of various totalitarian 'symmetries'. Judgements like this may be more or less accurate, more or less compelling – but they can and, in certain circumstances, should be made. And if they are to be based neither in a *posited* sense or idea of the original and of the procedure of translation (in the rigid, assertorial referring-function associated with the abstracted name) nor upon an *agreed* description of the historical circumstances of its production and on the cultural coherence of the natural language to which the translation is destined, then these judgements turn upon a particular *impossibility*: that of finding a ground for judgements (a form of expression; a grammar) that is general but proper to no natural language alone *and yet* untranslatable.

Let me return to Gaul to complicate the simple-minded Greco-Roman battle I have so far narrated, in order to give you a fuller description of this *impossible* ground: to present to you, if you will, Clio under the aspect of her *indecision*. In 'Des tours de Babel', Derrida concludes an analysis that is by turns philological and conceptual with this phrase: 'At the very moment when pronouncing "Babel" we sense the impossibility of deciding whether this name belongs, properly and simply, to *one* tongue'. The stakes here are naturally higher than one at first imagines. This is how Derrida has put it:

> Or un nom propre en tant que tel reste toujours intraduisible. . . . On serait alors tenté de dire *premièrement* qu'un nom propre, au sens propre, n'appartient pas proprement à la langue . . . par conséquent il ne peut s'inscrire proprement dans une langue qu'en s'y laissant traduire, autrement dit *interpréter* dans son équivalent sémantique: dès ce moment il ne peut plus être reçu comme nom propre. Le nom 'pierre' appartient à la langue française, et sa traduction dans une langue étrangère doit en principe transporter son sens. Ce n'est plus le cas pour 'Pierre' dont l'appartenance à la langue française n'est pas assurée et en tout cas pas du même type. Peter en ce sens n'est pas une *traduction* de Pierre, pas plus que Londres n'est une traduction de London, etc. . . . . *Deuxièmement,* le sujet dont la

langue dit maternelle serait la langue de Genèse peut bien entendre Babel comme 'confusion', il opère alors une traduction *confuse* du nom propre dans son équivalent commun sans avoir besoin d'un autre mot. C'est comme s'il y avait là deux mots, deux homonymes dont l'un a valeur de nom propre et l'autre de nom commun : entre les deux, une traduction qu'on peut très diversement évaluer.

[Now, a proper name as such remains forever untranslatable. . . . One would then be tempted to say *first* that a proper name, in the proper sense, does not properly belong to the language . . . consequently it can properly inscribe itself in a language only by allowing itself to be translated therein, in other words, *interpreted* by its semantic equivalent: from this moment it can no longer be taken as proper name. The noun *pierre* belongs to the French language, and its translation into a foreign language should in principle transport its meaning. This is not the case with *Pierre,* whose inclusion in the French language is not assured and is in any case not of the same type. 'Peter' in this sense is not a *translation* of *Pierre,* any more than *Londres* is a translation of 'London', and so forth. . . . And *second,* anyone whose so-called mother tongue was the tongue of Genesis could indeed understand Babel as 'confusion'; that person then effects a *confused* translation of the proper name by its common equivalent without having need for another word. It is as if there were two words there, two homonyms one of which has the value of proper name and the other that of common noun: between the two, a translation which one can evaluate quite diversely.][16]

Not, of course, that a simple *cordon sanitaire* drawn hygienically around infected terms, even 'master-terms' like 'translation' or 'Babel', can ever work: the common (and proper) term 'confusion', the term 'proper' itself (understood both 'properly' and metaphorically) reveal themselves, on Derrida's account, to be equally aberrant. The reflexive movement *from* understanding 'Babel' as both a proper place name and a common name synonymous with 'confusion' *to* converting the common noun 'confusion' into an allegorical, proper term – large case 'Confusion' – proceeds, on a different order of generality, to affect and infect the criteria according to which one would distinguish between the 'translated' or metaphoric or improper sense of 'translation' and its 'proper' sense. The 'Babelian performance' of indecision, as Derrida calls the order of translation that obtains between 'homonyms' or differently-valued names, serves as the occasion for a broader critique of metaphysical efforts to assert the primacy (the historical, genealogical, national, etc. pre-eminence) of one language over others. If no language or tongue, and in particular not the language of Genesis, the language of origins, is, on this account, decidably 'one' (in that it contains at least one term, the term designating and describing 'translation' that lies both within that language, as a 'common' and translatable noun, and 'without' that language as a 'proper' noun, stolid and fixed as a stone or an idea), then the (logically) secondary ideologies of unity built upon this fantasy of linguistic extension, coherence and completeness also harbour alien, foreign, *marrano,* colonial tongues.[17]

It would not be too surprising if 'Des tours de Babel' left matters here, having developed and deployed the 'Babelian performance' of translation as a concept or a para-concept for the deconstruction of 'secondary' ideologies of unity. The 'evaluation' of translation between homonymous common and proper terms within the same linguistic and ideological field would remain in this case the subject of permanent indecision; the economics of translation, without an index according to which to measure the 'diversities' at play; 'Babelian performance' would slide into the sort of inexhaustible 'play' of values that features so prominently in journalistic condemnations of deconstruction in the late 1970s and early 1980s. But this is not the whole story. Joseph Graham's exemplary translation gets at least one turn of phrase wrong, just where Derrida introduces the 'impossibility of deciding' whether 'Babel' in translation and in the original works as a common or as a proper noun. 'Now', writes Derrida in Graham's translation, 'this proper name [Babel] . . . also has, this is the whole point, as proper name the function of a common noun'. The phrase translates Derrida's 'Or ce nom propre qui nomme déjà au moins trois fois et trois choses différentes, il a aussi comme nom propre, *c'est toute l'histoire,* la fonction d'un nom commun'. The colloquial rendering of *c'est toute l'histoire* as 'this is the whole point' works without question, but it misses part of the polemic embedded in the deliberate 'confusion' played out in the balance of the essay between the 'choses différentes' that the word 'histoire' names: *allegorical* history, *religious* history, narrative, genealogy, tale, lie (these last as in the opening to Derrida's essay 'Mnemosyne', written in the first months of 1984: 'Je n'ai jamais su raconter une histoire'). 'That's all history', we might also translate; 'that's the whole of this particular, "Semitic" history', or even more grandly, 'c'est toute l'histoire', this is 'the history of Genesis, the history of the origin and totality of History', this time pronounced with the sort of ring that announces the capital letter, the entrance of the proper name of 'history' in its providential, Hegelian mode. Or put it like this: in 'Des tours de Babel' our turn towards 'toute l'histoire' serves as a means, if not for regulating at any rate for understanding and for 'evaluating' what Derrida calls the 'Babelian performance' of indecision between the 'proper' use of translation, and the improper or 'figurative one'. And if this is so, then 'the whole point' towards which we turn when we seek to understand this or that name in translation (say, 'Borges' or 'Quevedo' or 'Idéfix') is not only *one* turn towards 'histoire' but also *more than one* turn towards at least *three* common and proper uses of 'history': towards the 'history' of a word's usages in this or that material circumstance, the 'history' of linguistic practices and national conventions; towards the allegorical, religious, literary and other histories in which its appearance and uses are told; and most mysteriously towards the *idea* of History, understood with the sort of prospective hindsight we find in Hegel. The experience of being 'in history' is what

Derrida elsewhere in 'Des tours de Babel' calls the 'experience of the impossibility of deciding', the experience of being unable to decide towards which form of 'history' one has found oneself turning, in search of ground on which to 'evaluate' the sense of this or that event, act or utterance: or of this or that *translation*.[18] It bears remembering that this 'experience of the impossible' is the hallmark of the 'affirmative' moment in 'deconstruction' that Derrida begins to sketch in the middle to late 1970s, and which is generally construed to coincide with his turn towards understanding the *ethical* as a disposition towards the impossible.[19]

What would this 'experience of the impossible' amount to, properly speaking? For if we know anything about it, it is that this Derridean 'experience of the impossible' that serves as the ground for (judgements about) translation and for ethics (for ethical judgements) cannot be lined up with 'Idea' or with 'matter', with 'necessity' or with 'accident'. How does it then help us understand whether a translation is anonymous (i.e., to be viewed under the aspect of 'Histoire', under the aspect of the idea) or characterized by the proper name (i.e., to be understood as 'histoire', in the *hic et nunc* of particular linguistic practices) or in the domain of aesthetic history? Or how, in what grammar and with what criteria we make judgements *about* translations? Let me conclude with a glance at a text almost exactly contemporaneous with Borges's story, in which the terms 'translation', 'naming' and 'impossibility' are brought together, with determining consequences for the *history* of philosophical approaches to the problem of translation.

THE UNTRANSLATABLE NEED

Roughly in August of 1936, Wittgenstein impatiently strikes out his revisions to the German version of the *Brown Book* with the phrase 'all of this revision is worthless'.[20] He turns instead to a project that takes him through the 'dark times' of the war: the composition of the *Philosophical Investigations*. In Wittgenstein's opening story, a mason and his assistant are imagined to communicate on the job in a 'primitive' Augustinian language. The first calls out an order, in the form of a name of an object or a tool ('Slab!' or 'Pick!' or 'Axe!'), and the assistant, recognizing (according to the rules of the circumstance's language game) that the name is the elliptical form of a proposition or of a command ('Bring me a slab!' or 'Hand me the pick!' or 'I need an axe!'), then brings the tool or the object to the mason. The expanded rule of this language game runs like this: 'If you shout "slab!" you really mean: "Bring me a slab!"'[21] Wittgenstein's critique of the Augustinian position emerges in three sections, turning first on the question of whether 'thought' is shaped in propositions; then on the question of whether parts of arguments need to be simple propositions which are then coordinated according also to 'simple' rules; and finally on an examination of the criterion for determining the usefulness of names, in the face of the 'queer' [*seltsame*] connection that the philosopher seeks to establish between names and objects. This last 'queerness', in particular, Wittgenstein famously remarks, arises when the philosopher 'star[es] at an object' and repeats its name, seeking to discern thereby (or perhaps to generate) some intrinsic relation between object and name. When this happens, language and languages have 'gone on holiday' or they are 'idle' [*feiern*]. But when they 'work', languages generally define and relate to objects ostensively – as when we say 'this' and point to the object. In the visual register that Wittgenstein also employs, one might say that language 'works' when its relation to objects is imagined not as entailing my fixed or fetishistic or totemic gaze 'staring at an object', but rather as a glance, an overview, a looking over of a group of instances or cases arranged in a coherent space, in search of perspicuous resemblances or differences that can be pointed to. For the *Philosophical Investigations*, this is the work that language does: a set of tacit or explicit rules is deployed between two (or more) users of a language, who have agreed (again tacitly or explicitly) that for restricted purposes this or that name can be assigned to this or that tool, even in the absence of that tool (or providing a gestural or linguistic supplement to the name game so that the broken or absent tool, or the breaking or making absent of the tool, can also be communicated).

So far, Wittgenstein's account of communicative statements resembles closely the one we find in the *Brown Book*. Wittgenstein now notes, however, that disabling problems crop up in a number of circumstances, some involving directly self-referential uses of language, others only oblique ones. When we seek as it were to point to pointing, for instance, and require of language use that it explain or merely indicate its tacit or implicit rules (that it make the grammar of its language game an object in this game), then we soon lose sight of the 'use' of this or that language game (how are self-referring statements 'useful'? To what end?). Likewise, when we seek to make 'pointing' into an 'occult process', either by making the act of ostension 'point' at what Russell calls an 'individual' or at an 'object' in the *Tractatus'* sense or at a simple [*Einfach*] or a 'real name', or by imagining ostension to be an internal, intentional act; or to the contrary, by imagining ostension as an aspect of one natural language that we merely bear out (that works through us) – in this case, too, we are 'going on holiday' or are simply 'idling' [*feiern*]. Seeking to illustrate this second, obliquely self-regarding sort of 'idling' thoughts, Wittgenstein famously draws on this image:

For one is tempted to make an objection against what is ordinarily called a name. It can be put like this: *a name ought really to signify a simple*. And for this one might perhaps give the following reasons: the word 'Excalibur,' say, is a proper name in the ordinary sense. The sword Excalibur consists of parts combined in a particular way. If they are combined differently Excalibur does not exist. But it is clear that the sentence 'Excalibur has a sharp blade' makes *sense* whether Excalibur is still whole or is broken up. But if 'Excalibur' is the name of an object, this object no longer exists when Excalibur is broken in pieces; and as no object would then correspond to the name it would have no meaning. But then the sentence 'Excalibur has a sharp blade' would contain a word that had no meaning, and hence the sentence would be nonsense. But it does make sense; so there must always be something corresponding to the words of which it consists. So the word 'Excalibur' must disappear when the sense is analyzed and its place be taken by words which name simples. It will be reasonable to call these words the real names. (*Philosophical Investigations* ¶ 39)

[Denn man ist versucht, gegen das, was gewöhnlich 'Name' heißt, einen Einwand zu machen; und den kann man so ausdrücken: *daß der Name eigentlich Einfaches bezeichnen soll.* Und man könnte dies etwa so begründen: Ein Eigenname im gewöhnlichen Sinn ist etwa das Wort 'Nothung'. Das Schwert Nothung besteht aus Teilen in einer bestimmten Zusammensetzung. Sind sie anders zusammengesetzt, so existiert Nothung nicht. Nun hat aber offenbar der Satz 'Nothung hat eine scharfe Schneide' *Sinn*, ob Nothung noch ganz ist, oder schon zerschlagen. Ist aber 'Nothung' der Name eines Gegenstandes, so gibt es diesen Gegenstand nicht mehr, wenn Nothung zerschlagen ist; und da dem Namen dann kein Gegenstand entspräche, so hätte er keine Bedeutung. Dann aber stünde in dem Satz 'Nothung hat eine scharfe Schneide' ein Wort, das keine Bedeutung hat, und daher wäre der Satz Unsinn. Nun hat her aber Sinn; also muß den Wörtern, aus denen er besteht, immer etwas entsprechen. Also muß das Wort 'Nothung' bei der Analyse des Sinnes verschwinden und statt seiner müssen Wörter eintreten, die Einfaches benennen. Diese Wörter werden wir billigerweise die eigentlichen Namen nennen.][22]

It is hard to overstate the impact that Wittgenstein's example has had in the aftertimes of contemporary philosophy – an impact that flows not only from the philosophical development of the example in the paragraphs that follow but also from the work it does in registers other than the strictly logico-semantic one it seems on first blush to inhabit. In that register, Wittgenstein's sword becomes another, slightly more paradoxical version of the Augustinian tool of the early imaginative game, and the relation between sword and object becomes subject to the sort of contractual understanding between the worker and the foreman that opens the *Philosophical Investigations*. Even though there is no sword called 'Excalibur', outside of Malory's or Tennyson's works, the films of Walt Disney and the novels of T. H. White, or the broad literary-cultural tradition of which these are popular examples and so on, the sentence 'Excalibur has a sharp blade' *makes sense*. It *makes sense* in a way, for instance, that the phrase 'Jello has a sharp blade' does not or that 'Fghgmmh has a sharp blade' does not, and it makes a *different* sort of sense, and in a different *sort of way*, from the grammatically identical 'the wit of Browne's *Urne-Buriall* has a sharp blade'. On this description, sense-making, which is the function of propositions and is independent of the actual existence of 'objects' or 'simples', stands sharply distinguished from the *referential* function of words understood as names, which require the existence (or the possible existence) of the object.[23]

The *philosophical* uses of the example hardly exhaust it, though. Take for instance the work 'Excalibur' may be said to do in the aesthetico-literary domain. One suspects that Elizabeth Anscombe, Rush Rhees and Wittgenstein's contemporaries and colleagues, as attuned to Malory or Tennyson as the Austrian philosopher himself, would have heard a kind of rhyme sound between the 'vacationing' or 'idling' 'stare' with which Wittgenstein's philosopher improperly gazes at objects, calling out their name, and the fetishistic distraction with which Tennyson's Sir Bedivere gazes at the sword when the dying Arthur has asked him to 'take my brand Excalibur,/ . . . /And fling him far into the middle mere'.[24] Malory as well as Tennyson tinge Bedivere's moment of fascination with the colours of the Gospel: just as Peter denies Jesus in the Garden, so does the distracted Knight deny the request of his dying King:

> There drew [Sir Bedivere] forth the brand Excalibur,
> And o'er him, drawing it, the winter moon,
> Brightening the skirts of a long cloud, ran forth
> And sparkled keen with frost against the hilt:
> For all the haft twinkled with diamond sparks,
> Myriads of topaz-lights, and jacinth-work
> Of subtlest jewellery. He gazed so long
> That both his eyes were dazzled as he stood,
> This way and that dividing the swift mind,
> In act to throw. (437)

Or take a more ploddingly historical tack. In a time of crisis, we observe, certain names act as compensatory and therapeutic fantasies: names like 'Excalibur' or 'the Alamo', 'World Trade Center' or 'Hiroshima' establish and affirm the existence of an imagined community, in this case an imagined community of literate Britons with a shared cultural legacy, capable of recognizing a common allusion, and of recognizing themselves *as a community* in and by means of that name or allusion. And not just *any* cultural allusion, of course. Wittgenstein's English readers in 1939 and 1940 might have encountered Winston Churchill's assessment of Arthur, in *A History of the English-Speaking Peoples*, as a 'defender of the "sacred Flame of Christianity" and a promoter of world order'; they might have heard reports of Churchill's use of Tennyson's *Idylls of the King* in an address to the House of Commons, in June 1940. A radio listener in 1939 would have heard a six-part dramatization of White's *The Sword in the Stone*; between 1940 and 1942 she would have been treated to Clemence Dane's and Richard Addinsell's Arthurian extravagance, *The Saviours*. By 1941, he or she might well have read a poem by Edward Shanks published in the *Sunday Times*, which imagines Churchill wielding the contemporary version of Arthur's famous sword:

> The fire blazed up anew, the church tower crashed
> And threw a broader flame across the sky,
> Which caught our leader's bayonet and made it
> Bright with the magic of Excalibur.[25]

Even the resources of popular or semi-popular culture turn grimly to the task of national consolidation. Say that Wittgenstein's readers were furnished a compelling, much more light-hearted image of the sword's naïve use, by the young Arthur in White's almost contemporaneous *The Sword in the Stone*. *This* Arthur, as viewers of Disney's 1963 cartoon version will also recall, pulls the forgotten sword out of the anvilly morass of cultural overdeterminations simply to employ Excalibur as a tool for another who has called out 'Sword!' much as Wittgenstein's Augustinian persona at the opening of the *Investigations* calls out 'Slab!' Only a literary critic, or the venal Knights in White's tale, or a 'vacationing' philosopher, would dream of 'dividing the swift mind', as Tennyson's lovely line puts it, of gazing at Wart's sword with more attention, so as to find out its name, read its inscription and note or remember Excalibur's actual origins and function. The critic, vacationing philosopher or concerned Arthurian knight would also recall or discover in Tennyson's lines about the sword a particularly striking correspondence with Wittgenstein's text, in that they are themselves proleptically concerned with Excalibur's return, and with its uses in the popular memory. 'In those old days', Tennyson's dying Arthur remembers, 'one summer noon, an arm/ Rose up from out the bosom of the lake,/. . ./ Holding the sword--. . ./ And [I] took it, and have worn it, like a king;/ And, wheresoever I am sung or told/ In aftertime, this also shall be known' (436).

Tennysonian providentialism is partly a trope of epic self-consciousness, partly also a poetic fantasy expressing the poet's desire to control the circumstances of his work's future reception, of his poem's translation into historically alien lands and tongues ('Dividing the swift mind' has long been recognized as a close rendering of Virgil's 'Atque animum nunc huc celerem, nunc dividit illuc,/in partisque rapit varias perque omnia versat', *Aeneid* IV, ll. 285–86). It is importantly an aspect of imagining the 'history' of circumstance to be subsumed within a once-and-future 'History', the totality of effects perspicuously available, say, to Merlin (who lives it backwards) or to Hegel (whose Spirit does as well). In no way can the announced return of Excalibur be made to square with the radically different, accidental or materialist re-emergence of 'ashes', 'Urns', 'relics' 'bones' or mysterious Tlönite objects that we find in Browne, and then again in Borges. Rather, the providential return of the name 'Excalibur' serves to guarantee the solidity and coherence of the British monarchy, the solidity of national unity, its peculiar *destiny,* in time of need. When Rhees first undertakes his translation of the first part of the *Philosophical Investigations*, when Wittgenstein first corrects Rhees's manuscript, when Elizabeth Anscombe revises and completes the translation, England stands ready, like the narrator of Borges's story, to lose its language, its national autonomy, its freedom. The country has survived, barely, its first war, and finds itself on the edge of a second one recovering and reasserting a national tradition that seems as imperilled, as 'broken' or destroyed, as the sword itself. Little wonder that an Arthurian nostalgia suddenly suffuses this moment in the *Philosophical Investigations*! Little wonder that Churchill should now wield it (however peculiar the image may appear)! And in this context, Sir Bedivere's fetishistic attachment to the sword's *aesthetic* register threatens more than its use as a *sword,* more than its value as a good or useful *example* of a name that holds the place for an object, and more even that the *literary* return of the once and future King. The contemplative attachment to the *beauty,* aesthetic merit or allusive content of the name not only creates imagined communities, but it also threatens to *freeze* communal identification at the level of the imaginary, *understood as such.* Wittgenstein's logic demands what we may recognize as a *tractarian* sacrifice: in time of need we must cease 'dividing the swift mind' and, closing our eyelids, 'lest the gems/ Should blind our purpose', we toss out the name and the example, after we lightly use them. This is clearly no time for divided minds; now is not the time for philosophical vacations.

Of course, we shouldn't allow the name 'Excalibur' to blind us to our purpose, for after all we are only dealing with a *translation* of Wittgenstein's example – and the sword that Wittgenstein wields in the *German* of the *Philosophical Investigations* is not called 'Excalibur', but 'Nothung'. It is Siegmund's and Siegfried's sword rather than Arthur's that Wittgenstein unsheathes here, in his first drafts of the *Philosophical Investigations*; it is the community of Wagnerians and devotees of the *Nibelungenlied*, rather than the British Arthurians, that is here signalled to and reconstituted. The rendering of 'Nothung' as 'Excalibur' occurs in Wittgenstein's own corrections to Rush Rhees's translation of the first section of the *Philosophical Investigations*, corrections undertaken at some point late in 1938, when Wittgenstein is staying in Dublin with Dr Drury. In the corrected typescript, the German is changed to 'Excalibur' in manuscript and only where the sword's name first appears. The balance of the typescript retains the name of Wagner's sword.

The decision to switch 'Nothung' into 'Excalibur' is not really an obvious one, and the logic of the decision is not followed in other translations of the *Philosophical Investigations* (into Spanish or French, for instance). One reason – a tactical, rhetorical reason – strikes the eye immediately: by replacing 'Nothung' with 'Excalibur', Wittgenstein makes it impossible for his reader to confuse 'Nothung' with the word 'Nothing', a term whose *graphic, visual* resemblance to 'Nothung' could only 'blind [Wittgenstein's] purpose', prove distracting and draw the reader's eye from the concrete (if mythical) object towards the abstract name for the absence of every object.

Or then again perhaps the reason has less to do with the accidental visual similarity between the two names than with their *functional* similarity in the literary culture of each language. Say for instance that one wanted to argue that in translating 'Nothung' as 'Excalibur', Wittgenstein is 'pointing out a name' ('Excalibur') that 'holds a similar position to ["Nothung"] in the English language'. On what grounds is the judgement of 'similarity' made? And to what effect? Consider the 'position' that 'Nothung' occupies 'in the German language'. 'Nothung' is the name of the sword that Siegmund pulls from the trunk of the ash tree in Wagner's *Walküre*, the first 'day' of the *Ring* cycle, a sword that is broken and then reforged by Siegfried in the course of the cycle, after Siegmund's death.[26] The specifically biographical peg on which we hang an 'evaluation' of Wittgenstein's reference to Wagner is a fairly weak one. That Wittgenstein himself formed part of the community of Wagnerians seems more than likely (though his adherence to it was hardly uncomplicated). Although he has comparatively little to say about Wagner in general, in Wittgenstein's journals of 1931 we encounter this arresting observation about the *Ring*:

> Remarkable to see, how a substance sets itself against a form. How the Nibelungen-substance sets itself against dramatic form. It does not want to become drama, and does not become one (of those: does not become a drama, one of them), and only gives itself over to drama there where the poet or the composer decides *to become epic*. So the only genuine *passages* in the 'Ring,' the only ones that stay with one, are the epical (ones), in which text or music tell a story. And that is why the most impressive *words* of the 'Ring' are those of the stage-directions.

> [Merkwürdig zu sehen, wie ein Stoff sich einer Form widersetzt. Wie der Nibelungenstoff sich der dramatischen Form widersetzt. Er will kein Drama werden & wird kein's & nur dort ergibt er sich wo der Dichter oder Komponist sich entschließt *episch zu werden*. So sind die einzigen bleibenden & echten *Stellen* im 'Ring' die epischen, in denen Text oder Musik erzählen. Und darum sind die eindrucksvollsten *Worte* des 'Rings' die der Bühnenweisungen.][27]

Concerning Wagner himself and about his work Wittgenstein has little otherwise to say (this may or may not be surprising, given the controversies that already surrounded the figure) – but there is no question that he was familiar with his work.[28] It *is* worth recollecting that the most famous and influential of twentieth-century versions of the *Walküre*, conducted by the Vienna Philharmonic's main conductor, the famous Wagnerian Wilhelm Furtwängler, had moved from Bayreuth and Berlin, where it was performed in 1936 and 1937, to Covent Garden in London in 1937 and 1938. One need not stretch too far to imagine Wittgenstein, either in Vienna or in London, attending one or another of Furtwängler's performances.

But it would have been a far more dangerous thing in 1938 to gesture definingly towards the community of Wagnerians than to muse upon the matter of matter and the resistance to form in the *Ring* cycle, in 1931. For it would not do to forget what is happening on the Continent, precisely contemporaneously with Wittgenstein's corrections of Rhees's translation of the *Philosophical Investigations*. Wittgenstein's letters of 1938 refer tepidly to the possibility of what he calls 'a further compulsory rapprochement between Austria and Germany', a situation that causes Wittgenstein, as he puts it in a diary entry of February 1938, to 'think a great deal of a possible change of my nationality'.[29] The choice was soon made for him: on 12 March German troops entered Austria, at the invitation of the new Chancellor, and Wittgenstein became a *German* Jew, subject to the Nuremberg laws. He wrote to Keynes some days after the *Anschluss* confessing that 'the idea of becoming (or being) a German citizen, even apart from all the nasty consequences, is APPALLING to me', and asking for Keynes's help in applying for British citizenship.[30]

We surely find brief in both local and European history for reading the substitution of the Germanic 'Nothung' by the very British 'Excalibur' as representing, on the level of *philosophical writing*, the 'change in nationality' that Wittgenstein contemplates in these years. *This* Wittgenstein, who as an Austrian and a Jew finds himself willy-nilly *positioned* within the field of German culture, language and, most threateningly, legality, is less inclined to find a cognate position to 'Nothung' in English's 'Excalibur', than he is to repel, upon the battleground of the page, the occupying, imperial tradition represented by Wagner's work, upon the bayonets of an English tradition that did not 'appal' but rather welcomed him. And yet to make this argument means in part to sacrifice something that 'Nothung' brings to the text of the *Philosophical Investigations*, which is not reducible to the sociopolitical 'position' that the term occupies in German language and culture and which does not survive transport into English; something we glean from the term when we pause upon its 'position' in the *aesthetic* history from which it derives; when we fix our eyes upon the term, perhaps for too long; address it as we would an object; call out its name, and allow the visual, graphic matter of 'Nothung' to 'give itself over' to other, companion terms. And it may well be this indecisive aspect of the name that Wittgenstein *needed* most, but also most needed to give up (he himself having no 'position' within German culture any longer). If so, then Wittgenstein was only ever able to fix the indecisive muse of his translation (of his work's cultural migration from the European literary and philosophical tradition to the British and of his own) in the transitional 'translation' of the *Philosophical Investigations* found in his holographic, manuscript corrections of Rhees's translation, where the small battle between 'Excalibur', 'Nothung' and 'Nothing' takes place, materially, inked in once and then left implicit, like a stage direction, upon the page.

What then does 'Nothung' give the *Philosophical Investigations* that neither 'nothing' nor 'Excalibur' provides? Recall that the sword 'Nothung' crops up in the *Ring* cycle at the point of a triple or quadruple recognition scene where there's an almost comical stress on *naming*: the sword is named, Siegmund is named twice or three times by Sieglinde and by himself and Siegmund's father is named in two or three different ways. The recognition is complete when on hearing Walse's name Sieglinde finally gives Siegmund the name he will henceforth bear 'from her'. 'Was Walse your father', she sings, 'and are you a Walsung? Struck for thee was the sword in the ash-tree, so let me now name thee as I have loved thee: Siegmund, so name I thee!' On this, Siegmund dashes to the tree and draws out the sword, as he sings:

SIEGMUND (*springt auf dem Stamm zu und faßt den Schwertgriff*)

> Siegmund heiß' ich und Siegmund bin ich!
> Bezeug' es dies Schwert, das zaglos ich halte!
> Wälse verhieß mir, in höchster Not
> fänd' ich es einst: ich faß' es nun!
> Heiligster Minne höchste Not,
> sehnender Liebe sehrende Not
> brennt mir hell in der Brust,
> drängt zu Tat und Tod:
> Notung! Notung! So nenn' ich dich, Schwert -
> Notung! Notung! Neidlicher Stahl!
> Zeig' deiner Schärfe schneidenden Zahn:
> heraus aus der Scheide zu mir!

[Siegmund call me for Siegmund am I! Be witness this sword I hold now undaunted! Walse foretold me that in sorest need [*Noth*] I should find this: I grasp it now! Holiest love's most highest Need, love-longing's piercing passionate Need, burning bright in my breast, drives to deeds and death: Nothung! Nothung! So name I thee, sword – Nothung! Nothung! Conquering steel! Show now thy biting severing blade! Come forth from thy scabbard to me! Siegmund, the Walsung, seest thou here!][31]

The association between 'Nothung' and 'Noth' or 'Not', 'need', 'want', 'affliction' or 'necessity' is made already in the Grimm brothers' *Deutsches Worterbuch*,[32] and thus the name of the sword has the advantage, for Wagner as well as for Wittgenstein, of not just naming, but also describing the situation in which it arises, a situation of *need*, *Noth* (the pun description has a specific antecedent in Wagner's own career as well, an 1849-poem titled 'Die Noth'[33]). Still, the 'place' of 'Nothung' in Wagner's *libretto* is anything but assured. Imagine for a moment the flat, Freudian reading to which the scene lends itself – siblings beginning an incestuous affair, protected in some measure by their father's sword, protectively thrust through the tree of Sieglinde's failed home.[34] *What* 'Nothung' names here, and *how* 'Nothung' symbolizes, are both extravagantly overdetermined and underdetermined. The sword is indeed the father's gift, that is, it is a figure for a cultural and national legacy in which and by means of which an imagined community is constituted and recognizes itself; it is also a mark of 'need', the sign of a want that cannot be filled simply by the (cultural) gift of the father; and more: that 'need' is itself the gift that the father gives his son, the gift of his 'need' for 'Nothung', from which the son will derive the satisfaction of all his needs, a gift of 'need' intended to confirm Siegmund's destiny as the man who can rise from need into freedom. Wagner in this respect has not travelled far from his earliest poetic work; this is how his poem 'Die Noth' ends:

> Nature and Man – One Element!
> What had ever divided them has been destroyed!
> The dawn of freedom –, It was kindled by –, Need!

And yet, of course, the very circumstance of Walse's gift in *Die Walküre* is tainting: to be 'given' the experience of 'need' *as need*, in such a way that it can be translated, for instance, into a name, an instrument, a sword – to experience 'direst need' in the form of the redemptive promise of the father or of the national culture is already to receive 'Nature' under the aspect of 'Man' – and to lose the experience of forging freedom out of the destruction of their difference. Sibling incest is both the consequence of this loss and the sign that the opera attaches to it (a sign erased by, and translated, barely, into the only-slightly-more-remote incestuous bonds that bind Siegfried to Brunnhilde, his aunt). The 'kindling' of genuine freedom, represented not by Siegmund's mere acceptance of the given sword but by its reforging at the hands of his son Siegfried, entails figuratively making and receiving a sword without being told its name, without indeed being able to *read* its name as a description of the circumstances in which one finds oneself. The 'dawn' of genuine freedom, Wagner grandly suggests, is 'kindled' when one is *in need* without knowing that the experience of *need – Noth – has* a proper name that can then be turned into a weapon – *Nothung* – or for that matter into an aesthetic form: a poem like 'Die Noth'. For Siegfried, the 'gift' of *need* has no name (yet): what he (and, Wagner would argue, what every man) experiences, the affliction of historical subjection, is not understood as a gift, not received as a substance, not recognized as a tool or an instrument. And conversely, Siegfried's experience of his historical circumstances, of his genealogy, of the oppressive weight of a past he does not know and a present whose immiserations he cannot name, is thereby rendered unreadable and unthinkable *to him*: the name and the concept under whose aspect Siegfried's historical *need* presents itself to him is the only term he cannot *properly* apply to himself (without jeopardizing the totality of Wagner's cosmology). (Hence, we might observe, Siegfried's peculiar blockheadedness, his fantastical infantilism.)

A 'need' that has no name (yet), and in particular not the proper name 'need', *Noth*, which is strictly speaking 'nonsensical', and yet *works* to describe a human 'need' – but only as it severs the *historical* circumstance that 'need' names from the field of language, rendering it not only unthinkable but also *untranslatable*. Wittgenstein *needs* this construction of the name, one he can get only from 'Nothung', one he can derive only from dwelling and from inviting us to dwell repetitively, fetishistically, upon the word object 'Nothung', precisely because of the *type* of nonsense and the *type* of impossibility that Wagner's work embeds in it. 'Nothung' is the name that the *Ring* cycle gives to a translation that succeeds *too well* (it translates the 'need' felt by Siegmund successfully: it *redeems* that need), and fails on that account (only a 'need' that is not always already given up to translation, already destined for the redemptive promise of becoming-a-sword or becoming a proper name, can serve to 'kindle' freedom). Our gaze then pauses precisely *here,* as it were *between* 'Excalibur' and 'Nothung', and *within* the aesthetic history that 'Nothung' unfurls, *upon* the stubbornly nameless, untranslatable relation to need and affliction that Wagner's 'Noth' names and unnames, allow us to think and withdraw from our thought. It is here that we find we must precisely *not* 'close our eyelids' but instead dwell or 'idle' or 'vacation' or over-cathect in and upon the moment, circumstances, materials and determinations of translation and the untranslatable 'need' it names and conceals, 'dividing the swift mind' again and again. We dwell between these names, 'Excalibur' and 'Nothung', at the point where the translation between them is arrested, in order to 'evaluate' their different effects and their different felicities, in order to shape our judgements to the horizon of the translation's effects. At this idling point, we find ourselves unable to make the *tractarian* sacrifice of the aesthetics of the name, but interpellated, as ethical subjects, into a fetishistic, repetitive care for the names in translation, for names whose translating, back and forth, now threatens to find itself permanently interrupted by our attention. And on this score – on the question of whether our 'attention' is freely given to the name, as Bedivere's may be to 'Excalibur' – on this score, at any rate, we are not free. Wittgenstein is led away from 'Nothung' and towards 'Excalibur' for reasons we cannot know, not because they are indeterminate or because they are overdetermined or underdetermined, but because they are importantly *contingent*: nothing about 'Nothung' makes it kin to 'nothing', except the arresting graphic kinship the eye may or may not detect: 'nothing' comes of 'Nothung', and nothing that the philosopher can do will make it otherwise. This element of contingency attaches to the matter of the name, to the *Nibelungenstoff* itself: it is, indeed, what constitutes these names as *matter, graphic matter*, in the first place. The aesthetic fetish in translation attaches to this aspect of the name: our attention dwells *necessarily* upon what is unnecessary, on what makes up the name's contingent expression, its voicing, its graphic shape on this or that page, the resistance the name puts up to dramatic formalizations of all kinds, the accident of its historical inscription in this or that shape, here or there. To this extent, to the extent that the matter of any term in translation *necessarily* arrests our attention, it is incoherent to speak of a purely 'material' or 'materialist' account of translation. But the arising of the fetish moment in translation has no perspicuous coherence *within* the field in which it arises: the nature of the *necessity* of the arising of the aesthetic fetish in translation falls outside of translation (you might say: it is a proper name). And what is true for any particular phenomenology of reading or translating is true more broadly as well. The 'fetish-effect' 'divides the swift mind' and arises where the overdetermination and underdetermination of material 'history' by aesthetic history and by (the whiff of) providential History itself emerges as the criterion for understanding and evaluating the place of responsibility in translation. It forces on us the experience of the impossible: the ethical requirement that we dwell upon the name as such, in testimony to what it describes and inscribes in itself, *and* that we pass beyond it to what it designates, that we *both* choose our fetish *and* encounter it accidentally. On this rock we build the grammar of our propositions *about* the felicity and effects of translation: a stone we do not yet know what to call; our muse impossible, indecisive, divided; burdened or blessed with a proper and a common name. When we call to her, does she not answer, tendentiously *translating* the words that the 'unclean spirit' of madness offers Jesus in the gospel of St Mark: 'My name is Need, for we are many'?

Chapter 2

On Contingency in Translation

Here's how the story goes.[1]

Calixto, a young man of good standing in the city, is trying to find a way to make contact with a protected, beautiful young woman he's glimpsed accidentally and then spoken to, while chasing his hawk into an enclosed garden. One of his servants arranges for a notorious go-between to offer her services; when this go-between knocks on the master's door, another servant announces to Calixto that the first servant, Sempronio, is at the door with an 'old bawd hee hath brought along with him'. We are of course in the landscape of Fernando de Rojas's 1499 work *La Celestina*, or as James Mabbe's translation has it, the world of *The Spanish Bawd*.[2] Calixto worries aloud that this serviceable go-between will feel insulted at being called a bawd, *puta vieja* in Rojas's Castilian. His servant, Pármeno, answers him:

PÁRMENO: ¿Por qué, señor, te matas? ¿Por qué, señor, te congoxas? ¿E tú piensas que es vituperio en las orejas desta el nombre que la llamé? No lo creas; que assí se glorifica en le oyr, como tú, quando dizen: ¡diestro cauallero es Calisto! E demás desto, es nombrada e por tal título conocida. Si entre cient mugeres va e alguno dize: ¡puta vieja!, sin ningún empacho luego buelue la cabeça e responde con alegre cara. . . . Si passa por los perros, aquello suena su ladrido; si está cerca las aues, otra cosa no cantan; si cerca los ganados, balando lo pregonan; si cerca las bestias, rebuznando dizen: ¡puta vieja! Las ranas de los charcos otra cosa no suelen mentar. Si va entre los herreros, aquello dizen sus martillos. Carpinteros e armeros, herradores, caldereros, arcadores, todo oficio de instrumento forma en el ayre su nombre. Cántanla los carpinteros, péynanla los peynadores, texedores. Labradores en las huertas, en las aradas, en las viñas, en las segadas con ella passan el afán cotidiano. Al perder en los tableros, luego suenan sus loores. Todas cosas, que son hazen, a do quiera que ella está, el tal nombre representan. ¡O qué comedor de hueuos asados era su marido! ¿Qué

53

quieres más, sino, si vna piedra toca con otra, luego suena ¡puta vieja!?[3] (Rojas 2001, 256–57)

[*PÁRMENO:* You don't really imagine that the name I used for this one insults her ear? Don't believe it for a second: she's as proud of hearing herself called it, as you are when someone says: What an accomplished gentleman is Calisto! And what's more – this is the name she's known by, and that's her right title. Say that there's a hundred women, and someone happens to call out: Puta vieja! Without the least inhibition she'll right away turn her head and answer happily. . . . If she walks near a pack of dogs, their bark rings out: Puta vieja! If she comes near birds, their song is nothing but; if she happens on a flock, the sheep will baa it out; if near donkeys, their braying says: Puta vieja! Frogs in puddles have nothing else to say. If she strolls among blacksmiths, their hammers speak it out. Carpenters, builders, farriers, tinkers, coopers, every manner of tool forms her name in the air. Carpenters sing it, wool-carders card it, weavers, farmhands in the gardens, in fields, in the vineyards, in the threshing fields, spend their work-time with her. When folks lose at board games, her praises sound. All things that make sound, wherever she happens to be, make out that name. What a cuckold was her husband! What else can I say, but this: if one stone touches upon another, what sounds out is Puta vieja!][4]

This is grand fun – a rhetorical cascade, an escalation *a minore ad maiorem* towards the concluding, ringing 'if one stone touches another, what sounds out is "Puta vieja!"' That it is not *only* grand fun becomes apparent in the course of the work, as the movement *of* stones and *among* stones – as for instance when Celestina remarks that 'Las piedras parece que se apartan e me fazen lugar que passe' – and the consequences of things accidentally rapping upon stones take on an increasingly sinister quality, to climax with Calixto's accidental fall from a ladder: Melibea, rather too graphically, tells her father, just before dashing herself onto the same stones in imitation of her lover: 'De la triste cayda sus más escondidos sesos quedaron repartidos por las piedras e paredes' ['he pitcht upon his head, and had his braines beaten out, and dasht in pieces against the stones, and pavement of the streete' (196)]. It is also a remarkable staging of the problem of translation, taken in a number of its limiting cases: the matter of understanding, as speech, how the mere sound made accidentally by 'every manner of tool forms her name in the air' and, more strangely still, how natural phenomena, like the casual rapping or touching of one stone upon another, name and describe Celestina: '¡Puta vieja!'

The lumpy field of early modern translation is bounded by limiting cases – on one side, negative limits, cases of radical asymmetry or downright untranslatability, some of them on display in Pármeno's lines from *La Celestina*: the translation of God's word, the translation of the sovereign's command, translation from the language of the authorized and authorizing classical tongues, translations of the Aesopian language of beasts, translations from the languages of encroaching foreigners or resistant internal linguistic and ethnic minorities, translations to and from the languages of newly discovered American tribes. On the other side, the field of early modern translation is bounded by fantasies of universal languages and universal communication – again, God's word, the humanist Latin pedagogy, incipient formal-commercial languages like mathematics – cases where there would be no need for translation at all. The scene of the exclaiming stones from *La Celestina* carefully marshals both, often simultaneously, to scandalous effect – negative limits becoming positive ones and vice versa, the utterly foreign sound of the croaking frog suddenly sharing with human speech and with the ringing of hammers a single, rigid referent, as though '¡Puta vieja!' were the single expression that every manner of articulation, intentional or not, linguistic or not, shared, 'formed in the air'.

Two things about this scenario are scandalous, and they are quite different. The first is signalled by Rojas's daring translation of Christ's exclamation to the Pharisees when, in the Gospel of Luke, they ask him to rebuke his disciples for crying *Osanna fili David, benedictus qui venit in nomine Domini*! (Luke 19:40): 'And he answered and said unto [the Pharisees], I tell you that, if these should hold their peace, the stones would immediately cry out' ('Magister, increpa discipulos tuos. Quibus ipse ait: Dico vobis, quia si hi tacuerint, lapides clamabunt', as the Vulgate has it). It's futile to silence my disciples, says Jesus: 'The rocks and stones themselves would start to sing Hosanna', as the rock musical *Jesus Christ Superstar* famously put it – though in Rojas's startlingly heterodox translation, rocks, stones, animals, hammers and disciples all sing '¡Puta vieja!' The second occasion for scandal here comes from the strange analogy between modes of expression that this blasphemous syncretism produces: all sounds 'formed in air' call out in Castilian Celestina's name, or rather her eponym, her description and her social function – '¡Puta vieja!' The result is not to grant 'all things that make sound, wherever [Celestina] happens to be', the elevated status of articulated human language, but to point out that human language shares with mere sounds certain irreducibly material aspects, on the one hand, a wrought-ness that the *sounds* of artisans' tools borrow metonymously from the scene of those tools' instrumental use and, on the other hand, the quality of accidentality, of contingent occurring on which Rojas's catalogue concludes: 'What else can I say, but this: if one stone touches upon another, what sounds out is Puta vieja!' or in the Castilian, '¿Qué quieres más, sino, si vna piedra toca con otra, luego suena ¡puta vieja!?'

Let's ask four questions straight away. They have much less interest in themselves than in their relation to each other; none of them *alone* will allow us to approach Rojas's text, or understand the challenge it poses to our theories and practices of translation, but perhaps their combination will. In the first place, are there early modern *theories* of translation that could account for Rojas's translational materialism or for the scandalous pairing of linguistic materialism with parodic theology in this passage – and if so, what definition of 'theory' and of 'translation' are we employing to assert that this is so? Second, what is it that these theories, if there are any, or practices or systematic accounts of translation in the period of early modernity, can contribute to contemporary theory of translation? In the third place, what if anything do contemporary theories of translation – theories of translation developed in the wake of Herder, the Schlegel brothers, and the great projects of rational enlightenment; theories of translation that take account of the dynamics of decolonization, of technological innovations, of economic and mediatic globalization – allow us to see about the lexical culture of early modernity that was perhaps not clear in that period? Finally, in what way can theories of translation, or systematic accounts of translation, or descriptions of practices of translation, whether early modern or contemporary, help us to understand the chronological sorts of translation that my first questions envision?

These questions operate on different levels. They are genealogical as well as historiographical and methodological questions; their domains shift; they encroach upon each other, implying, presupposing and inhabiting each other. They express different disciplinary fantasies, agreements and desires. Addressing them requires us to put in place different protocols for argument, evidence and verification. My questions presume not just different definitions of translation, but also different ways of *defining* terms in general. We are never only talking *about* early modern translation, its practices or systematic articulations – we are also talking *in* translation, that is, performing an act of historico-imaginative reconceptualization of chronologically different cultural practices, amounting to a sort of translation. We are operating *from* conceptions of translation built about the great factors of modernization – technological shifts, denationalization, globalization, the loss of linguistic diversity and so on. How we conceptualize *what* we are doing when we talk about early modern translation is itself a theory of translation, call it a historiographical one, not to be confused with any of the other sorts in this determining, overdetermining and underdetermining circuit.

Nevertheless, with the exception of the last of my questions, the stickinesses I raise here would apply to any modestly self-aware form of historiography, which would want to be as clear-sighted as possible about the ways in which its object of inquiry might be the product of institutional and other desires at work at the moment of study and would want to take account of any deforming debts it might owe, conceptually and methodologically, to that object. But when we ask in what way theories of translation, or systematic accounts of translation, or descriptions of practices of translation, whether early modern or contemporary, can help us to understand historiography, we are making a specific sort of methodological assertion. We are claiming that 'translation' does not work *only* as the object of analysis, a cultural element among others, subject to description and interpretation in the way for instance that the fluctuating price of commodities in the early seventeenth century might be, or in the way that a particular work, whether a building or a poem, might be, or in the way that a practice might be, for instance a devotional practice in flux in the post-Tridentine period. When we ask in what way theories of translation can help us to understand historiography, or to understand a historiographical claim like 'Fernando de Rojas's *La Celestina* is a modern or modernizing work', we agree implicitly that historiography works as a *sort of* translation, and hence that 'translation' has a metadiscursive as well as a discursive function when we study early modernity. Pármeno's marvellous lines seem to provide an incontrovertible example of this folding in of translation's discursive and metadiscursive functions, since the 'translations' of barking, hammering, croaking, speaking and stones' knocking into the Castilian '¡Puta vieja!' also serve the heterodox function of commenting upon the translation of theological tropes into secular speech, of theological time into human time – and of transferring onto the latter the characteristics of the former – with far-reaching consequences for the theology of translation and for our conceptions of providence, determination and freedom. But is this folding of translation upon itself, as a discursive object as well as a metadiscursive syntactical element concerned with its material status, true of early modernity alone, or especially?

Allow me to answer this question with an example.

It is conventional to locate the emergence of modern Spanish grammar in the work that the great Spanish lexicographer and grammarian Antonio de Nebrija dedicated to Queen Isabel of Spain, in the signal year of 1492, some seven years before Rojas published *La Celestina*, the *Gramática de la lengua castellana*. This convention, however, is fairly recent, as the work itself had singularly little practical value, being published in one limited run in 1492, and then not again till the eighteenth century. (This is wildly overstated, in fact, since the work's influence was profound in humanist circles in Spain and out – its influence is simply not measurable in terms of print runs.) The critical consensus treats the *Gramática*, rather uneasily, as the anticipatory *symptom* of modernity precisely – a linguistic and national modernity accidentally underscored by the work's date of publication, which falls in the year of the expulsion of Spain's Jews, of the fall of Granada, of Isabel's patronage of Columbus and so on – a litany of world historical events. Nebrija dedicates his *Gramática* to 'la mui alta y assí esclarecida princesa doña Isabel' ['the very high and equally enlightened princess' Isabel].[5] The dedicatory prologue is of course best known for the famous, famously over-used proposition with which Nebrija opens, 'que siempre la lengua fue compañera del imperio: y de tal manera lo siguió: que juntamente començaron, crecieron y florecieron, y después junta fue la caida de entrambos' – the proposition that 'language was ever the companion of empire, and so follows it that they began together, grew and flourished together, and then declined together' (3).

'Siempre la lengua fue compañera del imperio' tends to be trotted out to underscore the imbrication of empires, for instance, Spain's soon-to-emerge empire in the New World, with early national ethnic and linguistic consolidation. And this is of course in part the case, and it is certainly the part most congenial to disciplinary practices that seek in early modernity the devices that consolidate a colonial-imperial regime whose endings, whether in 1898 or in 1975, they diagnose and celebrate. Sure enough, the ethnic-linguistic history that Nebrija tells leads, by historical *translationes imperii*, *from* 'el antigüedad de todas las cosas: que para nuestra recordación e memoria quedaron escriptas' (5) ['the greatest antiquity of all things, which remain written for our remembrance and memory'], from the empires of Assyrians, Indians, Sicinians and Egyptians, he says, *to* Isabel's own kingdom. The empire of Spain and Castilian Spanish that Nebrija seeks to describe and help found in 1492 looks within and without, and the project of national-linguistic consolidation is the place where the imperial and the national projects coincide. For at the same moment that Spain initiates the expulsion of its Jews and looks to the West for a trade route to the Indies, seeking the translation of empire across the Atlantic, Spain also, as Nebrija's text makes clear, begins to look within, to constitute itself *as* Spain (rather than semi-independent kingdoms allied by a common threat and purpose, the reconquest of Spain) by creating a nation of Castilian speakers composed of Biscayans and Navarrese as well as Aragonese, residual speakers of Arabic, Hebrew and merely regional languages. 'What will this book be for?' the Queen had asked him, and, responding to her in Nebrija's place, or so Nebrija says, the Bishop of Avila has answered:

Que después que vuestra Alteza metiesse debaxo de su iugo muchos pueblos bárbaros y naciones de peregrinas lenguas: y con el vencimiento aquellos ternían necessidad de recebir las leies: quel vencedor pone al vencido y con ellas nuestra lengua: entonces por esta mi Arte podrían venir en el conocimiento della como agora nos otros deprendemos el Arte de la Gramática latina para deprender el latín. I cierto assí es que no sola mente los enemigos de nuestra fe que tienen la necessidad de saber el lenguaje castellano: mas los vizcaínos, navarros, franceses, italianos, y todos los otros que tienen algún trato y conversación en España y necessidad de nuestra lengua. (8)

[That after your Highness had brought under her yoke many barbarian peoples and nations of foreign tongues [*peregrinas lenguas*], and after these peoples had been conquered they would have to receive the laws that the victor imposes upon the vanquished, and with these laws, our tongue. And then, by means of this my book they will come to understand it, as we now learn Latin from books of Latin grammar. It is true furthermore that it is not only the enemies of our faith who need to know the Castilian language, but also Biscayans, Navarrese, the French, Italian and all others who have any dealing and conversation with Spain, and need our language.]

But the historico-teleological story that Nebrija's phrase tells when taken in full, and which forms the core of the balance of the prologue, is much less familiar than its bald beginning. And taken in full, phrase and story do not quite lend themselves to the congenial fantasy they are most commonly made to serve, the story of a self-constituting linguistic-imperial and nationalist project taking on the translated mantle of antique or recent empires after the reconquest of Spain from its Muslim occupiers, then exporting this new hegemonic form Westward, and imposing it internally on recalcitrant communities.

Or rather, if Nebrija's Prologue *does* serve as the early record of this constituting device, the conjoining of national and imperial projects by linguistic means, it is on the back of a genuinely complicating factor. In order to assume the translated mantle of empire handed it by Romans, Greeks, Hebrews, Arabs and so on, Spain and the Spanish tongue, Castilian, must not only stand to these empires in the same relation as each stood to the other – their successor, by virtue of conquest. It must resemble them in form and custom. Because they shared a common linking of language and empire, Spain and Castilian can assume, by virtue of their similar linking of language and empire, the roles as imperial languages and state handed them in translation by their predecessors. Isabel's new kingdom must stand both inside and outside of this translated history and history of the translation of empires: like its predecessors, Spain's empire emerges primitively in hand with an equally primitive language ('tuvo su niñez en el tiempo de los juezes y reies de Castilla y de León', writes Nebrija: Castilian 'had its childhood in the time of the judges and kings of Castile and Leon') (5). Spain shows its nascent strength alongside the first great cultural products of and in the language ('començó a mostrar sus fuerças en tiempo del mui esclarecido y digno de toda la eternidad el rei don Alonso el sabio', writes Nebrija: Castilian 'began to show its strength in the time of the very enlightened and worthy of all eternity king, don Alfonso the Wise') and reaches its maturity in the reign of Isabel, when the combination of the monarch's labour and divine providence unites 'los miembros y pedaços de España que estauan por muchas partes derramados' ['the members and parts of Spain that were spilt in many places'] (6).

At this moment, then, if the translation is to stay consistent, Spain will begin its geopolitical decline along with its language. (These are companion

and correlative terms, so one could as easily say that the language will begin
to decline along with the empire.) And it is at this point that Nebrija, understandably uncomfortable to be seen prognosticating to its monarch the decline
of her empire just at the moment of its seeming linguistic consolidation,
does three things – none of them consistent with his project so far and, taken
together, not only subversive in the extreme but also exceptionally *modern*
or even *modernizing* in their consequences. Most strongly put, one could say
that European modernity hinges on these three gestures in translation, these
three decisive moves in the theory of imperial-linguistic translation, that we
find in Antonio de Nebrija's 1492 Prologue. For, anxious perhaps that the
ontogenetics of his historiography guarantees his patron's decline as well
as emergence, Nebrija switches the historiographical register, translating his
story into the idiom of providential historiography, or seeking rather to marry
or conjugate the two by asserting that Spain enjoys 'la monarchía y paz . . .
primeramente por la bondad y prouidencia diuina, después por la industria,
trabajo y diligencia de vuestra real Majestad' ['sovereignty and peace first
because of divine goodness and providence, and then on account of the care,
work and diligence of your majesty' (6)]. Isabel's empire will not suffer the
decline of previous empires because hers is a specifically *Christian* one, and
she is able to labour in consort with providence to elaborate a state 'La forma
y travazón del cual assí está ordenada que muchos siglos. iniuria y tiempos
no la podrán romper ni desatar. Assí que después de repurgada la cristiana
religión: por la cual somos amigos de Dios o reconciliados con él . . . no
queda ia otra cosa sino que florezcan las artes del paz' ['whose form and the
workings of which are ordered in such a way that neither the passing of many
centuries, nor insults, nor the change of customs will be able to break or untie
it. So, after the Christian religion has been cleansed, the religion through
which we are friends of God or reconciled with him . . . the only thing left is
for the arts of peace to flourish' (6)].

Thus far, then, an anxious move of supplementation, theology descending
to secure the exceptional, almost eschatological frame into which human
history is translated by 'el cumplimiento del tiempo: en que embió Dios a
su unigénito hijo' ['the accomplishing of that time, in which God sent his
only son']. There is nothing terribly remarkable to this, except inasmuch as
Nebrija's story has to this point been, if not exactly a secular one, at any rate
a story whose great laws, of emergence, consolidation and decline, are the
laws associated with natural bodies rather than divine ones.[6] But in order to
make this providential argument, a second one is marshalled alongside it: the
argument, as it were, from the book, from Nebrija's book and concerning his
book's role in securing that the old compact between state and language will
not be broken. This is the curious passage in which Nebrija asserts, with a

force in which we begin to see why he is so often identified as an early Spanish *humanist*, the value of his project:

> I por que mi pensamiento y gana siempre fue engrandecer las cosas de nuestra
> nación: y dar a los ombres de mi lengua obras en que mejor puedan emplear su
> ocio, que agora lo gastan leiendo novelas o istorias enbueltas en mil mentiras
> y errores, acordé ante todas las otras cosas reduzir en artificio este nuestro len-
> guaje castellano. . . . Por que si otro tanto en nuestra lengua no se haze como
> en aquellas [griego y latín], en vano vuestros cronistas y estoriadores escriven
> y encomiendan a inmortalidad la memoria de vuestros loables hechos, y nos
> otros tentamos de passar en castellano las cosas peregrinas y estrañas, pues que
> aqueste no puede ser sino negocio de pocos años. I será necessaria una de dos
> cosas: o que la memoria de vuestras hazañas perezca con la lengua; o que ande
> peregrinando por las naciones estranjeras: pues que no tiene propria casa en que
> pueda morar. En la çanja de la cual io quise echar la primera piedra, y hazer en
> nuestra lengua lo que Zenódoto en la griega y Crates en la latina. (6–7)

> [And because my thoughts and desires have always been set on exalting every-
> thing about our nation, and to give the men of my tongue works in which to
> employ their idle hours with profit, which they now spend reading novels or
> stories wrapped in a thousand lies and errors, for this reason I resolved, before all
> else, to bring into useful shape [*reduzir en artficio*] this our Castilian language
> . . . for if we do not do this same thing with our tongue, as has been done in Greek
> and Latin, it will be in vain that your chroniclers and historians will write and
> consign to immortality the memory of your praiseworthy deeds, as it will be in
> vain for others of us to try to transport into Spanish things wonderful and strange
> [*las cosas peregrinas y estranas*]. For this can only be the task of a few years.
> And one of two things will necessarily follow: either the memory of your deeds
> will perish with our tongue; or it will wander lost in foreign lands [*que ande per-
> egrinando por las naciones estranjeras*]; for it will have no proper home in which
> to dwell. And into the foundations of this home I wished to set the first stone, and
> to do for our tongue what Zenodotus did for Greek, and Crates for Latin.]

The second argument, which seeks to understand Nebrija's *Gramática* as the vehicle for the empire's preservation and Nebrija himself as the providential saviour of Spanish history as a result, sits uncomfortably next to the first. The third gesture has to do, not with the intervention of providentialism, not with agency and putting Nebrija's own interventions on a par with the intervention of providence – as though the human writer's intervention secured the memory of the queen's deeds from the inevitable drift into oblivion that providentialism *also* serves to ward against – but with this strange house that Nebrija seeks to build, out of language, for the memory of the queen's deeds, which will otherwise wander, *peregrinar*, in strange lands. As the parallelism between the phrases 'cosas peregrinas y estranas' and 'peregrinando por las naciones estranjeras' suggests, here the memorializing side of Nebrija's project becomes a means at once of securing the target language into which things wonderful and strange can be transported from other languages, and of ensuring that the queen's deeds do not exist merely in translation, wandering in foreign languages, but have a proper linguistic home as well. Nebrija is playing on the exquisite double sense of the word 'peregrino', which means, as Covarrubias tells us in the 1611 *Tesoro de la lengua* I discussed briefly in Chapter 1, both 'el que sale de su tierra en romeria a visitar alguna casa santa, o lugar santo', a pilgrim who leaves his land in order to journey to some holy house; hence one who wanders far from home; *and also* 'Cosa peregrina, cosa rara', a strange or unusual thing.[7] The etymology that Covarrubias gives for this strange word is 'Dixose en Latin *peregrinus à peregre, hoc est longe*, por andar largo camino' ['*Peregrinus*, from the Latin *peregre*, that is "far," because it entails covering a long road'].

We return to Nebrija's *Gramática*. The task of the grammarian, of the prescriptive as well as descriptive grammarian, is then not only to make it possible to translate odd or wandering things, odd or wandering terms, *cosas peregrinas*, into Spanish from other tongues, into a Spanish tongue that welcomes them into itself, but also to make it possible for Spanish to be translated into other tongues and into a national memory *from* a place where it is not 'strange' itself or strange *to itself*, not itself *peregrina*, but at home. Things, *cosas*, or terms can only be strange and wandering, *peregrinas*, if they have a home, a grammatical home, in the first instance. But Spanish becomes foreign and goes into translation, when it has none.

This picture of geopolitical wandering, of peregrine and homeless languages secured by the providential will of the humanist grammarian, is on the whole rather confusing, but it is a *systematic* confusion. In Nebrija, translation, the matter of moving 'things' or 'terms' between natural languages, operates as a term to describe both the things moved and the moving of the things, both the terms and the translation. Translation is both a noun or a substantive, and a verb, a verbalized noun; it occupies different discursive levels. One would of course be inclined to overlook this conceptual and syntactical slippage or folding of discursive and metadiscursive elements if the author were not so fine a grammarian, so clamorously committed to the regularization of usages, to the normativization of linguistic practice, and hence, one would suppose, deeply averse to these sorts of amphibian terms. In the *Gramática*, though, the grammatical transference between nouns and verbs for translation, the verbalization of the noun 'peregrino' into the form 'pereginar', is the marker of a drift internal to language, to a theory of language that moves from nouns to verbs, from a lexical to a grammatical conceptualization, from names to relations between names. This drift seems on first sight to match, to translate well from the grammatical to the geopolitical domain, the drift of empires that Nebrija is also treating in these lines – the drift of peoples from the enclosure of their borders outward, into commercial and other relations with others, a Babelian dispersal, the movement from localism to the grand grammar of international relations. The difficulties in all *this*, however, both in the grammatical case and in the case of the geopolitical imaginary that it seems to translate, finally come down to determining, in the first place, which comes first, conceptually as well as historically – the verb or the noun, the local or the global, state or empire and, in the second place, what force or agency compels this drift, grammatical as well as geopolitical, to occur at all.

In Nebrija's prologue, as we have seen, at the moment at which the question of the decline of the empire-language couplet arises, three writing or translating procedures or effects emerge – the strategy of providential historiography; the heroic strategy of the writer who seeks to secure the future of the queen's memory; and the discursive folding of grammar onto itself at the point of translation. At this crucial spot, translation is at the same time what guards the borders, what keeps 'peregrine' things from entering unannounced or untranslated; and the threat to the home, the threat that what is to be preserved within Spain's national-linguistic borders will find itself, even when it is notionally at home within its own national boundaries, in a peregrine exile, homeless. The humanist function of the heroic grammarian-translator, the providential saviour of an empire otherwise doomed to decline, emerges also as the engine of that very decline, of the dispersal or unrooting of language. By the same sort of metonymy that informs the displacement of levels between the 'peregrine' and the 'peregrination', noun and verb, state and empire, the translator and the translation exchange properties, neither prior to the other, each following the other. This moment of exchange, we might say, marks the simultaneous entrance of secular agency into the world of history and its exit. Secular agency enters the world by an act of providence, which provides the figure of the heroic grammarian whose epic task is to secure the reign of Isabel. Simultaneously, however, providence acts to remove *from* history the verb, the act by means of which the figure, the subject and the substantive, of the heroic grammarian enters history. The heroic grammarian is providentially called into history, as a figure and an example of secular agency; but his being called into history is itself envisioned, not as, or not only as, an act of providence, but also as mere happenstance, the mere touch of contingent occurring. Act and substance, translator and translation, now touch upon the contingency of mere occurring, upon what *La Celestina*, Rojas's remarkable and contemporaneous work, signals by the mere 'touching' of stone knocking on stone.

Nebrija's modernity lies in his willingness to entertain this double, contradictory thought about the history he is describing, and about his own relation to that history. We can now see that the etymology that Sebastián de

Covarrubias provides for the term governing and incorporating this strange logic, the word 'peregrino', serves in fact to foreclose a range of senses found in Nebrija's use of the term, and to foreclose more broadly the dangerous, modern logic that Nebrija's *Gramática* invents and discloses. For in the *Gramática* Nebrija is enacting and expressing, with unsparing clarity and rigour, in the mirror-structure linking the grammatical drift of peregrine translation to the geopolitics of imperial translation, the sense that the term 'peregrinus' had *in the empire*: the foreigner at Rome, the non-citizen among citizens. 'Peregrinus' is different, the Calepinus tells us, from the *hospes*, from the foreigner who comes to a foreign city, *qui aliena civitate est*, inasmuch as the *peregrinus, qui in sua civitate non est*, is he who is not in his city, he who is shorn of the positive predicate of being in another, even an alien city, he who is shorn of the positive predicate of inhabiting the alien city: the *peregrinus* lies within the borders of what he does not inhabit.[8] No, like the radically republican citizen that he also figures, Nebrijas's *peregrinus*, the figure of the translator, of the translating and of the translated term, is determined only negatively. This negative determination of the theory and practices of translation, in its grammatical as well as its political and civic senses, almost two hundred years before Spinoza, is the hallmark of the modernity that Rojas and Nebrija inaugurate, and which even so unusual a lexicographer as Sebastián de Covarrubias would find too threatening to face entirely.

It would require a different sort of writing to recapture this peregrine account of translation, opened briefly at the close of the fifteenth century and displaced and repressed, if not forgotten, over the course of the following century. It would require a writer like Cervantes, and a discursive form like the novel, able to capitalize upon the systematic strangeness of translation, emerging from that systematic, material strangeness, to sound again, in a different vein, stone on stone, letter on letter, the peregrine tones we find in Rojas and in Nebrija. I will close referring very briefly to a passage from *Don Quixote*, Nebrija's and Rojas's great heir. We know this scene of my story well, too well. It's a story told for us by the great cheerleaders of Spanish *convivencia*. In this scene, unmistakably, the matter of translation bears the full weight of the ideologies, of the fantasies, of *andalusi* cohabitation that the confessional Hapsburg state would be busily trying to replace and erase.

The story goes like this.

A man accustomed to reading all manner of odds and ends, distraught that a book he'd been reading dropped off midway, the manuscript apparently lost somewhere in the archives of La Mancha – this man, wandering the old Moorish-Jewish marketplace in Toledo, finds a manuscript destined for recycling in the shop of a silk manufacturer, notes that it's written in Arabic characters and finds someone who can read and translate the text. It turns out to be the manuscript of the second part, or second sortie, of *Don Quijote*. This is how the 1620 edition of Thomas Shelton's translation has it. I draw your attention to the date, and I'll come back to it in a second:

> Being one day walking in the exchange of Toledo, a certain boy by chance would have sold divers old quires and scrolls of books to a squire that walked up and down in that place, and I, being addicted to read such scrolls, though I found them torn in the streets, borne away by this my natural inclination, took one of the quires in my hand, and perceived it to be written in Arabical characters, and seeing that, although I knew the letters, yet could I not read the substance, I looked about to view whether I could perceive any Moor turned Spaniard thereabouts, that could read them; nor was it very difficult to find there such an interpreter; for, if I had searched one of another better and more ancient language, that place would easily afford him. In fine, my good fortune presented one to me; to whom telling my desire, and setting the book in his hand, he opened it, and, having read a little therein, began to laugh. I demanded of him why he laughed; and he answered, at that marginal note which the book had. I bade him to expound it to me, and with that took him a little aside; and he, continuing still his laughter, said: 'There is written there, on this margin, these words: "This Dulcinea of Toboso, so many times spoken of in this history, had the best hand for powdering of porks of any woman in all the Mancha."'[9]

This is Cervantes's Castilian:

> Estando yo un día en el Alcaná de Toledo, llegó un muchacho a vender unos cartapacios y papeles viejos a un sedero; y, como yo soy aficionado a leer, aunque sean los papeles rotos de las calles, llevado desta mi natural inclinación, tomé un cartapacio de los que el muchacho vendía, y vile con caracteres que conocí ser arábigos. Y, puesto que, aunque los conocía, no los sabía leer, anduve mirando si parecía por allí algún morisco aljamiado que los leyese; y no fue muy dificultoso hallar intérprete semejante, pues, aunque le buscara de otra mejor y más antigua lengua, le hallara. En fin, la suerte me deparó uno, que, diciéndole mi deseo y poniéndole el libro en las manos, le abrió por medio, y, leyendo un poco en él, se comenzó a reír. Preguntéle yo que de qué se reía, y respondióme que de una cosa que tenía aquel libro escrita en el margen por anotación. Díjele que me la dijese; y él, sin dejar la risa, dijo: 'Está, como he dicho, aquí en el margen escrito esto: "Esta Dulcinea del Toboso, tantas veces en esta historia referida, dicen que tuvo la mejor mano para salar puercos que otra mujer de toda la Mancha"'.[10]

I am hardly the first person to draw attention to this moment, which provides critics like Antonio Medina Molera with evidence that a 'mudejarismo cervantino' animates the novel – liberal and capacious in its disordered spirit, modern, an insurgent attack upon 'el ideal ascético cristiano viejo'[11] – and others like María Rosa Menocal with a symptomatic shorthand for describing the residual traces of Spanish *convivencia*, the outlines of its shape – a

Christian, Muslim and Jewish cohabitation, uneasily managed to be sure, but successful, in her view, over centuries – now, in 1605, under the most severe, Inquisitorial pressure, resulting in the expulsion of the moriscos from Spain some five years after the publication of this scene.[12] That the give-away line here – the line that identifies the manuscript for our narrator – should be the paratextual comment that 'Dulcinea had the best hand at salting pork of any maid in La Mancha' – tells us a number of things in this context. It is of course not accidental that it is pork that's being symptomatically produced here, as it is the marker, the dietary shibboleth, separating the three communities in a ritual of dietary exclusion that would make sharing food anything but a communal experience and would stamp any *shared* lexicon with division, dissent and dissimulation – 'pork' in one tongue would count, among its principal predicates, 'edible', and in other languages, 'not edible'. That a scene coding the transmission of cultural materials among the peoples of the book should turn on the recognition of the external marker of their differences, or one of them – the pig – need not mean that Cervantes is seeking to undercut the sort of transactional copresence of the three religions in this section. This might be easily understood as a dose of regional humour, indicating, as Eric Graf suggests, that

> The parodic and comedic tone of such episodes betrays a desire for social engineering; they are Cervantes's abstract ways of unveiling Spanish history as an absurd series of ethnic and/or cultural dialectics: Basque/Castilian, Moor/Spaniard, Leonese/Carolingian. In the end, Cervantes indicates that to be able to contextualize and to laugh at the tortuous complexity of Spanish history, so as not to become its pathetic protagonist, requires that one actively outmanoeuvres and defeats the fraudulent ideology of the ethnocentric Spanish national identity and replaces it with the hybridized truth of said history – that is, with more historically accurate, less ideal, identities. The identity displacements offered by Cervantes's vision open the way for the reader to recognize the incredulous and resistant perspective of the native Morisco, who is presently experiencing the ill-effects of Spanish nationalism.[13]

Finally, that what Dulcinea is so good at is the preserving of this pork suggests, with Cervantes's marvellous and typical humour, something about the preservation of cultural tropes or of historical residue: in the world of Cervantes's history, historiography too is a sort of salting away, for later consumption, of markers of difference rather than community alone.

Every detail of this famous scene, and of the ones directly preceding it (in which, as Graf suggests, the narrator's comment that Don Quixote and the Biscayan seem poised to slice each other up as you would cut a pomegranate, 'una granada', is also the gastronomic correlative of the violent exclusion of the Arabs from Spain, of their expulsion, in 1492, from Granada) – every detail of this famous scene is determined and overdetermined by cultural materials of which it is a symptom and a translation. The very accidental nature of the scene, then, is revealed to be ironic, or perhaps compensatory, or even, on a more Straussian note, defensive: nothing is accidental about the scene, or put differently, what appear to be accidental elements of the scene reveal themselves to be necessary and determined, determined for instance by a 'nationalist' cultural material in which 'pork' is never only pork, but also always a marker of ethnic and religious distinction; a pomegranate always also the symbol of the Kingdom of Granada; a silk merchant no doubt ancestrally linking the commodity 'silk' to the exotic circuits of Mediterranean trade. Even the location of the market, in Toledo's Alcaná district, reveals at the level of the name its peregrine genealogy and function. 'Alcaná' Covarrubias tells his readers, some six years after Cervantes publishes the first part of *Don Quixote*,

> es vna calle en Toledo muy conocida, toda ella de tiendas de merceria: nombre derechamente Hebreo del verbo. . . . Chana, que entre otras sinificaciones es vna *emere*, comprar, y cõ el articulo Arabigo al-Kana, y Cananeo es lo mesmo que mercader, que compra y vende. . . . El padre Guadix dize, que *Alcaná* es Arabigo de *alquina*, que vale ganancia. Bien puede ser, pero de la raiz Hebrea ya dicha. Esta calle antiguamente tenian poblada los Iudios tratantes: y en tiempo del Rey don Pedro, sus hermanos d[on] Fadrique, y don Enrique, queriendo encastillarse en la ciudad de Toledo, les resistieron la entrada por la puente de Sanmartin muchos caualleros: pero haziendo la desecha dieron la buelta y vinieron a entrar por la puente de Alcantara, y hizieron gran matança en los Iudios, que passaron de mil personas, y les robaron las tiendas que tenian de merceria en el Alcaná.

> [Alcaná is a well-known street in Toledo, lined with shops. The name comes directly from the Hebrew verb *chana,* one of whose meanings is *emere,* to buy. With the prefixed Arabic article it becomes al-Kana; Cananite is the same as 'merchant, one who muys and sells.' . . . Father Guadix says that *Alcaná* is an Arabic Word, from *al-quina,* which means 'profit.' It could well be, but it derives in any case from the aforesaid Hebrew root. This street was peopled in past times by Jewish merchants. In the time of king Don Pedro, his brothers don Fadrique and don Enrique, wishing to take the city of Toledo, were resisted by many knights at the bridge of San Martin. Taking a different route, however, don Fadrique and don Enrique went round and entered through the bridge of Alcantara, and slaughtered a great Lumber of the Jews, more than one thousand of them, and robbed their shops on the Alcaná.]

The Christian narrator who bumps into the manuscript, touches upon it as it were contingently, should appear to us contemporary readers but also to Cervantes's contemporaries to be a comic allegorization of the circumstances of everyday Spanish history in 1605, when it would be impossible *not* to encounter, among the detritus of Spanish society as in the lexicon of Castilian, the relics of the Muslim and Jewish past and of the Hebrew and Arabic languages it was trying so hard to repress at other, institutional levels. Under this description, then, Cervantes's theory of translation appears to us as particularly modern precisely because it is also an exercise, as it were, in the psychoanalysis of culture – an exercise in the exposure or translation of the determinations that underlie a circumstance or an accident of the text, or of a social symptom.[14] (What appears accidental, bumping into the presence of Islam or Judaism, Arabic and Hebrew, in a marketplace in Toledo, turns out to be determined: everywhere and necessarily, Islam, Judaism and Christianity clamorously touch upon each other in 1605, even or especially where this peregrine touch is made to seem the least plausible, the least necessary, the most accidental of circumstances.) But this would of course mean that Cervantes, like Covarrubias, has sacrificed to this culturally deterministic model of translation, however much it may appear to augur a psychoanalytic modernism at odds with other forms of determinism, the very peregrine form of translational modernity that Rojas and Nebrija seem to me to have discovered and disclosed a hundred years earlier.

Or perhaps not. For another way of approaching this matter would be to remind ourselves that Shelton's lines from the 1620 translation are not the first effort made to translate Cervantes's text into English, though they are the ones that have come down to English speakers, picked up and communicated in editions and adaptations for centuries on. The first edition of Shelton's translation, famously published in 1612 and working from the Brussels edition of *Don Quijote*, of 1607, had a number of small (and a few gross) errors, and the 1620 second edition of Shelton's translation introduced quite a few emendations in the original translation. Edwin Knowles, who first studied the two editions comparatively, noted that 'the superficial and careless quality of the job as a whole is definitely proved by the many mistakes common to both editions, both in the English per se and in the English as a translation'.[15] For this reason, Knowles concludes that 'the correcting [in the 1620 edition] was almost certainly not done by Shelton, for none of his mannerisms occur in the variant forms, and in general the new words are more modern English' (262).[16] The changes between the 1612 and the 1620 editions are in some cases primarily cosmetic and some are outright wrong, but others, particularly the changes to the first chapters of Shelton's 1612 edition, are more substantial, and at times they correct egregious errors.

At this juncture, then, in the Alcaná of Toledo, just at the point in Cervantes's own text where translation, the translation from Arabic script into Spanish, is made to bear the symptomatic and overdetermined weight that I have just been describing, just here where a translator is sought and produced, Cervantes's translator Shelton originally made quite a different translation from the one that the 1620 edition records. Cervantes's text, describing the moment when his narrator turns to look for someone who will translate the Arabic characters before him, reads in Castilian 'anduve mirando si parecía por allí algún morisco aljamiado que los leyese; y no fue muy dificultoso hallar intérprete semejante, pues, aunque le buscara de otra mejor y más antigua lengua, le hallara'.[17] The 1620 version of this phrase is 'I looked about to view whether I could perceive thereabouts, any Moore turned Spaniard, that could read them; nor was it very difficult to find there such an interpreter; for, if I had searched one of another better and more ancient language, that place would easily afford him' (63). But in Shelton's first translation, in 1612, 'any Moore turned Spaniard' read as 'any more translated Spaniard, thereabouts that could read them' (65), with the typesetter conveniently, driven by a typological logic that makes every sort of sense, having left the word 'more', 'Moor', shorn of one of the two letters 'o' it sports in 1620, and headed off by a lower-case 'm' rather than the upper case it garners in the corrected edition. A 'more translated Spaniard', in short, a Spaniard 'more translated' than the narrator, a Spaniard who has entered more deeply into the field of translation, who has travelled to more languages, across more borders, a more peregrine term, a 'more translated Spaniard'.

One sees why the correction in the 1620 edition is called for: this is a *lectio facilior* error, almost impossible to spot, pertaining to the phonic register of the word as well as to the visual one. And more: a 'more translated Spaniard' *makes more sense* or *at least as much sense*, and in certain senses it makes *better sense* than the more accurate 1620 emendation, and perhaps even than Cervantes's original Castilian. A 'more translated Spaniard' makes more sense not just because the comparative particle 'more' makes sense as a way of characterizing any other Spaniard who knew more Arabic than the narrator, hence a 'more translated' Spaniard, someone possessed of greater capacity to translate or someone who has himself been translated to more countries and tongues than Cervantes's narrator – and not only because it introduces the proper name, as it were, of the episode's action: it is *translation* that is the tenor of the 'Moor turned Spaniard', of the tropic 'turning' or conversion staged in the 1620 translation. The erroneous whiff of Shelton's 'more' is better than Cervantes's Castilian, or at least as good, precisely because we do not know whether it *is* a mistake, 'more' and 'Moor' being in one respect, phonically at any rate and in the loose typography of the time also visually, in at least this, the seemingly *material* sense, being at once the same and functionally and semantically entirely different. Shelton's 'more' is at least as good as Cervantes's original, precisely because its undecidable, seemingly *material* obscurity, reiterated and repeated across the history of its translations, preserved as it were in linguistic salt by the hand of subsequent translators operating like Dulcinea upon the contested consumable that is

Cervantes's language, reintroduces spectacularly the element of contingency, of aleatory touch, we found in Nebrija and in Rojas.

For this translation of the 'Moor' into a mere 'more' is an extraordinary error to make, but it is not clear *whose* error it is, Shelton's or the typesetter's, and it is not the last time that a translator, even an excellent one, will make a mistake at this point precisely. Tobias Smollett, for example, translates Cervantes's 'morisco aljamiado', Shelton's 'more translated Spaniard' or 'Moor turned Spaniard', like this: 'I was led by this my natural curiosity, to turn over some of the leaves; I found them written in Arabick, which not being able to read, though I knew the characters, I looked about for some Portugeze Moor, who should understand it' (Cervantes 1755, 45).[18] Not a 'more translated Spaniard', not a 'Moor turned Spaniard', but a 'Portuguese Moor' – an astonishing way to render Cervantes's 'morisco aljamiado'. And yet Shelton, and his typesetter, and Smollett after them had at their disposal at least one source that would have given them the sense of the word 'aljamiado' – Perceval's and Minsheu's *A Dictionarie in Spanish and English*, which gives for 'Aljama or Alçama' the definition 'an assembly of Jewes, or their synagogue' (Perceval), for 'Aljamia', 'the Moores call the Spanish toong Aljamia' (Minsheu) and 'Aljamiado, made into the Spanish tongue' (Minsheu) (all in Perceval and Minsheu).[19] Cervantes's 'aljamiado' is indeed an unusual word, a word in which, on the evidence of Minsheu's and Perceval's dictionary, the three cultures of the book crossed paths, as they do on the Alcaná of Toledo. It is a word that names at the same time 'the Spanish tongue', the 'assembly of Jewes, or their synagogue', and the *aljama* as Cervantes and Covarrubias would have thought it: as, in the words of Covarrubias's *Tesoro,* 'ayuntamiento y concejo', 'a town council or congregation', the administrative unit into which the *morisco* populations were organized in the course of the sixteenth century in Spain.

Covarrubias's definition of the term recalls that the philologist Diego de Urrea traced the word's etymology to 'Geamiun, del verbo *gemea,* que vale ajuntar, y puede ser Hebreo de *alliam,* . . . *iam,* vale mar, y congregacion de aguas: y metaforicamente congregacion de gentes, de donde se pudo dezir aljamia' ['Geamiun, from the Arabic verb *gemea* or *jemayaa,* which means "to gather together," and which may in turn derive from the Hebrew *alliam, iam,* which means "sea," and gathering of waters, and metaphorically the gathering of peoples']. And Covarrubias concludes revealing, by means of a different etymology, what we, and Cervantes, and in their symptomatic errors many years later Cervantes's translators as well, realize, record, repeat: that *aljamia* and *aljamiado* are not just discursive terms in translation, but they are also and inseparably names for the resistant materiality *of* translating terms, that is, discursive as well as metadiscursive operators. Covarrubias concludes his definition of *aljama* recollecting that for Juan López de Velasco, 'aljama' comes from '*al*, y *jamaha* lenguaje escuro en Hebreo', from '*al* and *Jamaha*, Hebrew for "obscure language".' Cervantes's novel captures narratively and turns to extraordinary advantage Nebrija's peregrine linguistic 'obscurity'. *Don Quixote* – and, in complexly irreconcilable ways, the novel's translations as well – wanders, peregrine, spreading narrative functions and their associated evidentiary paradigms and protocols for veridification across narrative voices and languages in translation among each other. Think of the novel's Castilian narrators; of Cide Hamete Benengeli, the *morisco aljamiado* who translates the lost and recovered manuscript; of the Hebrew language whose greater 'antiquity and perfection' still haunts the Alcaná in Toledo and despite or because of its absence can be read on every page of *Don Quixote* – this systematic confusion of languages and levels of expression capitalizes upon and generates the peregrine wandering with which this first novel of modernity recaptures and rethinks the drama of contingent translation radically set forth in Rojas's *La Celestina* at the dawn of the print age. In its translators' overdetermined, excessively motivated errors, in the symptomatic errors we detect at the moment when Cervantes's true subject matter emerges, when the peregrine obscurity of translation is itself *named,* we read, accurately to the symptomatic sense of Cervantes's work if also entirely falsely, entirely inaccurately, the *political* shape into which translational modernity can gather its late subjects.

Chapter 3

Nationum origo

What needeth a Dictionarie? Naie, if I offer service but to them that need it, with what face seek I a place with your excellent Ladiship (my most-most honored, because best-best adorned Madame) who by conceited industrie; or industrious conceite, in Italian as in French, in French as in Spanish, in all as in English, understand what you reade, write as you reade, and speake as you write; yet rather charge your minde with matter, then your memorie with words? And if this présent presènt so small profit, I must confesse it brings much lesse delight: for, what pleasure in a plot of simples, *O non viste, o mal note, o mal gradate,* Or not seene, or ill knowne, or ill accepted? (John Florio, *A Worlde of Wordes* (1598))

The Manifesto, says *The Manifesto* in German, will be published in English, French, German, Italian, Flemish and Danish. Ghosts also speak different languages, national languages, like the money from which they are, as we shall see, inseparable. As circulating currency, money bears local and political character, it 'uses different national languages and wears different national uniforms'. (Jacques Derrida, *Specters of Marx* (1993–1994))[1]

Globalization has taken our tongues from us – local, autochthonous, idiomatic, ancestral tongues. Its clamorous internationalism has hung critics on a mute peg, with no common voice or general vocabulary on which to string alternative international or transnational forms of work, thought and organization. We might expect – and most commonly do find – that this disarmed, heteroglot opposition takes shelter in various weak utopianisms (understanding the term 'weak' as it were *strongly*: in line with emergent forms of non- or anti-ideological 'weak thought'), weakly regulative images generally and understandably drawn from increasingly abstract domains (e.g., from reinvigorated notions of the 'human' and of 'humanism'). Consider these words from Michael Hardt's and Antonio Negri's *Empire*, in which not the 'human' but an active and complex ethic of circumstantial *translation* serves this sheltering, utopian function.

> There is no common language of struggles that could 'translate' the particular language of each into a cosmopolitan language. Struggles in other parts of the world and even our own struggles seem to be written in an incomprehensible foreign language. This too points toward an important political task: to construct a new common language that facilitates communication, as the languages of anti-imperialism and proletarian internationalism did for the struggles of a previous era. Perhaps this needs to be a new type of communication that functions not on the basis of resemblances but on the basis of differences: a communication of singularities.[2]

Not a little *pathos* inflects these lines, in which Negri and Hardt seek to recast the grammar of organic, critical intellectual discourse in the wake of the collapse of state socialism. Their acknowledgement that the global vocabularies of more-or-less orthodox, Internationalist Marxisms disastrously ignored every struggle's particularities quickly becomes a way of reflecting upon the increasing fragmentation of current critical idioms. For Negri and Hardt, the peculiarity of one or another circumstance requires – the injunction is distinctly an ethico-political one – an act of translation into a 'new common language', imagined here as a 'communication of singularities' in both senses furnished by the genitive: communication between radically particular, circumstantial 'struggles' and the communication of that particularity across national, linguistic, political and other frontiers.

Set aside the claims of novelty (the 'new common language', the 'new type of communication' that Negri and Hardt describe). A part of the appeal of Negri's and Hardt's trilogy, opened by *Empire*, surely comes from the odd *familiarity* of its prescriptions. Thus, the concept that *Empire* seeks to furnish for weak utopian 'translation', a vehicle for the 'communication of singularities', has the familiar shape of the general equivalent or index commodity value, though *Empire* shifts the equivalent's indexing function from the general economic domain to the critico-descriptive one.[3] So also the figure of the critic, whose new, singular 'translations' retain the roughly Gramscian shape of reasoned *sabotage* that Negri's early writing provocatively described. Even the notion of oppositional internationalism itself, one might argue, arises alongside the earliest understandings of the nation-form, as Europe reached in the course of the sixteenth century for a cultural, economic and political modernity whose defining description would not arrive until much later.

Say then that we seek useful, consequential discursive alternatives to globalization – a 'tongue', a cosmopolitan epistemology, a new international.

We ask in this context what might be the *genealogy* of the recent turn to 'translation', of its 'new' characterization as a communication of singularities, of its deployment as a weak utopian concept on which a critique of economic and cultural globalization can be mounted. We understand these questions to be prefatory but necessary to considering the ethico-political demand made for contemporary intellectuals in works like *Empire*, or by critics like Edward Said, Homi Bhabha and others. Even posing them requires of us a peculiar set of historical translations, however, among the contemporary moment, the defining and familiar nineteenth-century historiographic devices that continue to inform our postmodern vocabularies and the early modern historical moment when technological, demographic and other shifts bring the twin knots of incipient nationalization and *linguistic* translation to the fore and into explicit contact with each other.[4]

Let's open this genealogical avenue by observing that Ernest Renan's own, famous question of 1882, 'Qu'est-ce qu'une nation?' is already determined and overdetermined by a fantastical voluntarism built about and against an earlier understanding of linguistic identity that is troublingly fluid, or fractious, or heteroglot – in a word, an early modern form of collective and individual identity that cannot be *translated* into national or proto-national collectivities. But as he moves famously towards his definition of the nation as 'a soul, a spiritual principle', Renan appears untroubled. He considers and sets aside the concept's traditional vehicles: race, 'ownership in common of a rich legacy of memories', religion, common interests and geography.[5] Only when he takes up 'le langage' will Renan's most searching claim clearly emerge: 'There is in man something superior to language: and that is the will' [Il y a dans l'homme quelque chose de supérieur à la langue: c'est la volonté].[6] *La volonté*. For Renan, the notion braids together in time and act the juridical and the psycho-social domains, tidily gathered in this grammatical triplet: 'Current consent, a desire to live together, and the will to value the undivided heritage that one has received' [le consentement actuel, le désir de vivre ensemble, la volonté de continuer à faire valoir l'héritage qu'on a reçu indivis]. Note the distinctly pre-Nietzschean priority granted to the will over historical accidents, as well as the almost Scholastic certainty *Qu'est-ce qu'une nation?* expresses that the faculty can be cleanly separated from contiguous faculties and concepts (memory, desire, interest). Renan's earlier remarks 'Des services rendus aux sciences historiques par la philologie' (1878) make the point again, starkly: 'The nation is for us something absolutely separate from language' [chose absolument séparée de la langue]. 'There is something that we place above language and above race', Renan continues, 'and that is respect for man, understood as a moral being', a 'being' whose moral autonomy is manifested characteristically, as in Kant and in the ethico-political tradition that flows from the second Critique, as a 'will to continue living together' [volonté de continuer à vivre ensemble].[7]

For Renan, as for his contemporary Jakob Burckhardt, the highest *political* example of the superceding of linguistic particularism is Switzerland; the highest historical examples of the autonomous acts of will that constitute the decision 'to continue to live together' are to be found among the 'great men of the Renaissance, who were neither French, nor Italian, nor German. They had rediscovered, by means of their traffic with antiquity, the secret of the human mind's true education' [Ils avaient retrouvé, par leur commerce avec l'antiquité, le secret de l'éducation véritable de l'esprit humain].[8] Both the location and the period are unsurprising choices. We know that England, Spain and Italy saw a remarkable burst of published translations from the classical languages by the last quarter of the sixteenth century, but the emergence of what can fairly be called a *European* lexical culture dates perhaps to the appearance of Nebrija's influential 1499 *Gramática*, or to the publication in 1502 of Ambrosius Calepinus's *Cornucopiæ* (later reedited and better known as the *Dictionarium* or as the *Calepino*).[9] By 'lexical culture' I mean the loose subgroup of practices and ideologies that surround and concern the writing; copying; printing and transmission of lexicons; grammars; hardword books and dictionaries, both monolingual and multilingual, in the new print culture of the European elite.[10] What better evidence that language is imagined to serve the will than that provided by these various texts, intended as linguistic instruments for teaching oneself, or others, different languages? And I intend the stress on 'Europe': *pari passu* with recognizable *local* or even (proto-)*national* forms of identification (as speakers of this or that distinct and historically discrete language, under autochthonous political and economic regimes), the Renaissance's travelling books and manuscripts about words, *calepinos*, *trésors*, *florilegia*, *gramáticas*, primers on translation and assorted other metalinguistic texts furnish spectacularly deterritorialized, polyglot identities, gathered in increasingly broad, increasingly abstract ways.[11] This for instance is from Covarrubias's definition of *lengua*, 'tongue'. Remark the suturing work that the term 'human', *humano*, performs, as well as the characteristic stress on the *pedagogical* scene:

> La noticia de muchas lenguas se puede tener por gran felicidad en la tierra, pues con ellas comunica el hombre diversas naciones, y suele ser de mucho fruto en casos de necessidad, refrenando el furor del enemigo, que hablandole en su propia lengua se reporta y concibe una cierta afinidad de parentesco que le obliga a ser humano y clemente. . . . Yo tambien me contentaria con que los professores de qualquiera facultad supiessen y aprendiessen juntamente con la lengua Latina la lengua Griega; pues para toda diciplina seria de grandissima importancia.

[Knowledge of many tongues can be a matter of great happiness on earth, for with them man can communicate with diverse nations, which can be of great profit in case of need, as it dampens the fury of the enemy, for, speaking to him in his own tongue, he moderates himself and conceives a certain familial affinity that obliges him to be human and merciful. . . . And I too would be satisfied if teachers of any subject knew and learned the Greek language alongside Latin, for this would be of great importance for all disciplines.][12]

For the historiography of the late Enlightenment, then, the humanistic *internationalism* one glimpses here is both an effect and the primary source of early modern lexical culture. The knotted, fiercely overdetermined concept takes shape in association with the loose origins of modern disciplinarity, in hand with the work of (linguistic, cultural and historical) translation, inseparably from post-Tridentine philosophico-religious debates concerning the nature and attributes of the *will*, and braided with an ethico-organic 'conception of familial affinity' among 'humans' from which flow distinctly *political* forms of identity, association and obligation. Recall, too, in this sketch of the discursive *thicket* embrambling lexical culture with proto-national identification in early modern Europe, and in its defining historiographies, the double work that Renan's term 'commerce' carries out. The emergence of proto-national formations coincides not just with the rise of a speculative class of 'grands hommes' belonging properly to no particular nation ('ils n'étaient ni français, ni italiens, ni allemands', writes Renan), but also with the consolidation of a *commercial*, merchant class equipped (financially, technically, culturally) to negotiate the diverse requirements of different trading circumstances. More forcefully, the circulations of lexical culture and the earliest construction of an international commercial regime (inter-European, pan-Mediterranean or trans-Atlantic) cannot be separated from each other. Internationalist, lexical humanism arises with, conditions and enables (is conditioned and enabled by) commercial flows based in and profiting from increasingly differentiated commodity and labour markets – hence the peculiar ambivalence of all *recent* appeals to a 'humanist' alternative to the encroachment of globalization under information capitalism.[13]

Or put it like this. After Renan, Burckhardt and Marx, after the aesthetico-political concepts of the 'nation' and the 'civilization of the Renaissance' assume their well-known organizing function in the historical epistemologies of the mid-nineteenth century, as the notion that a 'new mercantilism' characterizing European trade between 1570 and 1620 comes to form the basis of 'modern', labour-based economics, we are free to derive from texts like Covarrubias's the determining image of a network of 'grands hommes' and great educators linked in a reciprocal commerce with antiquity when not with each other, a baggy network of scholars, merchants and courtiers trading texts, commodities and ideas across and against the grain of religious, linguistic and proto-national differences. Practically as well as conceptually this trading, translating or 'communicating' figure (it can be many-headed: think of Pico, Erasmus, Covarrubias, Marguerite de Navarre, More and others) represents the shadow form of a conciliar orthodoxy with equally internationalist reach and desires: indeed, the institutional history of the counter-Reformation Church after Trent cannot be understood except in light of the uncomfortable propinquity between conciliar ecumenicism and humanist internationalism.

Humanist internationalism preserves as a core and determining value the labour of deliberate and informed choice: the archaic function of the will, in its articulation with language and education, is the *minimum* that differentiates it from conciliar, corporatist internationalism, both in early modernity and in the mediatized postmodernity we inhabit. Think again of the heroic shape that the ethico-political demand takes in Negri's and Hardt's *Empire*. For them, as for the great nineteenth-century historiographies that they are seeking to renew, the modern subject's movement beyond a local, native language, beyond a received *legs de souvenirs* or a limiting autochthony is achieved just as the genuine 'spirit of a nation' must be for Renan: as a communitarian form of identification deliberately and repeatedly elected. As the stress in Renan's work on the Renaissance's 'grands hommes' suggests, the articulation of pedagogy, will and translation at the heart of humanist internationalism considerably precedes the formation of modern 'nations' that his work helped to diagnose. In certain respects, that earlier articulation presents a much more fluid shape than when Renan is writing, and *a fortiori* more recent critics, from Braidotti and Deleuze to Hardt and Negri – for different reasons (print culture is still not consolidated, ideologically or technically; easier communication has not yet meant a standardized pedagogy or a conventional 'commerce' with antiquity or with religious protocol; the definition of the will's freedom or servitude in the pedagogical, doctrinal and philosophical domains is sharply and explicitly divided). Indeed, our contemporary construction of humanist internationalism obscures – may in fact arise in order to displace or evade – a characteristic troubling of the relation between 'will' and 'language' to be found at work in the lexical culture of early modern Europe. So let me risk appearing to advocate a new return to the 'grands hommes de la Renaissance'. In the hesitant *translations*, in the linguistic troubles we encounter in the work of Covarrubias, Ascham, Minsheu, Verstegan – to say nothing of Machiavelli, Hobbes or Shakespeare – we come across the rough concept for a 'common language' for communicating singularities. The cost we pay for learning this language will be high, for in the lexical culture of early modern Europe the 'will' is invested elsewhere than in individuals: in accidents, contingencies, 'cases' both linguistic and historical.

The 'communication of singularities' on which early modern lexical culture turns blocks the articulation of individualism, the close cousin (to stay within Covarrubias's familial metaphor) of humanist internationalism, with will that comes to support the ethico-political project of the Enlightenment.

Here are two useful ways of approaching the matter. The first comes from the series of definitions that Covarrubias provides for the term 'translation' in his *Tesoro de la lengua castellana*. Glossing the hoary etymology that links 'traducción' and 'translation' to the Latin *trans* and *ducere*, to carry over or across, the Spanish lexicographer and seeming translator writes: 'lleuar de vn lugar a otro alguna cosa, o encaminarla . . . el boluer la sentencia de vna lengua en otra, como traduzir de Italiano, o de Francés algún libro en Castellano' ['To take something from one place to another, or to set it on a path . . . to change the phrase from one language into another, as when one translates a book from Italian, or French, into Castilian'].[14] The geographical vehicle is traditional and unsurprising: linguistic translation – 'traducción' – resembles for Covarrubias merely carrying or returning, 'llevar' or 'bolver alguna cosa' (a national language or idiom, say), from one spot to another. That this 'alguna cosa' remains the same from one language to another simply reflects a certain underlying sameness that links the *speakers* of these different languages as well – very much, in other words, as one's capacity to speak another language suggests to an enemy 'a certain familial affinity that obliges him to be human'. But linguistic translation *also* resembles, as the definition's odd, pseudo-appositive shape suggests, just setting something (an idiom, language, 'cosa') on the road, *en* and *caminar* – with no sense that one follows that road oneself or concerns oneself to ensure that 'alguna cosa' safely reaches the end of the road or has any stake in how, after all, 'alguna cosa' (a national language, again) might 'move' along this or any other road. One might make the point more forcefully by stressing the disjunctive aspect of Covarrubias's definition: translation is *either* a way for a subject to carry a particular, identifiable thing from one location in which it has one name to another in which it has a different one *or* it is the gesture of releasing a thing from its name, placing it as it were underway, upon the road, for any one to take. The stakes of this rather recondite grammatical point become clearer if we recall the explicitly *political* function of the conjunction 'o' in the title of Covarrubias's dictionary: *Tesoro de la lengua castellana, o española*. The project of national centralization initiated in Spain under the Hapsburgs, as well as the history of local and regional resistance to that project, might be said to hang on the status of this slight 'o', disagreements over different efforts to make 'lo castellano' synonymous with rather than alternative to 'lo español' showing no signs of abating to this day.

Or we might simply read on in the *Tesoro*'s definition of translation, where it becomes increasingly clear that Covarrubias isn't quite sure which road a *translation* actually 'takes', or who or what, for that matter, is taking that road:

> *TRADVCION*: Si esto no se haze con primor y prudencia, sabiendo igualmente las dos lenguas, y trasladando en algunas partes, no conforme a la letra, pero según el sentido sería lo que dixo vn hombre sabio y crítico, que aquello era verter, tomandolo en sinificación de derramar y echar a perder. Esto aduirtió bien Horacio en su *Arte poética* diziendo, 'Nec verbum verbo curabis reddere fidus Interpres'.[15]

> [*TRANSLATION*: If it is not carried out with care and prudence, knowing both languages equally, and translating in some places, not as the letter demands, but according to the sense, it would be what a wise and acute man once said, that this was to spill, meaning by this to waste or spoil, or to spill something. Horace warned of this in his *Ars poetica* when he wrote: 'Nec verbum verbo curabis reddere fidus Interpres'. [As a true translator you will take care not to translate word for word.]]

These are in most ways perfectly anodyne, even hackneyed injunctions, although the crossing of Pauline hermeneutics with these lines attributed to Horace is less than stable. Indeed, Covarrubias's image is in some respects quite opaque: just what is it that is 'spilled' or 'wasted' or 'spoiled' when one translates 'as the letter demands', *conforme a la letra*? Matters get trickier as one reflects more closely on the means that Covarrubias suggests for avoiding this wasteful 'spillage' – that one must know both languages equally, proceed with prudence and care and at moments translate 'according to the sense'. Here the 'faith' or 'faithfulness' of the translator or interpreter who is the custodian of the 'sense' or spirit as well as the letter of the text depends not only on his knowing both languages equally but also on his enjoying two distinct affective dispositions (*primor* and *prudencia*) that the *Tesoro* aligns elsewhere with two quite different class positions: 'primor', which the *Tesoro* uses (under *primo*) to describe artisans who do work expertly, is again not only a synonym but also a contrastive term to 'prudencia', a term associated with 'wise and acute or critical' hierophants, and which will notoriously come to characterize no less a figure than Philip II (remembered to this day as 'el rey prudente'). Recall for instance how the distinction between craft and art in treatments of Velázquez's work supports descriptions, ranging from the psychological to the materialist, of the painter's ambitions at court (his painting 'Las hilanderas', for example, has appeared to many an allegory of the relation between the material *craft* of tapestry-making, and the higher *art* of dramatic representation that true painting strives to capture): in the *Tesoro*, we might conclude, the translator, both craftsman and 'prudent' man, also works both as 'lengua', Covarrubias's term for a primarily *spoken*, mechanical 'intervention' ('lengua, el intérprete que declara una lengua con otra, inter-viniendo entre dos de diferentes lenguas') and as the 'intérprete', who works characteristically in writing, with the 'alusiones y términos metafóricos' of diverse languages (Covarrubias's example of bad 'interpretación' is a droll mistranslation from the Spanish of *La Celestina* into over-literal Italian). But Covarrubias's brief descriptions of the work of translation cannot proceed with the schematic hygiene one would expect, given all that seems to hang upon the term. 'Care and prudence', we understand, are needed not only in carrying over the sense of a phrase, whether 'according to the letter' or fol-lowing the sense of the sentence, but also in distinguishing those moments when one needs to vary from conformity to the letter in the first place. We are not free, in short, to align plain, workaday translation 'conforme a la letra' with an inflexible commitment to the letter or the old Law of the text, and the looser, 'prudential' translation 'según el sentido' with a new, Pauline atten-tion to its Spirit. Merely knowing two languages is not enough; to achieve the 'intérprete's' prudential understanding of the 'sense' of a text, and in order to distinguish when its translation is to be carried out 'conforme a la letra' or 'según el sentido', is a matter of education, of faith and of the will.

Now consider how Roger Ascham's very different *The Schole-Master* (1570) treats the articulation of translation and education in the production of what we are calling lexical culture. Ascham's concern in *The Schole-Master* is how best to teach 'children, to understand, write, and speake, the Latin tong, but specially purposed for the private bringing up of youth in Ientlemen and Noble mens houses'.[16] *The Schole-Master*'s argument against wholesale 'beating' has been a staple of progressive educational theory, in particular these lines, that bear on the formation of the child's will: 'Beate a child, if he daunce not well, & cherish him, though he learne not well, ye shall have him unwilling to go to daunce, & glad to go to his booke. . . . And thus, will in children, wisely wrought withal, may easely be wonne to be very well willing to learne. And witte in children, by nature, namely memory, the onely key and keeper of all lerning, is rediest to receive, and surest to keepe, any maner of thing, that is learned when we were yong' (10v-11r). Ascham further warns that the school-master must be gentle in order 'wisely' to work the young scholar's will towards learning and offers as the practical means and best example of this gentle work what he refers to, classically, as double translation. This is how Ascham puts it:

> Translate [some portion of Tullie] you yourself, into plaine naturall Englishe, and then geve it him to translate into Latin againe: allowing him good space and time to do it, both with diligent heede, & good visement. Here his witte shall be new set on worke: his iudgement, for right choice, trewlie tried: his memorie, for sure retaining, better exercised, than by learning any thing without the booke:

and here, how much he hath profited, shall plainlie appeare. When he bringeth it translated unto you, bring forth the place of Tullie: lay them together: compare the one with the other: commend his good choice, & right placing of wordes: shew his faultes iently, but blame them not over sharply: for, of such missings, ientlie admonished of, procedeth glad & good heed taking: of good heed taking, springeth chiefly knowledge. (31v-32r)

Ascham's strategy is a particularly humane one (note the palliative expressions: 'good space and time', 'commend his good choice, & right placing', show faults 'iently', do not blame 'sharply', admonish again 'iently'), though it turns on a rather problematical pivot: the supposition that the schoolmaster's first translation – into 'plaine naturall English' – will as it were vanish into Tully's text on being translated (back) into Latin. The schoolmaster's 'comparison', 'commending', 'showing' and so on depend upon his furnishing a 'plaine naturall English' version of the original from which the student can fairly derive an approximate retranslation, an ideal circuit closely reminiscent of the closed geographies we first found in Covarrubias ('lleuar de vn lugar a otro alguna cosa, o encaminarla' ['to take something from one place to another']). As to the possibility that the school-master may have lost his way, or that his translation may merely have set the Latin text as it were under way, *en camino*, or that he may have sacrificed sense or 'right placing' of words in his desire to produce 'plaine naturall English': in brief, as to the possibility that the *first* translation should also be the subject of 'comparison' with the original (and with the student's *second* translation), that the humane authority of the pedagogue, *lengua* or *intérprete* hangs in the balance here as well, Ascham's work is entirely silent.

It would be anachronistic, not to say absurd, to expect a pedagogy of the oppressed from Ascham, however 'progressive' or modern his tone may appear to us. My point is a different one. Note the genuinely remarkable lines with which Ascham closes his description of the pedagogy of double translation: 'Of such missings, ientlie admonished of, procedeth glad & good heed taking: of good heed taking, springeth chiefly knowledge'. Here Ascham proceeds with great subtlety, combining registers that stress, on the one hand, the school-master's disciplinary and monitory role (he 'compares', he 'admonishes'), while, on the other, they acknowledge that the pupil's knowledge itself 'springs' from other, mediating and consequent habits that the school-master may have encouraged but does not directly control. Just as the school-master's 'plaine naturall English' vanishes in the circuit of double translation, so too does Ascham's pedagogy itself seem to fade from an active, monitory role, becoming merely the occasion for the springing-forth of the pupil's knowledge. One is inclined to approve this almost Rousseauian account – with the sharp reservation that this double vanishing, of the translation and the translator, lesson and teacher, into the apparent knowledge and the spontaneous will of the pupil finally shelters the school-master (and *The Schole-Master*) from 'comparison', from 'blame', from admonishment and from judgements, however gentle, concerning his and the work's 'faultes' and 'missings'. In the humane scene in which the pupil's knowledge and will are fashioned, the technique of double translation vanishingly establishes and then protectively erases from view the school's mastery and its invisible persistence *as the will and very language* of the pupil.

My purpose is not to make Ascham and Covarrubias precursors of Althusser on ideological apparatuses (a grotesque but appealing thought) but to suggest the nature of the overdeterminations that the concept of translation suffers in early modern articulations of identity. Covarrubias and Ascham embed in their different, complementary descriptions of the translator and of the techniques and purposes of translation local anxieties concerning the translator's socio-economic status, concerning the stability of the translated work and the original, the legitimacy of the pedagogical enterprise to which translation seems intimately tied, concerning finally the 'freedom' of a will constituted in and by means of this pedagogical-linguistic enterprise. It lies much beyond the scope of this chapter to convey a full sense of the economic, ethico-political registers in which these 'local anxieties' operate in early modern Europe. We might productively complicate matters, though, by considering briefly two roughly complementary, roughly contemporaneous works, John Minsheu's 1599 *A Dictionarie in Spanish and English*, adapted from Richard Perceval's 1591 dictionary, and Richard Verstegan's odd and influential *A Restitution of Decayed Intelligence. In Antiquities. Concerning the Most Noble and Renowned English Nation* (1605), that more directly link the figure of translation to the consolidation of national identities and trading regimes.

The *Restitution* opens with a dedication to King James I, followed by an 'Epistle to our Nation' in which Verstegan, after noting 'the very naturall affection which generally is in all men to heare of the woorthynesse of their anceters' and 'seeing how divers nations did labor to revyve the old honour and glorie of their own beginings and anceters, and how in so dooing they shewed themselves the moste kynd lovers of their naturall friends and countrimen', deplores the prevailing confusion among both 'our English wryters' and 'divers forreyn writers' (Jean Bodin is Verstegan's example) between 'the antiquities of the Britans' and the 'offsprings and descents' of the English.[17] The balance of the *Restitution* will be devoted to recovering the 'true originall and honorable antiquitie' of the English nation, a project animated in seemingly equal parts by the wish to set 'the reverend antiquaries' of England straight and by 'the greatnes of my Love', Verstegan says, 'unto my most noble nation; most deere unto mee of any nation in the world, and which with all my best endevours I desire to gratify'. It is rather difficult to assess the value that these fulsome expressions of national pride and nostalgia might have had at the time of the work's publication. The dedication to James, whose Scots and Catholic roots placed him aslant of the dominant British tradition and in particular of Elizabeth's harshly repressive measures against English recusants, suggests Verstegan's quite understandable effort to enlist to his cause a monarch whose background seemed briefly to promise much to Catholics. The extent of Verstegan's own interest in Recusant politics, both within and without England, is still obscure – though it was by no means negligible.[18] Verstegan was the agent in Antwerp of the exiled English Jesuit leader, Robert Person (Parsons), and was charged by Person with translating and publishing Person's important *Responsio ad Edictum* of 1592; animated no doubt by a zeal no less commercial than religious, Verstegan also wrote two pamphlets serving in some measure to preface and advertise the *Responsio* or *Philopater*, as it came to be known (after Person's pseudonym: Andreas Philopater). The *Philopater* represented the most vigorous and consequential Jesuit response to the 1591 proclamation of Jesuit 'sedition', and more generally to the religious politics of Elizabeth I's treasurer, Lord William Cecil.[19] Verstegan's two pamphlets, published anonymously in Antwerp in 1591 and 1592, came in the shape first of a *Declaration . . .* and then of *An Advertisement Written to a Secretarie of my L. Treasurers of Ingland, by an Inglishe Intelligencer as He Passed through Germanie towards Italie.*

Verstegan illustrates the opening page of the *Restitution* with an emblem of his own devising, showing the tower of Babel and the dispersal of its builders into different linguistic nations. The emblem's *lemma* reads '*Nationum origo*'.

At the time, and reflecting the influence of Josephus's interpretation of Genesis 11, the story of Babel was understood as a parable of hubris and as the origin of linguistic variation from a common tongue.[20] The choice of image is of considerable interest, the emblem of Babel conceivably serving in 1605 as a sort of double warning to the new King – not only against provoking divisiveness within his kingdom, but also, perhaps more interestingly, as a comment on the policies of his predecessor Elizabeth, represented compactly both by the aspiring and by the quarrelling masses hubristically raising the tower of Anglicanism against the Roman church, *and* as the source of European and national division, of the edicts that provoke England's division into different (religious and linguistic) 'nations'. It is not I think far-fetched to imagine the distinctly physiognomic composition of the woodcut (a nasal, phallicoid tower, distant armies resolving into eyes and brows, a cluster of foregrounded squadrons in the triangular formation of a mouth and two cheeks) as a sort of landscaped portrait of the King, a looking-glass emblem

Nationum Origo.

Figure 3.1. Image from the opening page of the *Restitution*, showing the Tower of Babel. *Nationum origo*, the title vignette from Richard Verstegan's *A restitution of decayed intelligence* (London: Iohn Bill, 1628).

of James in the manner of the various chorographic portraits of Elizabeth associating her with her kingdom. Nor can it be discounted, given the peculiarly personal turn that the 'Epistle to our nation' takes, that this Babel-faced frontispiece also serves, fascinatingly, as Verstegan's effort at a self-portrait. Here is how the 'Epistle' continues:

> For albeit my grandfather *Theodore Rowland Verstegan* was borne in the duchie of *Geldres* (and there descended of an ancient and woorshipful familie) whence by reason of the warres and losse of his freindes hee (beeing a young man) came into *England* about the end of the raign of king *Henry the seaventh*, and there maried, & soone after dyed; leaving my father at his death but nyne monethes old, which gave cause of making his fortune meaner than els it might have bin: yet can I accompt my self of no other but of the English nation, aswel for that *England* hath bin my sweet birth-place, as also for that I needs must pas in the self descent and ofspring of that thryce noble nation; unto the which with all dutifull respect and kynd affection I present this my labor.

Victor Houliston has suggested that both Verstegan and Person conceive the Elizabethan repression of the Jesuit order (and of related events, like the foundation of the Jesuit colleges in Valladolid) on two competing models, a providential and a consequentialist one (providential, because divinely sanctioned, motivated and understood; consequentialist, because flowing from freely chosen human actions).[21] Houliston has in mind Person's and Verstegan's pamphlets in response to the 1591 edict of expulsion, but a similar hesitation between historiographic models is at work in the *Restitution* as well. Here, the story of the origin of nations that Verstegan tells accounts for linguistic variation, and for subsequent scholarly and doctrinal disagreements concerning that variation, by making the unexpected destruction of the original language parallel *both* to a form of cultural forgetting (nations and national languages drift apart 'naturally', forgetting an original tongue into which they can no longer translate their words) *and* to the effect of persuasion (by means of untruths, violence, coercion: nations and natural languages are separated by an act or acts of will, divine or human, from each other and from their common tongue). Verstegan's exile, we infer, is both a bit of Providence and a deplorable human act; he both can and cannot hold Elizabeth (and then James) to account for the repudiation of the Jesuits and for his own circumstances; nations originate in a catastrophic *decision*, or grow apart gradually, consequentially, without the direct intervention of any human or other agency. The 'Epistle's' autobiographical turn, as well as the odd compounding (if that's what it is) of the figures of James, Verstegan, the Biblical landscape and Verstegan's 'sweet birth-place', England, would seem to sit uneasily upon this double stool. And perhaps necessarily so, for the *Restitution* envisions a mythico-religious model of linguistic and national identity characterized by the very exilic insecurity that Babel inaugurates and that Elizabeth later imposes, a model of individual and collective agency built upon the same unresolved hesitation between Providential and consequential accounts of an event's origins (and of a person's: his own genealogy, for instance, syntactically atwitch between 'albeit' and 'and yet', the two grammatical horns of the Providentialist and consequentialist dilemma). The practice, history and theory of *translation* are for Verstegan the record of this insecure subjectivity.

Minsheu's situation is on its face much different from Verstegan's. A teacher of languages in London, he is not directly associated with the Catholic cause. There is some evidence that he was of Jewish origin (a significant detail, Jesuits and Jews being in different ways marginal populations under Elizabeth and James, and more than many others interested for obvious reasons in the economics and cultural-religious politics of translation). Minsheu seems to have led a rather hard-scrabble life, moving at one point to Cambridge so as to finish work on his 1599 *Dictionarie*. For so minor a figure he is not uncontroversial: the scale and audacity of his scholarly borrowings were such that to this day he is routinely referred to as an arch-plagiarist (Ben Jonson succinctly calls him a 'rogue'), though one with a famously enterprising and famously persistent side.[22] Finding it hard to find a publisher for his *Ductor in linguas* (1617), Minsheu sold subscriptions to the volume, which he then published – the first subscription publication in England; nonetheless, he is remembered by Edward Phillips, in the *New World of English Words* of 1658, as 'Mr. *Minshaw* that spent his life and estate in scrutinizing into Languages, still remaines obnoxious to the misconstructions of many . . . invading censurers'.[23] His *Dictionarie* and more obviously still his later and much better-known *Ductor in linguas* seem oriented towards just such a coherent articulation of the social sphere, based (like the project of subscription and the enterprise of teaching languages) on the tricky juncture between commercial and linguistic interests.[24]

Minsheu's Spanish-English lexicon appeared bound together with a collection of 'pleasant and delightfull dialogues in Spanish and English', which became strikingly popular on their own, were re-edited by Minsheu in 1623 and translated into French (by César Oudin) and edited separately in Spain as the *Diálogos apacibles. . . .*[25] The seven 'dialogues' bound with the *Dictionarie* (Oudin adds an eighth, which then becomes part of the tradition of these stories' reception) are models of language pedagogy and take their form from Noel de Barlement's (Berlaimont) *Colloquia cum dictonariolo linguarum* of 1536, a compendium of polyglot dialogues arranged in parallel columns.[26] A sort of precursor to Berlitz's dialogues, Minsheu's little exchanges are set in different useful venues: an *hidalgo* wakes and calls to his waiting man for his clothes, sword and dress; yet another *hidalgo* and his wife shop for silver and jewels; five gentlemen dine together, comment on their food and drink, then play at cards; two travellers, a muleteer and an innkeeper keep company and discuss travel and lodging in Spain; three pages meet after a trip to Court and tell tales; four friends, two English and two Spanish, meet and contrast the customs and language of their countries; and a Sergeant and a soldier discuss the qualities that make a good soldier. The motives of the didactic enterprise are clear, and appear, on the surface, distinctly different from the purpose that Roger Ascham's *The Schole-Master* advanced, some fifty years earlier, for learning Latin: one learns English or Spanish in order to facilitate economic and social exchange, and the works' readership is drawn from a merchant or a military class newly able to trade internationally, seeking every advancement in its trade with Holland, Spain, France, Italy and the Turkish empire and the Maghrebi monarchies.

It comes as no surprise to us that Minsheu's dialogues all concern sites of exchange and merchandising, for in his dialogues what Covarrubias calls 'La noticia de muchas lenguas', 'knowledge of many tongues', not only facilitates travel, the exchange of goods and social mobility, but it is also understood to be a commodity itself, both the means for facilitating the exchange and an 'object' with value to be exchanged. The duplicity of the language in translation thus makes these dialogues peculiarly reflexive, perhaps even allegorical: Minsheu teaches translation in dialogues that are in part *about* translation, which make of translation a place-holder for economic value and for economic exchange and which thus reflect throughout on the economics of translation (its value, its costs, its materials). Take the first two of the 'pleasant and delightfull dialogues'. The first opens domestically; ostensive designations abound as the characters call for the odds and ends to hand in any house. The scene then moves outdoors. In the second dialogue, an *hidalgo* and his wife go to purchase plate ('in nothing I spend money with a better will than in plate', opines Thomas, the *hidalgo*; 'that which is laid out in plate is not wasted, but to change small peeces for great peeces', answers Margaret, his wife) and then jewels ('now let us go to the place where they sell Iewells', suggests Margaret. 'This is a way that I goe unwillingly', says Thomas. 'What is the reason?' 'Because these Iewels are as maidens, that while they are maids, and kept in, they are of much value, and in taking them abroad they loose all, and are worth nothing'). Both the vocabulary and the nature of the objects named have changed. Minsheu's readers are no longer learning the sort of ostensive equivalents familiar from the domestic setting, and they are no longer reading about the highly instrumental objects described in the first dialogue – the clothes, shoes, hats, chairs and other useful matter of day-to-day trade. Between the first and the second dialogue, and between the scene in the silversmith's shop and the scene in the jeweller's shop, the squire and his wife move not only geographically, as it were, but also in increasing order of economic and linguistic complexity, calling for this or that instrument representing (as even in Augustine) the first order of linguistic acquisition, trading in substitutes (one bit of plate for another, just different sizes) representing a second order of linguistic complexity (in which words retain a substantial, material identity with each other) and trading in jewels representing a third, dangerously public, uprooted and exposed order of linguistic complexity (like a maiden's worth, the value of a jewel depends, as Thomas wryly notes, on another bauble, reputation). The risks of the market are here the risks to which the new speaker of another tongue also exposes himself: a loss of value, of sense, of dignity, of 'maidenhood' and of a private, linguistic and domestic domain in which to 'keep' them safe. It is no surprise that one requires a guide, a pedagogue or a *ductor*, as one ventures into the exile of the streets, of the market, of another language. The value of Minsheu's lessons is largely established by the content of his dialogues.

Or so it would appear. For Minsheu's first dialogue expresses rather more hesitation about the socio-economics of value (and about the value of the pedagogy of translation) than we might expect. The dialogue concludes with this exchange between the two servants, in which the virtue of knowledge finds a kind of check:

Alonso: O quanto polvo tiene esta capa!

Ama: Sacude la primero con una vara.

Alonso: Ama, más que vien hechos están estos calçones.

Ama: Tan bien entiendo yo de esso, como puerca de freno.

Alonso: Pues qué entiende?

Ama: A lo que a mí me importa si tu preguntáras por una basquiña, una sáya entera, una ropa, un manto o un cuerpo, una gorguera, de una toca y cosas semejantes, supiérate yo responder.

Alonso: De manera que no sabe léer, mas de por el libro de su aldea.

Ama: Quieres tu, que sea yo, como el ymbidióso, que su ciudado es en lo que no le va ni le viéne.

Alonso: Siempre es virtúd savér, aunque sean cósas que parece que no nos ympórtan.

Ama: Bien sé yo, que tu sabrás hazér una bellaquería, y ésta no es virtúd. . . . A ora hermano dexate de retóricas y has lo que tu ámo te mandó.

Alonso: Sí haré aunque bien créo que no por esso me tengo de asentár con el a la mesa.

Alonso: Oh what a deale of dust hath this cloke?

Nurse: Beat it out first with a wand.

Alonso: Nurse, how exceeding well are these breeches made.

Nurse: I have as good knowledge therein as a sow in a bridle.

Alonso: What have you knowledge in then?

Nurse: In what belongeth unto me, if thou hadst asked of a peticoate, a womans cassocke, a womans gowne, a mantell, a paire of bodies, a gorget, or a womans bead attire, and like matter, I could have answered thee.

Alonso: So then the Priest cannot say Masse but in his owne booke.

Nurse: Wilt thou, that I should be as the envious person which setteth his mind on that which belongs not unto him.

Alonso: Yet alwaies is it a vertue to know, although they be things which seeme not to appertaine unto us.

Nurse: I know well, that thou knowest well how to play the knave, and that I am sure is no vertue. . . . Now Brother, leave your Rhetoricke, and doe that thy Master commanded thee.

Alonso: So will I doe, although I beleeve, for all that I am not to sit at table with him.

The dialogue's brief turn at the end, the wry observation on the part of Alonso that he will not sit at the table with his master, has the effect of placing in question much of the value that the dialogue has rested on the transportability of knowledge – what the Spanish renders as 'sabe leer, por el libro de su aldea', and the English, rather more polemically, as 'the Priest, cannot say Masse but in his own booke'. Doing what the master commands will not bring one to the table, Minsheu's character says – but perhaps, we are left to think, a little bit of 'envy' will manage to do so.

What is the nature of this 'envy'? And why does 'envy', rather than any of the cardinal virtues, prove to be the ground for social mobility? In what ways are 'envy' and *translation* related? Set these questions aside for the moment. Minsheu seems to have been entirely aware of the provoking duplicity of his dialogues; indeed, he seems to take a particular pleasure in showing how translations suddenly acquire quite searching ethico-political implications. Take, in closing, his Spanish dedication to the suspiciously Shandean figure of Don Eduardo Hobby.[27] Minsheu opens relating a well-known story about Apelles:

que aviendo acabado de pintar una hermosa tabla, teniendola colgada en parte publica, inumerable gente de todas suertes combidada de la lindeza della . . . entre los de mas, se acerto a llegar un rustico labrador, y como todos alabassen grandemente el ingenio del artificio, iuntamente con la pintura: el villano, con boz roonca y mal compuesta, dixo, una gran falta tiene esta tabla; lo qual como oyesse Apeles, le pregunto qual fuesse esta? El respondio, aquella espiga sobre la qual esta aquel paxaro sentado, deviera estar mas inclinada, porque conforme al peso que presuppone el paxaro y la flaqueza de la caña, no podia sustentarle sin doblarse mas, oydo esto por el pintor, vio que tenia razon el villano; y tomando el pincel, emendo luego alla falta, siguiendo su parecer; soberbio pues el rústico con ver que se uviesse tomado su voto, passó mas adelante, y dixo, aquellos çapatos que aquella figura tiene no estám nuennos, a esto le respondió Apeles, Hermano, cura de tu arte, y dexa a cada uno el suyo. Esta figura, muy ilustre señor, he querido traer, por dezir, que si todos los hombres se conformassen con lo que saven y que su ingenio alcança, no quisiessen passar adelante, a saber lo que no es de su profession ny les toca, ni ellos quedarian corridos, como este villano, ni el labrador se entremetería a tratar de la guerra, ny el mercader

de la cavallería . . . sino que tratando cada uno aquello a que su capacidad se
estiende, y no mas, seria un concierto maravilloso, que resultaria en grande
utilidad de toda la republica, y para esto devriamos tomar ejemplo de las cosas
naturales, las quales perpetuamente guardan su orden y concierto, sin entreme-
terse las unas a hazer el oficio de las otras. . . . Pues aviendose de guardar éste
concierto y órden, a v.m. conviene y toca el juzgar de esta mi obra.

[[Apelles] who, having completed a lovely painting, hung it in a public spot,
where numberless people flocked, attracted by its beauty . . . among these, a rustic
peasant happened by, and as all those present were praising greatly the ingenuity
of the artifice, as well as the painting: the villain, with a hoarse and ill-formed
voice, said: this piece has a great flaw. When Apelles heard this he asked what the
flaw was. The peasant answered, that sprig of wheat on which that bird is sitting,
should be bent further, because if one takes into account the weight of the bird and
the thinness of the stalk, it could not hold the bird without bending further. When
Apelles heard this he realized that the villain was right; and taking up his brush, he
corrected the mistake, as he saw fit. The peasant, swollen with pride because his
advice had been taken, went a step further, and said, those shoes that that figure is
wearing are not [correct]. Apelles answered him, Brother, stick to your art [*arte*],
and let each mind his own. I have adduced this figure, most illustrious sire, so as
to say, that if all men confined themselves to what they know and to the reach of
their native wit [*ingenio*], they would not want to go beyond, and seek to know
what is not of their profession [*professión*] and doesn't concern them, and they
wouldn't be offended, as this peasant was, nor would the peasant intrude with
opinions concerning the war, nor would the merchant opine about cavalry . . .
but rather as each would treat only that matter to which his capacity extends, and
none other, a marvelous concert or harmony would ensue, which would be of the
greatest utility for the whole republic, and to this end we should take our example
from natural things, which keep their order and arrangement perfectly, and none
of them interrupts another seeking to do the other's job. . . . And since this order
and harmony must be maintained, it is your honor's part to judge this my work.]

The anecdote finds its way to Minsheu from Pliny, and by the time he employs
it the proverb embedded within the anecdote – *Ne sutor supra crepidam*,
roughly 'let not the cobbler aspire above his last', or in Spanish 'Zapatero a
tus zapatos' – has acquired a most respectable humanist genealogy, having
been collected and moralized in Erasmus's *Adagia* and largely glossed by his
followers. The 'Dialogues' follow a variant reading that if anything tightens
the slight conceptual knot in the scene.[28] What Minsheu's dedication refers to
as 'concierto', something like social harmony, effectively excludes the figure
of Apelles himself (he conceals himself, provokes comment in the street,
functions as a sort of permanent threat of duplicity and surveillance – a whiff
of Platonic indignation at the social role of art seems patent). This exclusion assumes a nearly paradoxical shape, however, when the dedication's

device is unpacked according to Minsheu's loose prescription: Minsheu, the work's hidden Apelles, presents his *tableau* to the patron, his judge ('and since this order and harmony must be maintained, it is your honor's part to judge this my work'), who is now under Pliny (and Minsheu's) warning not to overstep his competency. The entire edifice of social 'order and harmony' hangs upon the appropriateness, one might say, of the patron's experience and past knowledge to his current judgement: *Ne sutor supra crepidam.* The dedication appears in this way to anticipate the conclusion to Minsheu's first dialogue, in which the Ama's satisfaction with her own (social and other) limitations serves to contain the rather more subversive 'envy' expressed by Alonso, the page.

Two aspects of the scene disturb its satisfaction, its sense of 'concert'. Would one need to warn one's patron, as it were to prompt him not to stray above his shoes, if there were no danger that his judgement might not, after all, quite fit with his experience? Or say that one accepts this aesthetic 'concert' as a model of social and economic harmony, status and experience in perfect accord, the soothing fantasy of an entirely saturated, transparent polity whose 'parts' marry organically, working each with each. Where in this aristocratic fantasy would the marginal, scrabbly figure of the pedagogue, of the translator, of the enterprising salesman of subscriptions belong? More particularly, what would didactic texts like the 'pleasant and delightfull dialogues' and the *Ductor in linguas* actually *teach*? The *linguistic economy* of Minsheu's dictionaries and dialogues turns on an altogether different sense of the relation between 'experience', 'knowledge', class and 'judgment' than his 'Dedication' advances – and they furnish a radically different account of the mobile, 'envious' political economy of the early market. From its very opening, then, the work accosts the reader. *Either* the dialogues have no didactic function or have only the function of conveying the exact translation of an existing state of affairs (the rustic voice of the labourer remains just that, unimproved by works he cannot judge or understand); and the figure that Minsheu brings to bear in the 'Dedication' only 'teaches' Edward Hobby to recognize himself (in the warned figure of a 'judge' who must not stray outside what he already knows); and the 'pleasant and delightfull dialogues in Spanish and English' themselves 'please' and 'delight' without in any way facilitating social, commercial or international mobility (of the sort that would allow a 'villein' to become a 'shoemaker', or a shoemaker to 'set his mind on that which belongs not unto him', move beyond a local market, change his tongue, export his wares, eventually hope to aspire to 'sit at the table' of an Edward Hobby). *Or else* the 'figure' that Minsheu employs in his dedication is entirely improper to the 'Dialogues', slyly open to correction, calling for a figure – a humanist, a trader in cultural translations, a figure with a mobility of intelligence and experience to match the political-economic instability and *disconcerting* he will come to represent – able to understand the bent or veiled critique of aristocratic functionalism that the appeal to Sir Edward Hobby embeds.

Nothing in Minsheu's work serves to *teach us* which of these character-izations of his project, and of his readers, Minsheu advocates. Indeed, the stories that the 'pleasant and delightfull dialogues' tell embed scenes in which mistranslation and rhetorical misunderstanding, rather than resulting in disaster of one or another monitory sort, are prized and enjoyed and indeed are represented as alternatives to 'doing what thy M[aster] commands thee': the 'pleasantness' and 'delightfulness' of the dialogues, in short, comes into conflict with their explicit pedagogical role. I've mentioned in brief Alonso's brief resistance, in the first dialogue. By the time the seven dialogues con-clude, what seemed a monitory hesitation has become explicitly articulated with the linguistic project – as though the subtle articulation of reading with the Priest's saying Mass that occurs in the commerce between the Spanish and the English texts has become the structuring principle of the dialogues. One learns from these 'Dialogues' *because of* their errors (in and about trans-lation) – but *what* one learns can no longer in the same way be learnt; one cannot, for instance, 'learn' from them whether one should aspire to occupy the position of Edward Hobby, of Apelles, or of the sly Alonso, the new figure for mercantilist, envious mobility. To put it more polemically than a brief description can support: what one learns from the 'Dialogues' 'errors' and paradoxes is no longer the object of the reader's, or of the writer's, will.

Like Richard Verstegan, Minsheu thus lights upon a highly unstable account of social and economic 'concert' from which the aristocratic figure of *judgement* emerges dramatically changed. But Minsheu's project is not only, and not primarily a *critical* one (he has many projects, after all). Like Covarrubias, the English lexicographer, translator and pedagogue is also modestly a political philosopher with an affirmative programme to comple-ment a sharply critical one. Minsheu's radical pedagogy of translation washes the Enlightenment's fantastical construction of the early modern subject's informed *will* in revealing acids: the irreducibility of *envy*; the non-correspon-dence between judgement, 'taste' and experience; the provocative vulnerabil-ity of one's linguistic 'home' or 'nation' as one's language steps translated into the market. One can achieve a slightly clearer sense of the disconcerting political philosophy emerging from early modern lexical culture by returning very briefly to another scene of origins, where 'letters', 'ground', 'culture' and their various translations mythically meet. When Covarrubias defines the word 'letter' he reminds us that

> Otros sienten auerse dicho à *lite*, porque de las letras como de los primeros elementos se forman las silabas, y las dicciones: y para juntarse entre si tienen vna manera de contienda hiriendose vnas a otras. Y esta es la comun moralidad

en que se fundò la fabula de Cadmo, que auiendo muerto la serpiente, Minerua le mandò sembrar los dientes della: y dellos nacieron hombres armados, que peleando entre si se mataron, hasta quedar en cinco. Estas se entienden las letras vocales, que son el origen y vida de las demas, y assi le dan por autor de las letras.

[Others believe it to come from *lite*, because syllables and statements are formed from letters, as from primary elements: and in order to assemble amongst themselves they have a sort of battle, wounding one another. And on this common moral the fable of Cadmus is based. When he killed the serpent, Minerva ordered him to sow its teeth, and from those teeth were born armed men, who fought amongst themelves and killed each other off, until only five remained. These are taken to be the vowels, which are the life and origin of all others, and hence Cadmus is taken to be the author of all the letters.]

With this primal fight Covarrubias puts paid to the genteel claims of lexical humanism that he seems to advance in defining 'tongue', *lengua*: that speaking in another tongue 'dampens the fury of the enemy, for, speaking to him in his own tongue, he moderates himself and conceives a certain familial affinity that obliges him to be human and merciful'. At the heart of the word, embedded in the letter itself, lies not the 'concert' and aristocratic harmony of rhyming 'judgment', 'experience', self-identity and expression but fratricidal conflict, envy, murder, and warfare. Not natural *law,* but the claim of *jus naturale* or natural *right*, to turn to Hobbes's crucial and polemical distinction, makes up the matter of linguistic exchange.[29] Upon this torn lexical ground, this broken, translated culture, early modern internationalism generates models of identity based not on national fantasies but on forms of partial and conflicted linguistic – lexical – identification.

Or put it like this: Minsheu and Verstegan (and Covarrubias in Spain) share an understanding of the relation between 'will' and 'language' that places them, one might say, closer to Nietzsche than to Renan: for them, translation marks the spot where language paradoxically least lends itself to the will's use. And in both cases, as in the case of Covarrubias's enigmatic *Tesoro*, this torn spot is where a particular social freedom can be located: for Verstegan, the freedom of a certain kind of recusancy, of an exilic, compensatory and riven identity; for Minsheu, a political-economic freedom deriving from the disharmony between economic and epistemological interest. In a broader sense, the politico-historiographic tradition that so lionizes the Renaissance's 'grands hommes' as the models for the assertion of Machiavellian, individual autonomy arises so as to bypass these two arenas of freedom – precisely because the sorts of 'freedoms' they instantiate cannot be associated with the model of Kantian autonomy on which Renan's and Burckhardt's thought rests, and on which the discipline of modern Renaissance studies depends. Likewise, the utopian moment of intellectual internationalism that structures recent work as distant in spirit and argument as that of Derrida, or Negri and Hardt, or Bhabha, or Balibar cannot today be understood without reference to its hidden link with this reactive definition of early modern humanist internationalism. For at the moment of the emergence of the nation-form, the lexical culture of translation designates a specifically non-subjectivist form of cultural (self) resistance with consequences so radical as to have generated a whole sub-discipline dedicated to evading it, and a contemporary weak utopianism dedicated to reproducing it.

Chapter 4

Sovereignty *or* Translation

And I Solomon glorified God, and adorned the Temple of the Lord with all fair-seeming. And I was glad in spirit in my kingdom, and there was peace in my days. . . . I then, wretch that I am, followed her advice, and the glory of God quite departed from me; and my spirit was darkened, and I became the sport of idols and demons. Wherefore I wrote out this *Testament*, that ye who get possession of it may pity, and attend to the last things, and not to the first. So that ye may find grace for ever and ever. Amen. (*The Testament of Solomon*)[1]

A famous magician, by the name of Rousseau, succeeded in enchanting the Island Barataria in such a manner that all should be at the same time governors and governed, and he bestowed on this enchanted commonwealth the fantastic name of Democracy. Which name, if Don Quixote in his scholarship would recognize as meaning 'the power of the people,' Sancho in his simpler commonsense would certainly hold demoniacal and understand as 'the power of the devil.' (Salvador de Madariaga, 'Our Don Quijote')[2]

In this chapter, I'll be focusing on the relay system formed by the concepts of 'sovereignty', 'translation' and 'decision'. I'll be looking extensively at one of Cervantes's best-known stories. My argument concerns the philosophical bases for political subjectivity and political economy in early modern Europe. In its most polemical shape, it claims that Cervantes's work provides the defective concept of *identity* that allows classes of individuals to be imagined as constituting a *political* unit. In what sense does Cide Hamete swear ' "Como católico cristiano" ' that what he is narrating in the twenty-seventh chapter of the 1615 *Quijote* is *true*?[3] Some sense of what it means to speak *as* or *like a Christian* is entailed. A map of contiguous identities, of contrasting ways of speaking, truthfully or not, is entailed as well: to speak as a Jew, as a Muslim, as a *morisco* convert, as a *marrano* or crypto-Jew. How are such linguistic-religious-ethnic, even national, identities decided in Cervantes, and determiningly through Cervantes in Western modernity? They are decided *in translation* and *theatrically*. But what is a *decision* for Cervantes?

The relays and lines of force that link translation to early modern theatricality – by which I don't mean only works written for the theatre – and these to the concepts and fields that come to be called 'political subjectivity' and political economy are not obvious ones. A first way to formalize these relays and lines of force will insist on the *economic* structuring to which they're subject. Translated figures, commodities in transit across markets or cultural forms that work across linguistic and other borders acquire value as they move among markets, languages and expressive frames.[4] An orange that sells as a fruit in Seville in 1570 sells as a curiosity as well as a fruit in London – we might say that in London it *represents*, on the stage of the grocer's stand, its value as something edible and its value as something exotic; wool carded from Spanish sheep in the early seventeenth century returns to Spain as cloth spun on Dutch looms, its accent changed, value added to it, coloured by the circuit of its translation. Similarly this or that cultural product, for instance what the theatre critic Louise Clubb famously called a 'theatergram', or a *commedia dell'arte lazzo*, or a stage gesture, or a bit of clothing, or a concept like 'sovereignty' or like 'decision' – a cultural product too gains or loses value in translation and in transit, when performed or consumed as originating elsewhere but represented *for* a local audience or market.[5] Sovereignty *in* translation.

But I'm thinking now of sovereignty *or* translation: that's my formula, and it helps to tear up my first, primarily *economic* formalization of the relays and lines of force linking translation to theatricality, to 'political subjectivity' and political economy.

I'm setting on stage a small, grammatical perplexity: does the 'or' in 'Sovereignty or translation' mean, disjunctively, to oppose 'sovereignty' and 'translation'? Or do I intend my 'or' to mean something like Spinoza's *sive*, in the famous and much-abused apposition from the *Ethics 'Deus, sive natura'*, where it conveys something like 'that is': 'God, which is to say, nature', or 'sovereignty', that is, 'translation'? My point isn't just grammatical. He who decides what is, or is not, a translation, what is or is not translatable, what is or is not *in* translation, is sovereign – sovereign not only over one little discursive island, *in* which a word's sense is held to local uses, but also over that little island's relations to other language-worlds whose terms or concepts you or another subject might offer up as equivalents to those in the little discursive island over which I reign, in sovereign and untranslatable solitude. Carl Schmitt, whose famous phrase regarding modern sovereignty 'sovereign is he who decides upon the exception' I have been pirating, was a deep student, through Donoso Cortés and through other routes, of the confessional Spanish monarchy. I'm translating Schmitt so as to have him say *first*, 'Sovereign is he who decides on the translation, sovereign is he who decides what is or is not a translation, who decides whether a translation will or will not stand in place of the word or the world translated'. 'Sovereign', my Schmitt says, 'is he who decides what is untranslatable'. And my translation of Schmitt has an important, reflexive, *second* corollary: 'Sovereignty is untranslatable inasmuch as it is a quality that resides with one, indivisible, singular term. The sovereign is he who is possessed of that quality, of sovereignty, inasmuch as he decides how sovereignty is to be translated or distributed'. The conceptualization of modern *imperial* sovereignty, with its delegated, distributed and bureaucratized translations of unitary sovereignty, emerges together with modern practices and understandings of 'translation': they come on stage together. Sovereignty, that is, translation.

But 'translation' is also, in the emerging market economies of early modernity, an alternative to imperial sovereignty: it is the locus, not of the bureaucratic and disciplined distribution of sovereignty but of the dispersal of the 'one'; translation is something that occurs transactionally, something that happens where I forget something, where my speech and I are used and passed from hand to hand and tongue to tongue, like merchandise that's examined by hand, *tratado*. Translation in early modernity is what happens where and when my speech and I reach the market – and we do, always. Nothing, in the emerging market system or the emerging world system, is untranslatable or regulated by a sovereign and untranslatable term: everything is always, already, on the market in translation and everything bears, always and already, the mark of its prospective value. Like my bale of wool or my Seville orange, a story about the decision that a Jewish king makes reaches from Judea on the shoulders of translations through Greek, into the Vulgate and to the European popular traditions, thence into the theatre, across borders and genres and languages into the early novel, and from there to our days through the theatre again, or in different genres entirely. A kind of value attaches to each of the story's translations in this new market system, as it moves from hand to hand, and as it erases or forgets elements of its embeddedness in an originating context: the story as a commodity. The universalization of translation is an alternative, opposed paradigm for the motion and the accumulation of the value of commodities, as well as the means for both. The dispersed sovereignty of the market system, the forerunner of the headless sovereignty of capital, is at odds, inasmuch as it is *systemic*, with the theologico-political consolidation of sovereignty into the untranslatable *one*, the forerunner (on the philosophical stage) of autonomy and, on the stage of political economy, the forerunner of Lockean possessive individualism.

The point I'm making should be controversial in three ways. The first, because I'm stressing that, whatever the relation that each term, 'sovereignty' and 'translation', entertains with the concept of 'decision', there is some way in which it is impossible to decide *between* thinking of 'translation' and 'sovereignty' as synonymous, and thinking of them as radically heteronymous, disjunctive, privative, even adversarial. The second, inasmuch as I'm linking the three-part system, 'Sovereignty', 'translation' and 'decision', with the stage. Finally, note what's implied by my introducing a temporal element into the scheme, an element of radical potentiality or modality. This is the third point of controversy – and, I think, the most problematical by far. A cultural product bears the prospective marks of the languages and axiologies into which it will move, and from which it may derive values, now and then, or on whose account it *will* lose, or *does* lose value, here and now. Let's say we agreed, notionally, *concesso non dato*, that the normative understanding of an established cultural framework provides, here and now, a way to assess the value of this or that object, commodity, sign and so on. (We would say, imagine that we could agree on a general equivalent against whose normative value we would index the relative values of commodities we seek to market.) When we open matters to the standpoint of potentiality, to the contingencies of possibilities, to the logical frame of modality, we seem to deny ourselves the redemptive promise of a normative frame. The mediation of possible markets-to-come, of possible languages-to-come, makes it impossible for us to decide, here and now, what value this or that commodity has not just in itself (this was, in any event, too strong a requirement), but also relatively – in part because the mediation of markets- and languages-to-come dispossesses us of the sovereign right to make such a decision. Untimeliness is a structural element of cultural commodities, including the cultural commodities we call 'sovereignty' and 'identity' or 'political subjectivity', and this structural untimeliness dispossesses us of our sovereign right to decide on their translatability or untranslatability across languages, cultures, markets and times. And by 'dispersed sovereignty' I intend something quite specific. The frames that assign value to this or that commodity or cultural object are always simultaneously underdetermined and overdetermined by the dispersal of the circumstances of production, in the past, and by the uncertain light the contingent future casts back as well. We will see the disturbing, profound formula Cervantes supplies: we can, it appears, never close or finish, or stop, *determination*: 'no acabar de determinar'.

This is all rather abstract, so let me tell you a familiar story. Somewhere in La Mancha, or in a province not far from it, a rather cruel play is being staged. The year – sometime before 1615. One of the people we see does not know that many of the other figures around him are playing parts. He has been imported into a dynamic, differentiated scene, where his acts and statements will be valued, assessed, rejected or accepted, according to rules he and many others in the scene only partly understand. Some of the audience know that our protagonist is being abused and that they are spectators at a cruel trick; others do not, and believe themselves instead to be present at a piece of what we can call political theatre, the act of investiture of their new governor, appointed to rule by the distant feudal owner of this little territory. We're in chapter 45 of the 1615 *Quijote*. Sancho has been named governor of the Baratarian Island by the Duke and Duchess whom the Squire and Knight encountered some chapters before. Like many characters in the second part of *Don Quixote*, the Duke and Duchess are readers and lovers of the first part of the novel. They, however, have at their disposal the means to see Sancho's long dream fulfilled and to deliver to him the governorship of the island promised to him by Don Quijote, and by the chivalric tradition. Their cruel joke braids together Sancho's fantasies of wealth and sovereign authority, the spectacle of political theatre, even the strange homology between the distribution of political power and the circulation and consumption of cultural commodities. Barataria, the land *baratry*, of *simony*. A 'barator' is a 'Symonist', one early British wordbook says, 'called of the Italian word (*barrataria*) signifying corruption or briberie in a Iudge giuing a false sentence for mony'. And the word 'Baratar', Sebastián de Covarrubias tells us in 1611, derives from 'barato', *cheap*, probably dropping the agentive prefix *a-*, 'abaratar', to cheapen – but the link to fantasy and to the theatre is even tighter. 'Baratar', he writes, means 'trocar vnas cosas por otras, y de aqui se dixo baratillo, cierta junta de gente ruyn, que a boca de noche se juntan en vn rincón de la plaça, y debaxo de capa venden lo viejo por nueuo, y se engañan vnos a otros' ['Baratar means to exchange or replace one thing with another, hence the word *baratillo,* an assembly of base people who, in the dead of night, will assemble in a corner of the marketplace, and under cover will sell old things for new, and trick one another'].[6]

The Dukes' joke goes awry, as such things do in Cervantes. The Squire steps onto the stage and into the market prepared for him by the aristocrats, who have charged one of their servants to record what they expect will be the Squire's homely malapropisms. What follows is legendary.[7] Our fat peasant, having drunk deeply in the waters of humanist political wisdom delivered him by the knight; armed with the precepts that Don Quijote furnishes him and with his native, rustic wisdom; bringing to the stage and to the market of which he is unaware the resources of popular intelligence for which the first part of the novel made him famous; believing himself to be performing in one sort of political play, while actually performing in another sort of spectacle altogether; our fat peasant, I say, thinking he has one sort of tradeable value, when in fact he has another, performs for a divided audience, part of them aware that it's a sort of farce they're witnessing, part of them believing themselves to be present at the theatre where their political future will be decided. Sancho pronounces himself with such intelligence and to such great effect that 'he that wrote down Sancho's words, deeds, and behavior', the transcribing witness, the Duke's and Duchess's recording narrator, 'could not resolve whether he should set him down a fool or a wise man' ['el que escribía las palabras, hechos y movimientos de Sancho no acababa de determinarse si le tendría y pondría por tonto o por discreto'] 'No acababa de determinarse': the imperfect and imperfective formula of cultural, economic and political judgement in Barataria.

All this indeterminacy, this unresolvability, this imperfective 'no acabar de determinar', turns out to threaten the languages of civil society in the Baratarian Island, and in Cervantes's novel generally. Sancho's decisions are played for a divided audience, by actors divided on whether they know what play they are in. The scene of political representation doesn't *know* that it is political, or that it *is* political not only where it represents itself explicitly *as* political, that is, in the decisions of the 'governor', but also *elsewhere*, where it isn't decidable or determinable, on first sight, whether what we're seeing and reading is real, a real case brought before a fake governor, or false, a mere representation of a case brought before a fake governor. The Baratarians don't know whether the majority of the cases brought before Sancho are true or false, actual cases or samples of paradoxical cases drawn from the reservoir of literary and religious *exempla* and staged with Sancho cast, absurdly, in the role usually played by a figure like Solon, or Socrates, or Christ, or Saint Nicholas, or Salomon. And 'we' who read or see this cruel play – are we sure that we know, firmly, what our role is? What we read, and what the assembled subjects in the Insula Barataria see, may be political in one rather obvious sense – it is the performance of political power accompanying an investiture; but it may be political in another as well, since the episode reads easily as representing the unfoundedness, the indeterminacy, the ephemerality or dreaminess of *all* politics.

At the heart of this little play, the highest example of Sancho's canny intelligence, beats this scene.

Two ancient men appear before Sancho. One of them leans on a light cane, a *cañaheja*; the other tells the aspiring governor that he lent the man with the cane ten pieces of gold, which have not been returned. The man with the cane says he's prepared to swear that he did indeed return the gold, hands the first man the *cañaheja* which hinders him, and, unhindered, swears on the cross formed by Sancho's staff of office that he did, indeed, return the gold. The old man is largely believed, is given permission to go, retrieves his cane and sets about hobbling off. Sancho deliberates, calls him back, and has him hand the *cañaheja* to the first old man, saying to this one, 'There, you're paid'. 'What do you mean – could this light cane be worth ten gold pieces?' And yes indeed, the crafty, second old man had hidden the gold in the hollow cane, and was able to swear truthfully and literally that he'd returned the money when he had handed the cane over.

The story's rich allegorizations stand in part on existing stories, on existing values, on agreed cultural tropes that determine and overdetermine it, like 'old things' being sold for, with, and as a way of adding value to or of subtracting value from, the 'new' story that the Baratarian actors stage for Sancho. The Duke's and Duchess's actors are echoing, without perhaps knowing it, one of the stories told in Livy's *History of Rome*, regarding another brute, a Brutus, Lucius Junius Brutus, the son of Tarquinia, 'a young man of a very different mind from that which he pretended to bear', that is, a young man of canny intelligence who allowed himself to 'assume the appearance of stupidity' and even 'accepted the surname Brutus, that behind the screen afforded by this title the great soul which was to free the Roman People might bide its time unseen', a Brutus who once took to the oracle at Delphi as a hidden gift a rod of gold encased within a wooden staff, *is tum ab Tarquiniis ductus Delphos, ludibrium verius quam comes, aureum baculum inclusum corneo cavato ad id baculo tulisse donum Apollini dicitur, per ambages effigiem ingenii sui.* The old, sanctioned, *secular* and political tale beats under the Baratarian episode: the great, hidden soul in the brutal exterior; the political saviour subtly awaiting, in rustic disguise, the decisive moment.[8] The subjects of the Duke and the Duchess are also adapting, schematically, a *religious* story that finds its way to La Mancha from Jacobus de Voragine's *Legenda aurea*, passing in all probability through a number of Castilian filters and translations where it is popularized and standardized, then collected in works like Clemente Sánchez Vercial's *Libro de los enxiemplos por A. B. C.* of about 1400, or the anonymous, slightly later *Espéculo de los legos.*[9] The stories are a staple of the repertoire of many 'vicars' in La Mancha *ca.*1615, so it is not improbable that Sancho recognizes the old story in its new version. It also wouldn't be absurd to recollect just here, where Cervantes sets onstage the effectiveness of humanistic precepts in forming the education of the most unlikely of princes and governors, that the most famous of the humanist adaptations of Plato, the Erasmian Silenus of Alcibiades, concerns the golden figure of Socratic wisdom hidden within the philosopher's gnomish body. With Erasmus's *Enchiridion* and the *Adages*, *that* little Platonic fable becomes, translated, the gold of Pauline Christianity hidden within the rude literalism of the Hebraic Law and of Catholic orthodoxy – and also, as Erasmus definingly notes, an allegory for how we can read *all* rude fables, an allegory of humanistic allegory. Fables, this one for instance: the story of two old men handing one another a hollow cane filled with unexpected gold; fables carry, hidden, the gold of revelation, and we need just to crack the container, the *cañaheja*, that carries it.

Now, Cervantes's story does indeed take shape against a standing reserve of 'old things' and old stories, golden political legends from Livy, or Platonic or Erasmian fables that Sancho's subjects and Sancho himself keep before them. But the point is stronger. In this Baratarian insula, the sovereign learns how to decide cases by recalling these 'old things'.[10] He treats their meta-allegorical content as a procedure for governance and as a technique he can translate to his circumstances – he treats the cases before him as further cases of the *exempla* he has been taught at the knee of the local vicar or of the wandering Knight. They are examples of examples. This exemplary translatability is at the same time a technique, and the core of the 'old things'. Gold is gold, after all; it is the standard of value; it not only survives translation, but it is also the basis upon which translation among natural economies occurs. At the core of any particular story in the reservoir lies the universal gold of theologico-political revelation; its universality shines, once the local containers bearing the accidents of culture, language and time are cracked.

Remark the fantasy I am indulging. I am following one direction of Cervantes's story: the temptation to make all and every hermeneutic or theologico-political gold out to *be* gold, as if at heart every 'new thing' that the market of culture produces beats an 'old thing' which, in its core, in the heart of its heart, is substantially identical with the heart of the heart of any other story, of whatever-story. I'm not straying far from humanist orthodoxy: find the capable, even the inspired sovereign, by looking inside the Silenus figure of the rustic peasant; find the single, archaic and ideal source of value, manifested prefiguratively in pre-Christian texts and then, syncretistically or typologically, translate it into particular circumstances. This is the very stuff of humanism, after all, the very stuff of humanist pedagogy.

But the old stories, the golden legends that this new Cervantic story capitalizes upon don't in fact share a core structure or substance – and this dissensus unravels spectacularly throughout the episode, producing opacities and untranslatabilities in the conceptualization of value, sense and sovereign decision that Cervantes offers us. European political modernity would have been a very different thing indeed if these opacities and untranslatabilities, rather than the compensatory universalisms built to evade them, had crossed the fictional boundaries of the Baratarian Island onto the mainland of European culture.

Consider the episode's most obvious source, de Voragine's *Legenda aurea*. Sancho is remembering – with some stark differences – the so-called miracle of the cheated Jew, who in de Voragine's compilation is cheated, like the old man in the Insula Barataria, by means of what Caxton's translation calls 'an hollow staff' in which the 'deceiver' hides the gold. If Sancho's audience had also heard this story, if their memory is to be solicited by this story as well – and we're to recall the monstrous influence of the golden legend in this time, of hagiographies and *exempla* – if the audience remembers for instance the versions found in the *Libro de los enxiemplos por A. B. C.* or the *Espéculo de los legos*, then it recalls that the moral of the *Legenda aurea*'s story regards the ultimate conversion of the Jew. In the exemplary tradition, the deceiver, carrying the gold-filled staff, is run over by a cart that kills him and spills the gold from within the staff. The defrauded Jew, in William Caxton's translation of the *Legenda aurea*, 'saw the fraud, and many said to him that he should take to him the gold; and he refused it, saying, But if he that was dead were not raised again to life by the merits of St. Nicholas, he would not receive it, and if he came again to life, he would receive baptism and become Christian. Then he that was dead arose, and the Jew was christened'. This is a different scenario from the one enacted in Sancho's theatre. Voragine's story makes the unexceptional theological point that the miraculous rising from the dead is the index of and catalyst for conversion. Perjury punished divinely, resuscitation, restitution – these are exemplary *for the Jew*, who learns from the example of the perjured and punished Christian, and from the miracle of his resurrection by Saint Nicholas, the truth of the resurrection on which Christianity stands, hidden like gold inside of the story of the perjured debtor. But Cervantes's version has secularized the story: matters now concern the restitution of property, and redemption in an entirely economic sense; the gold that the staff contains does not stand in for an even more golden moral attribute, like faith or the soul; the story's allegorical content concerns, not the gold of conversion, but the clever translation of moral allegory into secular circumstances. In this courtroom in the Insula Barataria, the drama of conversion has been translated into a drama of jurisprudence and of distributive justice. The sovereign has stepped into the role vacated by the miraculous saint; conversion becomes the restitution of property to its rightful owner. The moral 'gold' of the golden legend has become the social faith necessary to a society in which economic transactions are carried out by people who are faithful to contracts. In this new society, God is a useless witness. In his place, Cervantes furnishes a corpus of existing knowledge, humanistic or doctrinal, that allows the wise and prudent governor, the Solomonic governor, to cut to the heart of the case and guarantee that the capital flows to its rightful owner.

But Sancho, the new sovereign, foreign though he may be to many of the Island's inhabitants, novel, unparalleled in general – Sancho, the gathered audience seems to agree, *is not unique*. He *can* be translated into the cultural landscape of the Island, because the cultural lexicon *does* provide a sovereign analogue to the fat Squire. *We* don't know, and the Cervantic narrator and the Duke's witness don't tell us, whether anyone at the scene recalls Saint Nicholas's story from the schematic variations of the tricked-Jew story common in early modernity. But the subjects of the Insula Barataria – *all* of them, those in the know regarding the Dukes' cruel trick and those simply present at what they believe to be the new governor's investiture – *all* of them, as a single political and interpretative unit, *do* hold Sancho to be what the narrator refers to as 'a new Solomon': 'Quedaron *todos* admirados, y tuvieron a su gobernador por un nuevo Salomón', the narrator tells us: '*All of them* were dumbfounded, and held their governor to be a new Solomon'.

'A new Solomon' – Sancho?[11] The consolidation of the disaggregated, divided public and audience as a political group, a 'todos' bearing appropriately a single, collective pronoun, occurs here, when the Baratarians, those in the know and those not, 'admire' Sancho together, and together recognize in him the ghostly antecedent of the story's Saint Nicholas. That is, the disaggregated Baratarians come together in name, as a 'todos', when they recognize in Sancho the Jewish king whose wisdom in seeing to the heart of the case and in deciding matters has been translated figuratively, the letter of the Solomonic story becoming the golden spirit of Saint Nicholas. Now, passing through this older recollection, the story of the conversion of the Jew found in the *Legenda aurea* and in the exemplary tradition has been reversed: Saint Nicholas has been converted, or translated, back into his model or prototype – the figure of Solomon. And the collective identity, the *political* identity of the subject-audience viewing Sancho's mock, or real, play, passes through this retranslation, this unconversion, of the governor, appointed by the Dukes, through Saint Nicholas, and on to Solomon. The true 'gold' of the Christian legend is the Solomonic decision; the ground of the New Law and its charitable interpretation, its vaunted spirituality, is attainable only by turning Sancho into Nicholas and then *back* into Solomon, and by seeing and admiring the sovereign under the aspect, not of the merciful king of Christianity, not as the saint who figures in the golden legends, not as the Christian prince, but rather as the Solomonic, ancient prince whose prudential decision, whose ability to cut through to the heart of the case, is tied to a pre-Christian literality. It's on these grounds that modernity, and in specific a *political-economic* modernity, can be envisioned. In this anachronistic Insula Barataria, to be truly modern, to achieve the headless, dispersed sovereignty of the modern mercantile system, we must forget the intervening Christian epoch, and translate the story of our decisions, however new or strange they may appear, into whatever it is that the name 'Solomon' represents. The exemplary value of the case we are deciding and the grounds on which we make our decision follow from an archaic, even mythological frame whose value is redeemed under the dispensation of a new, Christian frame that is yet to come, but which only works politically when it is recognized as an 'old thing' under the new, as Solomon hiding under the cloak of the new governor. From this preposterous temporality, something like a civil society will emerge in this insular republic, a civil society based on contracts, on the combined theatre of law and spectacle, on the regulated exchange of money. Civil society will emerge on and in this cruel Solomonic spectacle where the value of our examples, where the theatre of our affects and passions, is translated through the letter of the Hebrew scripture. Here Sancho-Solomon, the judge or governor who may not in fact *be* a judge or a governor but who also does not know that he is not, and thus cannot be said to be only *acting* the part of the judge or governor, decides cases that may not be cases but citations from legendary works, in which plaintiffs and defendants may be acting parts or not, for an audience some members of which understand themselves to be at the theatre, at the cruel theatre of the aristocracy's last pleasure, and another part of which understand themselves to be present at the serious spectacle of the investiture of a political sovereign. The Jewish Ethic and the Spirit of Capitalism.

So who – or what – was 'Solomon' for Cervantes's audience? To this point, I've made the name out to be something like the staff in which modern theologico-political secularism is held – the container for the hidden Weberian gold of cultural values we can now disclose, centuries on, as if by splitting the allegorical Solomonic stick. Not *faith*, but collective admiration, lies here, at the heart of Cervantes's story: charisma. (Weber: '[The Prince who intervenes at will in the administration of justice] treats the grant of legal remedies to a large extent as a free gift of grace or a privilege to be accorded from case to case, determines its conditions and forms, and eliminates the irrational founs and means of proof in favor of a free official search for the truth. The ideal example of this type of rational administration of justice is the "kadi-justice" of the "Solomonian" judgment as it was practiced by the hero of that legend – and by Sancho Panza when he happened to be governor. . . . The specific form of charismatic adjudication is prophetic revelation, the oracle, or the Solomonic award of a charismatic sage, an award based on concrete and individual considerations which yet demand absolute validity. This is the realm proper of "kadi-justice" in the proverbial, not the historical sense'.[12]) I've made the name 'Solomon' out to be a metonym for the literality of value, for which the universal value of gold is a first trope. I've made the name, 'Solomon', into a concept, whose sense and value translate like gold, with losses and gains to be sure, but predictably, across languages and across times. A gold standard; a golden legend.

But this is simple-minded: our drive to settle, to decide, whether Sancho is to be taken as a fool or a wise man leads us too quickly away from Cervantes's imperfecting, even imperative formula: 'No acababa de determinarse si . . . tendría y pondría [a Sancho] por tonto o por discreto', he says of the story's witness. 'No acabar de determinarse', yes, of course, meaning 'he could not decide, he could not stop deciding, he could not reach the end of the decision', but also flickering between the impersonal and personal forms of 'determinarse', and allowing Cervantes's readers to understand, in this proxy reader they are witnessing, the full force of the reflexive 'determinarse'. Not to be done with a decision: not to be able to determine *oneself*. The cultural material to which the story refers is resolutely indeterminate. In Cervantes's time, Solomon was a figure of prudence, certainly – a figure associated not infrequently with the late Philip II. But of what else as well? What would the audience in Sancho's island have remembered, when they translated or converted Sancho's admirable novelty back into the familiar 'old thing' from which its value and sense derive? What values attach, in the cultural tropology into which Sancho is imported, to the name 'Solomon'? And let us not forget the preposterous, redemptive temporality that Cervantes's work exploits as well. What does the name 'Solomon' borrow from its past uses and from its future ones? Or, to put matters more precisely, how does the proper name 'Solomon' become, or become translated into, a *concept?*

This is a complicated question, and methodologically productive just where it is most difficult. There are four principal aspects to this difficulty; I'll close by running through them in order of interest. They are, not surprisingly, difficulties that afflict any dialectical approach to literary historiography, but they are also, I'd like you to note, the difficulties we encounter when we consider how a phrase may be *translated* from one natural language to another, or from one period to another. When we ask, 'What value attaches to the name that seems to bring the audience together, that seems to create the conditions for a prudential governance, the name "Solomon"?' we're asking after the uses of the name in roughly 1615 – and we run immediately into *practical* complications, since the name "Solomon"'s uses are manifold, an open archive we'd be hard pressed to complete. Since we would want to have some sense of the range of the archive in whole before deciding to what *concept* the name 'Solomon' corresponds, we'd want to be able to account, not just for the use of the name 'Solomon' as the figure of prudent and just sovereign decisions, but for the name's use in pre-national mythology (the strange fable of the 'mesa de Salomón', which is supposed to lie under the city of Toledo), in farces (as in Sánchez de Badajoz's extraordinarily weird *Farsa de Salomón*, from before 1549) and in popular romances. The catalogue of these uses being both infinite and incomplete, we'd be forced to proceed relatively blindly, and designate as 'the Solomonic in 1615' some portion of an archive whose range we ignore, based on a decision taken on practical rather than immanent or definitive grounds. This in itself is not concerning – it is, after all, what we do in common usage, when we translate among languages or when we speak to one another – but it becomes more worrisome, of course, when the concept of 'the Solomonic' is meant to replace a transcendent, theologico-political ground for sovereign decisions.

The second methodological difficulty deepens the pragmatic dilemma. Say we succeed, minimally, in mapping some portion of the uses of the name

'Solomon' *ca.* 1615. We may well find that these cultural uses are not coherent – and have never been, really. We recall the apocryphal *Legend of Solomon*, source for the controversial, companion tradition standing alongside the story of Solomon's wisdom and prudence – the tradition that has him trade in diabolism, go mad, become a figure for sorcery and imprudence. Understanding what 'un nuevo Salomón' is will prove consequently more difficult: not only are we not sure what the archaic sense of the name or the concept 'Solomon' is, but the notion of the 'new' or of the *novelty* of the archaic figure will apply *differently* to different uses of the name, some admitting of a Christian eschatological sense, others not.

Our third difficulty bears on the procedures we would use, *today*, for determining what is, or is not, a figure of 'Solomon' in 1615 or so, or for determining what the principle of coherence is that makes the name 'Solomon' exemplary, that is, our difficulty bears on the procedures we use today for *deciding* what makes 'Solomon' a concept rather than a proper name. For these procedures are hopelessly linked to contemporary fantasies and protocols regarding identity that falsify, or at least alter, the *historical* object. The Island of Barataria, like that other one on which it may remotely be based, the Island of Utopia, is located in the twenty-first century as well as in early modernity – and in times to come, and in intervening times that unsettle its borders as well.

This anachronic, untimely aspect to our decisions is deeply unsettling. When, for instance, this episode of *Don Quixote* is translated, into English and into the eighteenth century, the concept of community on which Sancho stands changes dramatically. Was this different community present already in the 1615 text? The question is much harder to answer than would at first appear. Take Thomas d'Urfey's 1694 translation into English and dramatization of *Don Quixote*, titled *The Comical History of Don Quixote*. D'Urfey's version of the Baratarian scene dispenses with the analogy to Solomon entirely, in part so as to emphasize Sancho's doltishness, even his clownishness. Here is the scene where Don Quixote instructs Sancho in the relation between the people and the sovereign.

Don Qu.: Your hat, *Sancho* your hat, 'dsdeath, don't you see they are all bareheaded: Come, come look grave and speak after me, we'll imitate·the *Polish* Election, and give it them in Latin, – *Sit bonus Populus.*

Sancho: Sit bonus Populus. (Speaks loud and Clounishly.)

Don Qu.: Bonus ero Gubernator.

Sancho: Bonus ero Gubernator.

They shout.

> *Duke:* So then, since all things move in their right order, here now let's part, and *bonos nocios* Governour.
>
> *Sancho:* The Governour is your Grace's Footstool, my Lord.[13]

In this scene, d'Urfey delivers the sovereign-subject relation in macarronic Latin, pronounced by Sancho, who without, manifestly, knowing what he is saying, is imitating Don Quijote, who is imitating, as he has it, 'the *Polish* election'. It is a tricky moment. The Latin of the 'Polish election' – more on what this historical analogue might be in brief – is itself mocked in the Dukes' intralinguistic pun. 'Bonos nocios', they say to the Squire and Knight, and to the Baratarians, and they mean in part 'buenas noches', 'good night', but some portion of d'Urfey's audience would have heard also the echo of *nescios, necio* in 'nocios', Spanish and Latin for 'ignorant' or 'foolish'. This intralinguistic playing wishes the Knight and the Squire good night, mocks their ignorance and also brings 'right order', a principle of cosmological sovereignty, into the picture. This mocking, garbling, makes the subjunctive 'sit bonus populus', which might roughly mean, 'inasmuch as', or 'were the people good', then the governor will be good, a future that says, to the extent that the 'populus' is good, the sovereign will be good too – this is made to depend on the 'noscios', on the *necedad* or stupidity, or even better, on the incapacity of Sancho to understand what he's saying – not inasmuch as he's sovereign, but inasmuch as the Duke is creating, in a kind of collusion with Don Quijote, a community of audience members who watch the audience within the play ridicule Sancho and the knight. It is not, as in Cervantes's work, *admiration* for the naïve Squire's 'Solomonic' prudence that produces a general political identity, but rather a universal contempt for the Squire, inasmuch as he cannot pronounce, or understand, the formula of sovereignty. So the political community here is doubled – the audience watching the play at which Sancho's lack of knowledge of Latin puts on stage a principle of reciprocal governance, between the subjects who are good, and the sovereign who is as well. And of course the 'Polish election' the Knight is imitating, a prospective imitation of late seventeenth-century events, is precisely the epitome, not of political consensus but of radical *dissensus*, d'Urfey having in mind, with breathtaking anachronism, the elevation to 'elector of Saxony' in 1697 of Frederick Augustus I, which scandalously required his *conversion* to Roman Catholicism, that is, required the Latinization of the Protestant duchy of Saxony.

Clownishness at the level of language – Latinizations, garbling or gobbling of languages – is unpredictable when it's translated into theatre, when it's gesturalized and acquires the temporal specificity of a performance.[14] A review by the remarkable Tony Aston of a performance of d'Urfey's adaptation, published in London in 1808 in *The Cabinet, or, Monthly Report of Polite Literature*, noted that the actor playing the role of Sancho, whose stage name is Cave Underhill, 'though not the best actor in the course of precedency', had 'no rivals in his dry, heavy, down-right way in low comedy'.[15] This of course makes him an excellent choice to play Sancho – a role which Underhill was famed for, along with the first gravedigger in *Hamlet,* Iacomo in the *Libertine* and a few others. Underhill, it appears, 'was about 50 years of age' at the time, 'about six foot high, long and broad-faced, and something more corpulent than this author', Aston tells us. 'His face very like the *Homo Sylvestris* or *Champanza;* for his nose was flattish and short, and his upper lip very long and thick, with a wide mouth and short chin, a churlish voice, and awkward action, (leaping often up with both legs at a time, when he conceived anything waggish, and afterward hugging himself at the thought). He could not enter into any serious character . . . and was the most confined actor I ever saw: and could scarce be brought to speak a short *Latin* speech in *Don Quixot*, when *Sancho* is made to say, *Sit bonus Populus, bonus ero Gubernator;* which he pronounced thus:

> *Sh[it] bones and bobble ar[se]*
> *Bones, and ears gobble nature'.*

Aston is offended, but it is not clear just *why:* is Underhill acting particularly *badly*, garbling or gobbling d'Urfey's version of Sancho's words or is he acting particularly *well*, and performing, to carnavalesque and uproarious effect, the sort of 'clownishness' that d'Urfey's stage direction calls for? It's even hard to tell how soberly the effort to classify Sancho works. He is *Homo Sylvestris*, an early version (indeed the earliest recorded version) of the chimpanzee—thus *Champanza*, a sort of portmanteau name, a hybrid or a chimera mixing the chimp, the French wine, and the name of the Squire, Sancho Panza. Thus Champanza, as if Aston himself were drunkenly (champagne!) gobbling and garbling the Squire's name in the same apish way that Underhill is said to be garbling or gobbling d'Urfey's translation, or version, of Cervantes's words. Here it is impossible to decide whether Aston is acting Underhill acting d'Urfey's acted-out version of Sancho, or whether simply by propinquity to the name, Sancho Panza, Acton's Latin becomes translated, despite itself and despite our best efforts to keep chronology and taxonomy straight, into something like *Homo Sylvestris*' language. To what, then, does 'homo', the human, remit, in this anachronic chain of translations? The "redemption" of Sancho by the clownishness of the possible future enactment is not a future value we can use *necessarily* or even *predictably* to redeem the present or to set boundaries for what we call (in what language?) the human animal.

This is grand fun, but the stakes are obviously very high indeed, since what's being decided is the status of the human animal. Two ghosts haunt our scene straight off. The first is colonial: just *where* was this primate drawn from, extracted, to be set onto the metropolitan stage for profit and entertainment? What routes did the animal follow en route, acquiring and shedding values as it approached the stage? To what other commodities was the primate analogized so as to provide it with a general value – from which abstraction could be made, a general equivalent offered? Champagne, Panza? Not just a primal scene of value production is played: a *primate* scene, the conversion or translation of the most-proximate non-human animal into humanity, of brute to human or to Brutus, from its primary colonial ecology to the metropolitan market. The second ghost that haunts our reading of Aston's little scene is Darwinian: Sancho Panza, the *champanza*, the *chimpanzee*, valued retrospectively as the evolutionary precursor of the human animal. Of course this Darwinian ghost contends for us with its own precursors – archaic ghosts that establish the merit of the human animal in contradistinction to the demerits of the primate who merely apes insight or consciousness or thought, who lacks a soul, who cannot speak and so on.

And this seeming undecidability in the chrematistics-taxonomics-chronology has a further domain of complication. Let's return to Cervantes's text. When we ask what 'Solomon' might mean, what work the name does here, how it works to constitute the field of the audience as a political field, we are pointing to the place in which the figure of Solomon becomes tied to the concept of interpretation or translation as decision: Solomon is a figure for prudential decision, which is to say that regarding the semantic overdetermination of 'Solomon', regarding just what 'Solomon' means, and when, and for whom, and with what foreseeable consequences, we have to be 'Solomonic', we have to be 'new' Solomons with regard to the structure of the 'old' Solomon we are reading in *Don Quijote*. Precisely *because* the name 'Solomon' is overdetermined and under-determined in its uses, and precisely because it takes its overdetermination and underdetermination both from the past *and* from its future, the reader or the spectator is put in the position of needing to make a sovereign decision, a taxonomic decision, to say: 'The name "Solomon" has as a conceptual equivalent this or that range of senses; it can be translated in this way and not that into a concept'. This way, but not that; a sovereign decision; a cut, a judgement, whose authority resides finally in the untranslatable act of making the decision. 'Solomon' is the name for the figure from whom we derive the sovereign procedure used in establishing 'Solomon's' sense and value; 'Solomon' is also a concept whose historical uses we assess, taxonomize, collect, interpret, in admiration and in contempt, eventuating in political community and in radical dissension, in the archaic Hebrew of political modernity and in the humanist Latin of theologico-political Election.

Let me close. My brief in this chapter was to think through three related questions. How do we understand the way in which a cultural network receives, transforms, is transformed by an import – a new cultural commodity, a new theatergram, a new governor, a new term? I was also interested in understanding how we might begin to historicize what I'm calling the second-order use of the concept of translation – those uses of the figure of translation to describe and regulate the movement of cultural materials among markets and along trade routes more generally. Finally, I was interested in seeing whether the association of translation with sovereignty in early modernity provided us with ways of thinking about the regulative relation that the second-order concept of 'translation' has with regard to first-order uses of the term. My suggestion was that the theatre emerges as the space on which the relation between these concepts is displayed, in the period of early modernity. I've focused on the compact, symptomatic way in which the name 'Solomon' is used as the figure for translating the language of religious identity and of religious conversion into a politico-economic language, and for translating the literary-cultural-political figure of Sancho into the cultural landscape of the Baratarian Island. The fourfold methodological complication I have outlined shapes the concept of sovereign identity on whose defective core modern politics and modern political economy stand. The path that leads from Machiavelli to Hobbes and on to Weber and Schmitt crosses the Baratarian Isle, where its contours, edges and direction will be imperfected on the Cervantic stage. Cervantes's staging of Sancho's admirable, Solomonic decisions – stagings that stretch in space from the colony to the metropolis and back, and in time both backward and forward, into the moment when the taxonomic status of the human animal is being decided in *scientific* rather than in religious terms – this staging is constitutive of the relation between the good subject and the good sovereign. The brute becomes Brutus, or Solomon: that *every* brute might become Brutus, *could* become Brutus or Solomon – this is the fantasy of *republican* governance in modernity. But it will no more do to stand our notional republic on the conceptualized name 'Brutus', the brute becoming the foundation of the republic, than it will to stand it upon the conceptualization of 'Salomón': one Brutus, concealing the golden heroism of republican virtue, will be indistinguishable from another, who conspires to murder Caesar in the republic's name: *Et tu, Brute?* One Solomon, wisely governing, from another, mad and ruled by passions. Cervantes's formula or imperative of imperfective decision – 'no acabar de determinarse' – offers up and shapes the fantasy of distributed republican governance and subjects it by the same stroke to a harsh counter-factuality. The future performance of a sovereign decision as well as the overdetermined value system of the past; the heroic eschatology and chrematistics of governance in modernity – these are always open to mistranslation, to being garbled, clowned, aped: *every* Brutus become brutal, become *champanza*. This: the republic of brutes under Solomon's decisive hand. To govern and to interpret entail, in Cervantic modernity, taking on as the condition of political relations what Barataria dramatizes as the spectacle of intolerable indeterminacy: *No acabar de determinarse,* which we can also render as *No acabar de traducirse* – not to finish translating/being-translated/translating oneself.

Chapter 5

What Is *Possible* in Machine Translation

Once adopted into the production process of capital, the means of labour passes through different metamorphoses, whose culmination is the machine, or rather, an automatic system of . . . set in motion by an automaton, a moving power that moves itself; this automaton consisting of numerous mechanical and intellectual organs, so that the workers themselves are cast merely as its conscious linkages (*die Arbeiter selbst nur als bewußte Glieder desselben bestimmt sind*). . . . In no way does the machine appear as the individual worker's means of labour. (Karl Marx, *Grundrisse*)

Dear Dr. Seitz: In April of 1964 you formed an Automatic Language Processing Advisory Committee at the request of Dr. Leland Haworth, Director of the National Science Foundation, to advise the Department of Defense, the Central Intelligence Agency, and the National Science Foundation on research and development in the general field of mechanical translation of foreign languages. We quickly found that you were correct in stating that there are many strongly held but often conflicting opinions about the promise of machine translation and about what the most fruitful steps are that should be taken now. ('Language and Machines: Computers in Translation and Linguistics', a Report by the Automatic Language Processing Advisory Committee Division of Behavioral Sciences (ALPAC Report), National Academy of Sciences [1966])

A question that is of considerable interest is the optimum combination of man and machine. It has come to be generally recognized that machine translation with intensive human pre- and post-editing is hardly worthwhile since this method is largely concerned with remedying the defects of the machine. A far more satisfactory concept is that of companionship. An efficient translating machine that can operate whenever required, can continue when its human partner is fatigued, can instruct its partner without the wearisome labor of consulting dictionaries and grammars, and can retire quietly into the background when the human partner desires to exercise his powers unaided qualifies in considerable measure as a good companion. (R. H. Richens, 'Preprogramming for Mechanical Translation')

Cervantic modernity, then, sets on stage translation as the condition on which there is governance and interpretation: as a political concept, but political inasmuch as it is a defective practice, inasmuch as it is unending, over-determined, radically indeterminate, brutish and brutalizing, inhuman and dehumanizing, taxonomically aberrant. Translation in Cervantic modernity is a political concept for governance and interpretation, in short, inasmuch as it is inhabited by a radical untranslatability.

In this chapter, I'll try to formalize the notion of 'inhabiting'. Contemporary approaches to the philosophy and practices of translation displace the relation onto a disabling, if (or because) authoritative, distinction between instrumental and non-instrumental uses of language. Translations may thus be relevant or not, technical or poetical, practical or literary, idealizing or materialist, they may be domesticating or foreignizing.[1] Can we set that archaic distinction aside? What contemporary concepts will step in to organize the complex, discontinuous, antagonistic semantic fields designated by the term 'translation'? In what way will these contemporary concepts of translation be 'political'? How is what we call 'politics' transformed – translated – when 'translation' becomes a 'political concept', along the lines I sketched in chapter 4 (and joins terms we might more readily be willing to call 'political': a *people,* a *tongue, representation, interest*)? In order to parse what the 'inhabiting' of translation by radical untranslatability amounts to, with a view to understanding how that couplet moves towards the end of what I've called global thought, I will first sketch the outlines of the prevailing, but conceptually trivial, sense of translation we might be tempted to press into service as a political concept. I'll then turn to the languages of so-called machine translation (MT), which organize the semantic field covered by the term 'translation' today, to describe a different sense of translation and of the limits that inhabit it and which provide different futures as a political concept. Finally I'll return to early modernity and, with the help of different sorts of machines entirely, or different sorts of mechanical entities, I will hope to show how these two senses of 'translation' should be thought in relation to one another and then reworked into our understanding of the practices and politics of translation we encounter today.

It is no secret that the group of phenomena that we call *globalization* today takes shape around the differential flow of people, labour, commodities and capital among different regions, along axes that line up not only North to South but also East to West, and which might be charted politically on a slightly different map, in which domains of protectionist legislation, specific labour practices, relations to colonial tradition or access to natural resources are the organizing devices, rather than national borders or strictly geographical ones. 'Translation', the conveying of information between natural languages, is a political concept in this sense: it is at the same time one of the instruments that make possible certain of the flows, and it is itself what one might call a second-order commodity practice whose value is established in relation to the flow of capital and of first-order, material commodities. I am using the rather special term 'commodity-practice' where others would probably use the expression 'immaterial labor', so as to decouple, sharply for the sake of brevity, the notion of value from the scheme of 'material labor' on which it classically depends.[2] 'In no way does the machine appear as the individual worker's means of labor', says Marx in the 'Machine Fragment' from *Grundrisse*. This is the tendency I would like to stress: in no way does *translation* appear today as a worker's 'means of labor'.

Something like this articulation of commercial production and translation has of course obtained for a very long time indeed. Translation and mercantilism emerge hand in hand well before the modern concepts of 'market', 'commodity' and 'value' are agreed, and well before translation joins its other hands to religious evangelization and to colonial administrative practices. The situation today inflects that longer, geocultural picture with the particularities of labour-export manufacturing, a highly articulated global transportation and communication system and a system of global credit and finance that makes both possible. If I want to locate my widget-making assembly line in Nicaragua or my iPad factory in China, where labour laws are lax, environmental regulations negligible and the cost of labour sits at about one-fifteenth of what it might be in the European Union or in the United States, then I'll need to understand Spanish or Mandarin, or hire a translator who does, in order to transact business; the value of the practice of translation is indexed among other things to the worth of that business, and not only to the supply of speakers of Spanish or Mandarin who can serve as translators, or to the supply of labourers who speak only those languages, and who must be convinced in them to work on my assembly lines.

The governing fantasy of this sort of translation is the fantasy of strict or rigid designation, a 'widget' and an iPad being rigidly designated or, minimally, designable in all natural languages. We understand this fantasy of strictness or rigidity in two complementary though quite different senses. I say to my Nicaraguan partner, 'Let's make widgets', and for him or her to understand me, my partner must first understand that what I am saying is, in fact, intentional and communicative speech, an expression with some sense to it and not just gibberish. In this bare, stipulative sense, it is necessary that my partner grant that in my phrase there is sense, and that this sense is sufficiently independent of my 'expression' and of the words themselves, that the sense of whatever it is that I'm saying, for instance, 'Let's make widgets', is transferable to Spanish. This bare double stipulation, that we are engaging in communicative, intentional expression, and that what is being expressed can be severed from whatever it is which expresses it, is necessarily true if there is to be translation, or so we believe. It is at any rate a condition for my seeking the services of a translator, whom I would not require if no communicative situation of this sort were stipulated or envisioned. (We could put it like this: for there to be translation, we have to agree, in some shared language, that there *are* 'natural languages', always more than one.)

Remark that *this* version of the widget story has an important kinship to the stories that underwrite *some* theologies of translation, Pauline ones specifically: the severability, the circumcision, of letter from spirit is underwritten by, and in turn comes to underwrite, a tradition severing expression from content that may date to Socrates.

The second way in which we should understand the 'strict' or 'rigid' designation of the term 'widget' is related to this theological strain, but derives most closely, of course, from Saul Kripke's early work in what comes to be called modal semantics, where some linguistic unit, a name or a demonstrative, is said to be a rigid designator 'if in every possible world it designates the same object'.[3] In the world of the global factory, we are in the presence of a highly simplified version of 'identity across possible worlds'; perhaps, even, we are in the presence of the type or archetype of such identity across possible worlds. This is our ecology: the world of Mandarin or Spanish, the world of English, an object common to both, and two names, one in English, one in Mandarin or in Spanish, designating that object.

But it could even be slightly different. Let's say that there are no widgets in Nicaragua, and that there's no name for a widget in Spanish. My translator will produce the object that I have handed him or her, show it to my partner and describe its uses: my translator will then say in Spanish something like 'In English, this is called a widget, and Jacques proposes that we should make them'. 'Widget' in the target language now means: 'The object called "widget" in English'. A description of the object might follow, its uses enumerated and so on. An ostensive act – showing the object – is linked to an act of naming, or rather to one explicit act which serves to designate the object and to an implicit act of ostension, the metalinguistic designation 'in English'. At this point, and perhaps to my distress, my Nicaraguan partner might possibly strike off on his or her own and do business with a Portuguese company, also perhaps lacking the word and object called in English a widget and in Spanish 'the object called "widget" in English'. He or she employs a Spanish-Portuguese translator, who will call the object he holds, in Portuguese, 'The object called "The object called widget in English" in Spanish', and perhaps describe in Portuguese its uses, even its colour and possible benefits, attending to the different uses that an object of that description might have in Portugal (where circumstances of culture, geography, climate or circumstance might dictate different uses for a widget than might seem appropriate, or even conceivable, in different circumstances, conditions, times, etc.). The whole eventual, global edifice stands on two bases: on the regressive, metropolitan stipulation that in English the object is called a widget and on the supposed commonality, the zero degree of linguistic expression, in which ostension and designation are linked *before translation* and *as the condition for* translation, in English, in Spanish, in Portuguese, in Mandarin and so on. (Explicit ostension, as regards the object I seek to designate; implicit or metalinguistic ostension, as regards my designating the language or the designation practices in which I make that explicit designation.) In the political economy of 'possible worlds' philosophy what is designated by the notion of 'possibility' is the universal of an index for value and of a naked anteriority in which such indexing may rigidly occur, the 'real' time of the designated entity, of the potential commodity before, and as the condition of, its stepping into the market. Here, 'possible' means 'bearing ostensibly a value that is translatable across possible markets'. Whatever the term 'widget' may be in Mandarin, and even if there is no term in Spanish or in Portuguese for the object my translator is holding, there is some sense, and beyond that sense some real thing, to which the English 'widget' refers, and the Mandarin or Spanish for 'widget' refers rigidly to that referential or baptismal moment, as does each subsequent translation.

A visual analogue may help here. Recall the 'stone which Euripides calls a magnet' [ὥσπερ ἐν τῇ λίθῳ ἣν Εὐριπίδης μὲν Μαγνῆτιν ὠνόμασεν], used by Socrates in Plato's *Ion* (533d) to describe the inspiring power of the Muse. The magnet 'not only attracts iron rings but also puts power in the rings so that they also have power to do the same thing the stone does and attract other rings. Sometimes quite a long chain of iron rings hangs suspended from one another; but they're all suspended by the power derived from that stone' [πᾶσι δὲ τούτοις ἐξ ἐκείνης τῆς λίθου ἡ δύναμις ἀνήρτηται].[4] But the 'real' things designated in the 'possible worlds' scenario, or in the global 'possible-markets' scenario, need not be real in the sense of 'really existing in the world right now or at one time': we do not mean that what 'widget' designates is real in the way that the magnet that imparts the charge to the chain's rings must be real, or must, to impart the charge, have been materially real, the charge imagined now as the subsisting trace of that initial *touch*.[5] We do not mean that this or that thing must have a value in a market, before it can acquire a different one in another market: we mean only that it *might* have a value, because the concept of valuation or the mechanism of valuing pertain in this or that thing's home ecology, even if that thing itself isn't immediately understood in that ecology as being the sort of thing that has value. And we mean this because the stipulative phrase 'this or that thing' (or something like this phrase), however different the 'thing' it designates may be in one or another world, works to designate in all possible worlds. (Designation conventions are, if not identical across all possible worlds, at least sufficiently *analogous* to be translatable across all possible worlds: this is a fact of all possible worlds, even if the conventions of each world differ. Modal semantics stands upon the stipulation that 'possible world' designates a possible world in all possible worlds, that is, that the convention of designation is itself *rigid*.)

We say that 'the king of France' designates something that is real but does not necessarily exist, or that a 'widget' designates something that *could* have a value. Now we mean by 'real' a complex of things – we mean that it is not analytically impossible that there be such a thing as a 'king of France' (a 'king of France' is not a round square); we mean that there have been kings in France historically; we mean that we can imagine a world in which there is a king in France, even though there is none in this world, the one we share; we mean that we rely, in making an argument concerning the special reality of widgets, upon a mediating allusion to Russell's arguments regarding denoting, which I use here to baptize or magnetize my widgets with a further, philosophically regal surplus value.[6] We also mean that a 'widget' is something that *could* have a value, whether of this sort or of that, in this market or another. When it comes to widgets themselves, there is even some lexical support for this seeming casuistry. Generally, when we use the word 'widget' and if we are speaking before 2002 or so, the date when electronic machine programmes called 'widgets' entered the lexicon, then we are referring to what the *Oxford English Dictionary* defines as the 'indefinite name for a gadget or mechanical contrivance, especially a small manufactured item'.[7] *Before* 2002, a 'widget' is a real, but indefinite, place-holding term for any manufactured gadget, but it is not a 'really existing' gadget that I can hold in my hand and pass to my Nicaraguan translator. Absent a 'real' thing (though not necessarily a really subsisting thing or a material thing) designated by the English, the Spanish and the Mandarin, it would be meaningless to speak of translating the term 'widget' into Spanish or Mandarin, or indeed to speak of translatability in general. Absent this reality principle, this principle of 'identity across possible worlds', or more properly this principle of the sufficient analogy of 'identity' and the sufficient analogy of 'designation' across all possible worlds, we would be unable to compare the worth of this or that commodity across frontiers – including the second-order commodity practice of 'translation'.

I have been speaking so far about direct instrumental translation practices – of technical documents, business contracts, restaurant menus, travel schedules and the like: the transference or transport of this bit of information, for instance, the information that 'Jacques wants to produce widgets', which is accidentally expressed in one or another natural language, English in this case, into a different natural language. Now let us consider those practices – of literary translation principally – in which the supposed worth of the aesthetic dimension of the original language and of the translation is part of the value accruing to each. Here the relation between the bit of information and the 'natural language' in which it is expressed or into which it is cast is not imagined to be accidental, though it may not rise to the Aristotelian level of an 'essential' or undisseverable relation, in which case translation would simply not be possible. Very little else about my widget scenario changes, however. A communicability agreement seems to be stipulated strictly. In place of a real, though not necessarily existent, object underlying the rigid designation of the term 'widget' or the term 'translation', I now imagine a real, though not necessarily existent concept called 'aesthetic value', which is rigidly predicable of my expressions, whatever they may be. That bare predicate is then undisseverably, rigidly, characteristically applied to the specific translation of my expression or my poem, from English to whatever other natural language I may envision, whether I am reciting a poem that begins 'Let's make widgets', or one that sings 'Love is not love/Which alters when it alteration finds'.

We might comfortably imagine the long history of translation, the practices as well as the theory or conceptualization of translation, in terms of these two poles or foci, which are also paradigms for valuing one translation over another, even for deciding what counts or does not count as a translation. We might remark that at different times and under different economic, political and cultural pressures, the comparative value of the instrumental form of translation on one side, and of the aesthetically inflected sort on the other, will fluctuate in relation to one another and to different criteria. We might believe ourselves to be working on the ground of a three-way analogy or a *ratio* – a natural language is to a term in that language, say 'widget' or 'translation', *as* the ecologies in which it is to be valued and marketed are to a real object; the movement from one natural language to another in which 'widget' or 'translation' is to be expressed is like the movement from one ecology or one market, in which a widget or a translation is to be valued, to another. In this imagining and remarking, we establish the genealogy of the concept and practices of translation and we globalize the ecology and the market in which these concepts and practices obtain. We reassure ourselves in doing so that after all we are, still and always, the expression of the word despite ourselves, the animal or *zoon logon echon* who in the course of forgetting its archaic relation to the word becomes the rational or the marketing animal.[8] And in this remarking and imagining we remain, always and necessarily, at sea in the modern political economy of possible markets.

In all this remarking and imagining, however, we will be overlooking two related matters. We will be overlooking, in the first place, something that appears in some respects entirely new: the epochal shift introduced in the standing map of practices and theories of translation by the advent, in and following the Cold War, of MT.[9] No longer do *workers* translate; the task of the translator is no longer primarily a human, even a humanistic task. The paradigm of Babel, turning in the ellipse formed by the two foci of instrumental and aesthetic translation, underwriting but also expressing a distinction between technical and intellectual labour, a conception of the human as *homo laborans* or *homo faber*, has given way to what one might reasonably call the Babel Fish paradigm. Or the Babel Fish epoch, Google Translate's time, the age of a double displacement: on the one hand, the displacement of what might allow *logos*, the flashing-forth and gathering-in of Being as unconcealment, Heidegger would say, to flash forth in otherwise technical expressions like 'natural language', 'linguistic difference', 'information' or 'semantic distinction or drift'.[10] But on the other – and this is what would make the story something other than the account of the advent of a technological world picture – the simultaneous displacement of the characteristically inessential, mystified dimension of linguistic expression that, in Heidegger's telling, steps in where *logos* is forgotten. Google Translate's time; the Babel Fish epoch marks, simultaneous with the displacement of whatever in language attends to what Heidegger calls 'the being that was originally opened up in gathering', the displacement also of language become 'mere hearsay', the work of *glossa*, language become the mechanical organ of the tongue, language inasmuch as it represents the 'loosening' of 'truth', that is, Google Translate's time marks also the time in which language becomes, both gradually and catastrophically, the expression of a machine, 'the act of speaking, the activation of the organs of speech, mouth, lips, tongue'.[11] Google Translate's time – the Babel Fish epoch – not only takes from us our tongues, the act of speaking, expression inasmuch as it pertains to the articulating machine we call our body; indeed, but it *also* takes from us whatever relations to more authentic, primary, archaic terms the long history of metaphysics has sought to employ to designate what is not merely expressible and yet makes the human animal properly and distinctively human.

Google Translate's time; the Babel Fish epoch: a different keying of value to time and to labour than obtained before the advent of MT; a different indexing of labour to human action, intention, body[12] and, as a result, a different concept of the human altogether. Witness, for instance, the fate of the metaphor that governs the conceptualization of MT in 1956 – the cosy figure of the collaboration between the human translator and his machine aide: 'An efficient translating machine [is] a good companion', writes R. H. Richens. But when Franz Joseph Och, the lead developer of Google Translator, was asked in 2010 by the *Los Angeles Times* about the 'training of the translator', it was not companionship between human and machine translators that was envisioned. Instead, it is the combination of statistical-machine-translating algorithm, database and search engine that the word 'translator' referred to, and the three forms of labour the question rather foggily envisioned – the 'training of the translator', the 'searching' and the 'translating' – were to be understood as instances of the same process, a process camped out in anachronistic metaphors as the most primitive form of extractive manual labour, mining, carried out by entirely non-human means. This is Och, in answer to the question 'When you train the translator, you've got to get so-called parallel data sets, where every document occurs in at least two languages. Where do you get all of those translations from?' Och says:

> When we started, there were standard test sets provided by the Linguistic Data Consortium, which provides data for research and academic institutes. Then there are places like the United Nations, which have all their documents translated into the six official languages of the United Nations. And there's a vast pool of documents available there in the database, which has been very useful because the translation quality has been very good. But then otherwise, it's kind of 'the Web.' . . . Our algorithms basically mine everything that's out there.

To this, the interviewer remarks, 'So it's sort of analogous to the way Google's Web crawler spiders Web pages?' And Och answers:

> It's similar. While the Web crawler is mining the whole Web and indexing it, then for the translation crawler is the subset of documents that include translations [*sic*]. The challenge is to find which texts are translated into another language – and where to find the corresponding translation.[13]

Note the outrageously anachronistic use of the term 'mining'; the wonderful and symptomatic verbalization of the noun 'spider'. Remark the awkward anacoluthon in Och's answer. We are watching the interview's language strain to express a state of affairs for which there is not yet a lexicon or a syntax. Something, and it is neither *logos* nor *glossa,* flashes. We are, it appears, in the event.

Of course, when we tell the story in *this* way, we are surrendering to a different sort of temptation. We imagine that an event has occurred or is occurring, and we stand in its shadow or at its advent, we moderns, like bold Cortez upon a peak, or Zarathustra at the opening to his cave or like Captain Kirk on the deck of the Starship Enterprise. Nothing about this new, adventitious time is or will be translatable into its forerunner; our world has changed; the linguistic function of 'referring' differs, and what we refer to does as well, semantically and syntactically – a spider now 'spiders', an algorithm mines, and the search for 'a corresponding translation' to a string of words is carried out neither instrumentally nor aesthetically, but mechanically. When we say 'language', or 'translation', different things, unimaginably different things, are designated than when the same words were used *before* Turing, and *before* the Cold War.

The temptation, then, is twofold. In the first place, to imagine the advent of MT in the breathless light of the messianic – or its proxies, the robotic, the inhuman. 'The Android version of Google Translate allows the user to speak to the application, and have his or her words translated', says the *Los Angeles Times* interviewer. 'Is it', he continues, 'just one short step from here to real time, speech-to-speech translation, a la "Star Trek's" universal translator?' And Och answers: 'To really do the integrated speech-to-speech translation, where you can have a phone call with someone and it would [be] interpreted live? I believe that based on the technology that we have, and the improvement rate we have in the core quality of M[achine] T[ranslation] and speech recognition, that it should be possible to do that in the not-too-distant future'.[14] The garishness of this science fiction scenario tends to obscure the second, related mistake, which is to imagine that the advent of MT does indeed mark an epochal break with the Babelian paradigm, whose humanist heroics and whose elliptical circuit, defined by and mapping the fluctuation of value invested in the foci of technical and aesthetic labour, would seem untranslatable into the emerging lexicon and syntax of MT. Each, we like to think, is cut from the other by a historical caesura every bit as sharp, as unbridgeable and untranslatable, as any we might find in the Christological imaginary.

But is this indeed so? Might there be other ways of rethinking translation, the concept, the history and the present of translation?

Which brings me to the second thing we will have overlooked in all this imagining and remarking. Let us say that MT has always and already inhabited the Babelian paradigm. You can imagine already the consequences this might have for the various maps in which we've settled what we call 'translation' – the map of the market, of evangelization, of the long-cherished definitions of the human animal as *homo faber* or as the animal that produces art. You can imagine what it might mean for the long linking of value to material production to claim that an inhuman commodity practice has always and already spidered away in the texture of what seems to be most proper to human animals, to *zoon logon ekhon*. We can imagine these consequences of claiming that MT has always spidered away at natural languages, at an angle to the twin foci of instrument and aesthetic enjoyment that I've graphed – we can imagine the consequences of the claim, but what would it mean to claim such a thing? Not, of course, offering some sort of time-travelling marriage of Google with Heraclitus, the mere reverse of the science fiction scenario I have been evoking, peopled with Androids and Star Trek translating devices. What we mean by a 'machine' will have to change; what we mean by 'translation' too; 'history' as well – not to the point where the *modern* 'machine' cannot serve us as a translation of the older one but also in a way that does not stand or fall upon the fantasies of designation, of possible world economies, that I have been outlining. To claim that MT has always and already inhabited, worked or spidered away at natural languages would mean claiming that the difficulties the concept of translation entails work, silently or clamorously, or occur, not just across societies and at different historical moments, but structurally in natural languages, and in the space of single, determining descriptions of the processes of translation.

To say that 'difficulties' of this sort occur 'structurally' in natural languages, and that they crop up across historical moments and locations, would not *seem* terribly different from the rigid fantasies of designation and of value-indexing attached to the 'possible worlds' of the global market and of the commodity practice of translation. But it is. Let us say that in place of widgets, in place of the commodity I hope to produce with my Nicaraguan partner, my translator and I are discussing the related commodity that my translator is hoping to produce for my consumption, the second-order commodity or commodity practice that is his or her translation. We are not talking about an object either of us can hold or produce as one would a widget (presuming for the moment that a 'widget' is a really subsisting, material object): what we are discussing, roughly speaking, is the object we call 'a natural language' or two such languages and the relation between them. We are discussing the uses to which that relation is to be put; the costs associated with moving between them; the value of the product my translator delivers and so on. The Mandarin or Spanish translator and I will have to agree that we are engaging in some sort of intentional, communicative expression, and we will have to have a minimally similar understanding of what it means to 'translate' when I set about hiring him or her. Here, where the object under discussion is not a widget but the means of designating a widget in two different languages, that is, where the object designated is what we call 'translation', the threat of a poisonous regress is unavoidable. This poisonous regress distinguishes this level of discussion concerning this sort of object-which-is-not-an-object, called a 'natural language', from the discussion my translator and I might have regarding a widget, however the reality of such an object is to be imagined. And note that, poisonous though it may be, this threat of regress is also, crucially, the source of unassimilable values and designation effects, values and effects immeasurable according to the ecologies of *either* language and of *either* market, original or target. When we say that some word or expression in Mandarin or in Spanish is a translation of the English 'widget', and that this holds true in all possible worlds because of the logical requirement imposed by the notion that we are indeed 'translating' between languages, then we seem to be required to stipulate that designation conventions are, if not identical, then sufficiently similar among natural languages that 'widget' may be said to designate in much the same way in the original language as in the target – independently of what, in fact, is designated by 'widget' and its translation in Spanish or Mandarin. What obtains for the concept of 'designation convention' is also true for the concept of 'translation', and in general for metalinguistic terms that natural languages use to designate themselves, and which may indeed be said not just to 'designate' but also to 'translate' the natural language into the condition of being a discursive *object* (composed of statements, a lexicon, conventions of usage, syntax and so on) named or designated by a metadiscursive statement, or a name, *in that same natural language*. As you might suppose, what's happening here – whatever process I am designating when I describe this objectification of a language from within that language, this metaphoricization of the language by means of itself – this process is neither instrumental nor aesthetic simply. As to its strictness or rigidity across the possible world, you will get a sense of how tricky the situation can become when you note that metalinguistic terms are not always and exclusively metalinguistic in a given context (metalinguistic statements, like performative utterances, are always, an early Derrida might put it, parasitized by context); when you note that certain 'object' terms can be and often are used tropically with a metalinguistic function; and that the rules for deciding when a term is being used in one way or another are themselves conventional, partial, changing and contentious, when not contradictory, and when they are not also the consequence of such metalinguistic uses.

Let us call the widget that produces intra-linguistic translation and designation effects of this sort *Machine Translation*, the spider in the linguistic cup *before* Turing and *before* the Cold War. This widget produces the flickering, undecidable movement between statements' (or names' or terms' or metaphors') linguistic and metalinguistic status. It works between statements and what they designate; it spiders away to tip a particular thing designated into the ensemble of designation conventions, lexicon and syntax that make up the natural language within which such designations take place. It is internal to the metalinguistic statement or term, its designation and the object it designates. What does this sort of MT look like?

I will give you an example taken from the canon of phrases regarding translation, repeated mechanically since Quince, one of the 'rude mechanicals' of *A Midsummer Night's Dream*, first uttered it some four centuries ago, in an infamously haunted forest, treading heavily among fairies, monarchs and translated lovers. We are the audience at Shakespeare's most subjunctive play, his most extravagant exploration of the fantasy of possible worlds, the most radical staging of philosophical modality in the theatrical canon. (Prose is another matter.) Shakespeare peppers his text with the most severe marker of unconditionality, the word 'never' – used here over thirty times, more often than in any other comedy (with the exception, oddly, of *Much Ado about Nothing*). 'Never' – yes, but set against the most basic and pervasive form of counterfactual wondering. What if the woodland held a Fairy court? Is a world possible in which a weaver can become an ass and stay a Bottom; where domestic dilemmas of Athenian politics are solved extramurally by sprites, mechanicals, actors; where senses become disjoined and garbled, voices can be seen and faces heard ('I see a voice: now will I to the chink,/To spy an I can hear my Thisby's face', says Bottom's Pyramus (5.1.192–93)? The theatre, of course, is always structurally counterfactual, a staging of modality – but this is Shakespeare's most alarming, seductive and rigorous enacting or *translating* of that staging.

And so, when Quince says to Bottom's Pyramus in *A Midsummer Night's Dream*, 'Bless thee, Bottom! bless thee! thou art translated' (3.1.119), the poor ass-headed weaver, Nick Bottom, hears, we presume, that he is 'transformed' as well as 'translated', even though he does not realize just how translated, or in what ways transformed, he is (and this perhaps should be a sign to his audience that Bottom is, at bottom, already and always an Ass, although and because he is unable to recognize himself as one).[15] This, after all, is the double sense Shakespeare's audience has learnt to expect in *A Midsummer Night's Dream*, Helena having told Hermia that, 'Were the world mine, Demetrius being bated,/The rest I'd give to be to you translated' (1.1.190–91). Quince's famous line follows, as if glossing or translating it, Snout's much less famous exclamation, to the same effect, 'O Bottom, thou art changed! what do I see on thee?' (3.1.114–15). Shakespeare's audience might well have heard the same synonymy of 'change' or 'transformation' in 'translation', though they, unlike Bottom, would have also heard the linguistic 'translation' of 'change' into 'translation' and of 'Bottom' into 'Ass' and they might well have registered the additional metalinguistic value of Quince's word, 'translated', which also designates and describes what has happened between the partially synonymous expressions 'O Bottom, thou art changed!' and 'Bless thee, Bottom! bless thee! thou art translated', as it also designates and describes what has happened between the terms 'Bottom' and 'Ass'. (Analogues? Translations of each other?) For a contemporary public, a public at the Public Theatre in New York in the year 2012, for example, the archaic sense of 'translated' as 'changed or metamorphosed' would be largely lost, as would the old sense of a 'Bottom' as a 'skein' or ball of thread, or a nucleus on which thread or cord could be wound, in order to produce the warp of a fabric. Today's public would render 'translation' 'conformable to *our* manners', as Cicero might say, *verbis ad nostram consuetudinem aptis*, and hear, minimally, the flicker of an interlinguistic pun opening from the scabrous play on ass-bottom onto the wonderful resonances between the transformed Bottom's human speech and a donkey's braying.[16]

To us today, as to Shakespeare's audience but *not* to Bottom himself, or not *yet* to Bottom himself, or not in a way that the play registers *as* the character's 'knowing' this, to us and to Shakespeare's audience Bottom's words from this point forward sound in both registers, in English and in Ass, though of course without our being in any way able to say what, precisely, Bottom's words or near neighs designate *in* Ass. (Rather, to the extent that we understand Bottom's words, we find that we may be able to understand, not just English alone but Ass as well – with the consequent rather demoralizing realization about our own intelligence.) As for what it is that Titania hears when she's roused from sleep by the sounds of Bottom's singing, before she sees him even, plucked from her midsummer night's dreams by an 'angel' who 'wakes [her] from [her] flowery bed' – this remains forever foreclosed to us. We, and Shakespeare's Elizabethan audience, hear the mechanical sing, and some of us hear also the extraordinary metalinguistic surplus value that 'translation' adds to 'change', and Ass to Bottom – but who among us is '[moved] perforce/On the first view,' or on first hearing the weaver, 'to say, to swear, I love thee' (3.1.137–41) to an Ass? His Ass-head having scared away the other 'mechanicals', Bottom sings to scare away his fright just after his translation, 'The finch, the sparrow and the lark,/The plain-song cuckoo grey,/Whose note full many a man doth mark,/And dares not answer nay' (3.1.130–33).

We hear Bottom's 'nay' not once but twice, here and in answer to Titania's professions of love: 'Nay, I can gleek upon occasion' (3.1.146–47). But what do we hear? Onomatopoeically, some sort of utterance in Ass, of course – a 'neigh', what man 'dare not answer', an expression of a man's asininity, what one might call an example or a *use* of the language Ass. A man 'dare not' 'neigh', because he understands a 'neigh', whatever it may designate in Ass, to be uttered *in Ass* and to designate collectively the natural language I am calling, rudely and mechanically, Ass. To answer 'nay' is to 'neigh', or to be an Ass: the 'neigh-ness' of 'neigh' removes 'nay' from the language human animals can use without losing their humanity, in whole or – like Bottom – in part. But 'nay' lines up also, syntactically, in the parallel shape the little ditty takes, with the 'plain-song' of the cuckoo, an adjectivized noun-phrase first characterizing the cuckoo (the bird that sings in plainsong) and then becoming, tremblingly, the antecedent, with that cuckoo itself, of the cuckoo's 'note'. A man's 'nay' is not just *what* he dare not answer: for example, I'd like to say 'Nay', or no, to the note that the cuckoo-cuckold calls to me, but I dare not answer 'Nay' to that call because in my heart I believe or fear myself to be a cuckold, to be a cuckoo, that is, I fear myself to be the bird that calls its own name and calls me by that name, a name that names *and* describes me. A man's 'nay' is not just *what* he dare not answer, it is the name of the language in which he *dare not* answer: *either* the 'plain-song . . . note' of cuckoo, which makes him out, as the utterer of notes in the language onomatopoeically named 'cuckoo', to be a cuckold himself; *or* the plainsong note of 'Neigh' or 'Nay', which designates him an Ass for denying, *in Ass*, that he is, indeed, a donkey and cuckold to boot. It's hardly a coincidence that Titania refers to Bottom's speech in the same way as Bottom does to the Cuckoo's 'note': 'I pray thee, gentle mortal, sing again,/Mine ear is much enamored of thy note' (3.1.137–41). Here much of Shakespeare's humour stands upon the uncontrollable translation between discursive *use* and meta-discursive *mention*, between languages – the English language of weavers and other mechanicals, the languages of Asses and cuckoos, of Fairies and spirits like Puck – and metalinguistic terms designating languages, English, Ass, Cuckoo, 'Neigh', note, plainsong or language uses. Extraordinarily *threatening* humour, however, and not just for the poor man, unmanned at finding himself unable to say 'Nay' to being cuckolded – unable to say 'Nay' for fear of losing his tongue and speaking 'Neigh' in Ass, and thus, silent, assenting to the plainsong of the cuckoo, which not only calls to but also *names him:* 'Cuckoo', cuckold, it calls to him. If Nick Bottom's man answers 'Yes', he has agreed to the cuckoo's designation and to the bird's description of himself, and the man thus answers *in cuckoo*, with his name. ('Cuckoo!' says the bird. 'Yes?' answers Bottom, or any other man – 'Yes, that's me, I am Cuckoo, a cuckoo, inasmuch as I understand your call, in the language that calls me and to me that, and calls itself "Cuckoo," inasmuch as I understand that your call designates me. And it is in that language that I answer you, cuckoo to cuckoo or Cuckoo to cuckoo, my "Yes?" in English serving to confirm that yes, I am (a) Cuckoo, that my English is also the natural language called cuckoo, spoken by cuckolds and cuckoo-birds alike'.) If he answers 'Nay', he answers in Ass, and reveals that he is an ass for not knowing that he is, at heart, a cuckold, who should have answered, also or instead, in cuckoo. Bottom must, perforce, keep silent – and what sort of theatre is it that enjoins silence upon its characters, that calls upon them to 'Love, and be silent', for example, as Cordelia calls upon herself to do? (*Lear* 1.1.62). The designation of a language *as* a language, that rigid condition on which translation among possible worlds stands or falls, frays: is 'Neigh' a word in Ass or in English? (Is a 'word' in Ass even a word? Is it not, rather, a 'neigh'?) Is 'neigh' a word in *both*, as Bottom seems to be both human and Ass? Does 'Cuckoo' designate the language, the bird-speaker, the husband, the Ass-Man? Among the first things to fail: the identity of the designation 'natural language', parasitized by the language of birds, donkeys, to say nothing of Fairies.

So threatening, so possibly *tragic*, is this little comic scene, that even the most loving, the most charmed audience, Titania herself, cannot bear to listen to Bottom's speech, to his frenetic riffing on the senses of her retinue's proper names, Cobweb, Peaseblossom and Mustardseed, names suddenly translated into Ass, as it were, by Bottom, demoted from proper names to descriptions of different mechanical or natural functions much as the name 'cuckoo' passes from the bird that utters the plainsong note in cuckoo, to designate the object it calls to and who marks himself in it. *So* disturbing is what the Queen of the Fairies hears in her beloved Bottom's voice, a voice she praised absurdly not a hundred lines above, a voice whose angelic notes she wished to hear again and again; *so* shaken is fair Titania that (whether out of fear some like fate will befall her own name or perhaps out of fear or awareness that her 'love' for Bottom will indeed produce at least one more 'cuckoo': Oberon himself, cuckolded by the Ass-headed weaver) the Fairy Queen orders Cobweb, Peaseblossom and Mustardseed to 'tie up my lover's tongue, bring him silently' (3.1.201). Titania, deprived of the sweet neighs of her lover's voice, thus confirms for herself, in compensation, that it is she who gets to determine what functions her servants have, and not their names, and not the translating voice of a mere mechanical Ass – and that she will be able to cuckold Oberon with an Ass without having the Faerie King's shame designated and neighed about openly, in Cuckoo, in Ass or in English.

So disturbing is this mad scene that the crowned king of Shakespeare's translators, August Wilhelm Schlegel, that Fairy King on whom the plays, and this one in particular, exercised a charm with far-reaching consequences in European modernity, finds it impossible to translate Bottom's translation literally. About the transformation scene Schlegel writes, in the *Lectures on Dramatic Art*, that 'the extremes of fanciful and vulgar are united when the enchanted Titania awakes and falls in love with a coarse mechanic with an ass's head, who represents, or rather disfigures, the part of a tragical lover. The droll wonder of Bottom's transformation is merely the translation of a metaphor in its literal sense' ['Das scherzhafte Wunder der Verwandlung Bottoms ist eigentlich nur die Uebersetzung einer Metapher in ihren buchstäbli-chen Sinn'].[17] The translation of a metaphor. This is promisingly abyssal, easily reversed into the metaphor of a translation, a translation of a translation and a metaphor of and for a metaphor, and these nice reversals immediately throw into question the notion that the Ass-head's 'literal sense', *buchstäbli-chen Sinn*, can be determined rigidly. In Schlegel's words, we appear to be, in other words, very much in Shakespeare's threatening lexicon and wood, where the antic widget of intra-linguistic translation between discursive and metadiscursive statements threatens to lead to silence or to tragedy. But when Schlegel *translates* the scene he tends to silence this strange and threatening aspect of Shakespeare's text. Snout's 'Changed' is rendered, unexception-ably, *verwandelt* ('O Zettel! du bist verwandelt!'), but the not-quite-synony-mous, because immediately and dangerously metalinguistic, 'translated' with which Quince translates 'changed' is translated not through *übersetzung*, as the *Lectures on Dramatic Art* would seem to urge, but through the slightly different *transferiert:*

> *Zettel:* Warum laufen sie weg? Dies ist eine Schelmerei von ihnen, um mich fürchten zu machen.
>
> (Schnauz kommt zurück.)
>
> *Schnauz:* O Zettel! du bist verwandelt! Was seh ich an dir?
>
> *Zettel:* Was du siehst? Du siehst deinen eigenen Eselskopf. Nicht?
>
> (Schnauz ab. Squenz kommt zurück.)
>
> *Squenz:* Gott behüte dich, Zettel! Gott behüte dich! du bist transferiert.
>
> (Ab.)
>
> *Zettel:* Ich merke ihre Schelmerei: sie wollen einen Esel aus mir machen.

Transferieren does mean, Grimm tells us, 'verteutschen', an archaic form of *verdeutschen*, 'in ein andere sprache setzen', and it's used, for instance by Luther, to designate 'translation'.[18] But Grimm tells us that such metaphoric – translated – meanings are distinctly secondary to *ein ding von ein ort zum andern tragen*, the literal sense, 'to carry a thing over from one place to another'. And as if to confirm that this translation, willy-nilly, ties up Bottom's tongue, Ass and Bottom become *Esel* and *Zettel*. Each of these transformations is amusing in its way, the Ass-*Esel* perhaps echoing in Titania's word about the music that she hears, the word Angel, *Engel*; and *Zettel*, which Schlegel gets from Wieland's earlier translation, losing much of its physicality, its association with stupidity and doltishness, its synonymy with *Esel*, but gaining a peculiar compensatory metatheatricality, a *Zettel* being, not just a piece of paper or a chit, but also a playbook or a script. The metalinguistic function of our weaver's 'Nay', opened by the linguistic sense of the word 'translation' in the English, is absent from the German – Bottom's little cuckoo song now goes: 'Der Kuckuck, der der Grasmück/So gern ins Nestchen heckt/Und lacht darob mit arger Tück/Und manchen Ehmann neckt'. The German for *neighing* is *wiehern* – so although 'necken' may *sound* like neighing to us (speakers of English), and to Schlegel's readers and audience, the word's function of naming its onomatopoeic function is lost, as is, of course, the play on negation and expression we saw in the English 'Nay'.

All of this goes far to paint Schlegel as a latter-day Titania, a translator who ties the tongue of Shakespeare's play, and seeks to keep at bay the English play's riotous transformation of statements, syntax, lexicon and names into functional elements taking as their designation and object the ensemble of statements, syntax, lexicon and names from which they derive – and back.

Schlegel appears to silence Bottom-Zettel as Titania does, Bottom's tongue chained to the chit of paper or to the playbook, speech become writing, the play become a playbook, the translation-machine become a sort of transcription machine. But this is not quite right, or not sufficient to this strange translation scene, where instrument and aesthetic enjoyment meet Shakespeare's rude mechanicals. Schlegel, and before him Wieland, captures marvellously something that is almost silent in Shakespeare's text, but which the German gives us loudly: it gives us the connection of 'change' and 'translation' to the practical and repetitive crafts of the mechanicals – precisely under the aspect of the machine. For a *Zettel* or *Zettelmaschine* is also the name of the weaver's and the carpet-maker's so-called 'warping machine', the cylinder or framework on which the thread or the cord is turned so as to make it into the warp for the woof to cross, themselves the support and structure of the textile.[19] This translation of Bottom's mechanical 'bottom' into a full-fledged machine, we might say, is the widget of MT that Schlegel's version of *A Midsummer Night's Dream* discloses for us – and discloses precisely where the translation fails to translate Shakespeare's own translation machine. This *disclosing* of the translation machine, however, is not to be conceived as the appearing of a historical invariant, a general equivalent or a universal index of value that would apply across markets, like the word of archaic being in language, *Logos* in its lying-before-to-be-collected, *Logos* flashing forth in *Glossa*. In Shakespeare a translation machine moves the hand of the weaver, the eye and ear of the Faerie Queene and the ear and the eye of the audience, bottom to Bottom, 'nay' to 'Neigh', cuckoo to Cuckoo, word to the eye-machine and to the ear-machine. There, as in the early industrial lexicon, the translation machine translates the material supports of linguistic expression, warp to the woof of expression – but always conditioned by the surplus enjoyment, and the conceptual risk, posed by its being produced or scrambled, 'I see a voice: now will I to the chink,/To spy an I can hear my Thisby's face'. It is a different matter in our days than it is in Cicero, in Heidegger himself, or today, where I have been giving it the strange and indeterminate name of a 'widget'.

To return in conclusion to my charges: to thinking through how translation is inhabited by untranslatability; and to think this inhabitation as a political concept for the age of credit capital and MT. To tell the history of the differences I've been charting – the history of the literalizations of the translating machine and of MT – is to tell the history of post-war, postcolonial capitalism over, in a peculiar, even queer way. This history allows us to give a longer arc than has previously been possible to the seemingly postmodern phenomenon of the dematerialization of labour; this history allows us to rethink and distress, transversally, on a bias, the informing foci of the labour-value ellipse, instrument and aesthetic enjoyment; it allows us to account for labour time differently, by bringing into our accounting the inhuman spidering work of translating machines at different times; it allows us to think differently the nature of labouring machines. But most importantly, reworking the nature of political thought and association through the concept of translation conceived in this way, inhabited by an extimate untranslatability, allows us to disengage the language of the 'possible' – in the modal, philosophical sense and in the revolutionary sense – from the silencing binds in which the postcolonial export labour imaginary has tied it, as Titania's labourers once bound Bottom's tongue.

Chapter 6

The Animal in Translation

The title of this chapter, which echoes Temple Grandin's remarkable 2005 bestseller *Animals in Translation*, puts on display the crassest sort of disciplinary commercialism, since I am provokingly astraddle two of the hottest subfields in the humanities today, animality studies on one side, translation studies and translation theory on the other. I am not interested in asking why, today, these two subfields sell more than others, and I am not interested in producing out of the contact between them a hybrid disciplinary commodity that would sell in any market – animal translation theory, if that is even conceivable. My interest, however, is indeed disciplinary – at least in part.

I have three goals in this last full chapter of *Untranslating Machines*. I want first to suggest a definitive way in which each disciplinary formation – animality studies and translation studies – may serve to limit the other but may also disclose aspects of that field which remain otherwise obscure. Each inhabits the other; each unfinishes, untranslates the other; each provides for the other a way of avoiding the disabling conceptual traps set by seemingly necessary essentialisms, institutional-disciplinary, linguistic and species-ist. Animality studies and translation studies provide these limiting-disclosing functions for each other just where they come to rely on accounts of mediation in order to produce rules for conduct or for thought more generally.

My second goal, approached less frontally, will be to show how these two mutually limiting-disclosing fields can be *exemplary* and provide in their mutual incompleting and untranslating a way to imagine the sort of defective political, juridical, academic-disciplinary institutions, that will serve to produce and guard what Marx calls 'real communality and generality' [*wirklichen Gemeinschaftlichkeit und Allgemeinheit*].

My third goal will be to take up directly the submerged argument I have been making throughout – concerning the imbrication of the humanist definition of the human animal; the conceptual and economic paradigm of global translatability and the limits both find in what is, to them, irremediably *untranslatable*.

In what follows I will have a little more to say about Grandin's book, but I will turn for Grandin's properly philosophical bases elsewhere: to Vicki Hearne's work and to W. V. Quine's. I'll characterize the position they share as *empiricist* and mean by this that Grandin, Hearne and Quine place an abstract notion of immediate *stimulus* at the origin of their consideration (variously) of the varieties of human attention (Grandin), the ethics of animal training (Hearne) and of radical untranslatability (Quine). I will contrast the (suitably complicated) empiricist position with one I will attribute to Jacques Derrida, and which I characterize as mediationist. I mean by this that Derrida's consideration of the 'relation' between human and non-human animal never settles into a concept that is immediately at ease with itself. My point will not be to promote the latter over the former, but rather to describe, first, their shared, if quite different, engagement with normativity, and, second, the productive conflict between the two.

I'm interested in two sorts of paradoxes. Here's the first sort. Say I assert that my animality is what is most immediate to me. Nothing stands between me and my circumstance as an animal; my animality is precisely that, perhaps that and only that, in respect to which I entertain no mediation, no conceptualization: it is a synonym of the facticity of my human being, my form of being in the world, my life form. What and how I may think about my animality is subsequent to this state of affairs and perhaps to my realizing this state of affairs to be primary and immediate. But, on the other hand, there is nothing about which I can think, no concept or problem more heavily overdetermined, more historically saturated than the 'animal' I may or may not be. Even to characterize my animality as the facticity of my human being is to position my assertion, my characterization, in a historically dense, shifting and fractured discursive field. Nothing is less immediate to me than my animality, which comes to me conditioned by the genealogy, the history, the differential drift of the correlative and mutually limiting concepts of the animal and the human.

And, on the other side, the second sort of paradox, in the shape of these two assertions: everything can be translated, give or take, of course, and not just from one natural language to another, but even within a language: I have a notion, I express it in English, and beyond the specifics, beyond whatever it might mean to me in private to say the words 'house' or 'car' or to mention the colour 'red', whatever associations I might have from early experiences with the terms 'house' or 'car' or with that colour, you understand them well enough, we arrive at a practical exchange of information, the right or the expected things happen when I say, 'I have painted my house red' or

'Hand me the red jar' or 'I drive a red car'. But, on the other hand, nothing can be translated, properly speaking, not just between two national or natural languages but within any language. I say 'I have painted my house red', and you understand me and say, 'How nice' or some such, but only because you and I have set aside the criterion of exactness or the consideration of the intentional force of my utterance, in favour of the criterion of practicality, which amounts to acknowledging that 'I have painted my house red' can only be 'translated' inasmuch as each term has been abstracted of its historical embeddedness for me and for you. Both of us now say 'I', 'my house', 'I have painted my house red' or 'I say to you that it's nice that you've painted your house red', in a phatic, indexically neutral sense. No expression is translatable if it is not separated (or, minimally, separable) from its circumstances of utterance, from its history, unless it is immediately abstract. Our register is now tragic, where it was comic; by 'translatable' we now mean 'properly translatable', and we have in mind something like a formal procedure that converts, without loss, sense into sense: a mathematics of translation. A mapping. Nothing moves from this map to that, from this space to that one there, unless it first sheds the complexities of circumstance and ascends again, utterly naked, into the idea which is its home, from which it can pass, trailing, into another location, language, map.

How do these two limiting descriptions of 'the animal' and 'translation' line up?

Say that we claim to be able to 'read' the expression on an animal's face, or to guess what our companion animals are thinking, or to understand the pain they feel when they are mistreated. Such translations, we might maintain, are possible because animals belong properly and already within the field of translation, because they are sufficiently alike to human animal users of natural languages to permit analogies or outright, Aesop's fables-ish allegorizations of animal speech. That is why we can analogize 'speaking' *to animals*, and perhaps more broadly speaking about them, with speaking *to someone*, to a human animal, whose language we don't yet know. Non-human animals are 'in translation', as Grandin has it, when and if the field of translation encompasses their communicative disposition, which is not linguistic.[1] We could say that this or that primate, call it or her Koko or Quigley, may not know what her trainer's gestures mean to her trainer, that no non-human animal poses to itself the question of the 'meaning of meaning' and that for this reason no non-human animal can, strictly speaking, be said to 'intend' this or that communication. And yet there is communication. Say then that two human animals who don't share a natural language encounter each other. Inasmuch as they are animals they share a relation to the matter of translation. The relation need not be identical or symmetric as to the circumstances of the act of translation, but we might non-trivially maintain that as to its structure or type it is both. For instance, it may be that I think of translation from English to Japanese under the aspect of a commercial advantage to myself, whereas my Japanese interlocutor imagines learning to translate English as a way of gaining access to a cultural sphere. (My example squarely shoulders the coarsest of cultural clichés, quite deliberately: examples too are intra-linguistic translations; when they work to give an abstract argument concrete shape they trail, even sometimes turn upon, often-unremarked common-places.) 'Translation' would be a term and a practice mediated differently for my Japanese interlocutor and for me, and yet we could, perhaps, agree that what we are doing when we seek, each for his reason, to understand what the other is saying, is something we could both call 'translation', a limit-term or horizon or type-term that falls apart as soon as we seek to specify, each on his side, what it means.

This is controversial. The poet, animal trainer and philosopher Vicki Hearne famously defended a vigorous trainer-to-dog anthropomorphism in her account of 'How to Say "Fetch!"'[2] There is a crucial moment in her training of Salty, a 'year-old Pointer bitch' that Hearne invents for us. The dog has learnt to 'obey' the trainer, but the trainer does not yet 'obey' the dog – which is to say that although the dog obeys the command 'Salty, Sit!' the 'looped thought' between trainer and dog is still unidirectional: 'the flow of intention', Hearne says, 'is, as it were, one way. In my account the dog doesn't initiate anything yet. She obeys me, but I don't obey her'. And then one day, Hearne says:

> Salty gets my attention by sitting spontaneously in just the unmistakably sym-metrical, clean-edged way of formal work. If I'm on the ball, if I respect her per-sonhood at this point, I'll respond. Her sitting may have a number of meanings: 'Please stop daydreaming and feed me!' (Perhaps she sits next to the Eukanuba or her food dish.) Or it may mean, 'Look, I can explain about the garbage can, it isn't the way it looks.' In any case, if I respond, the flow of intention is now two-way, and the meaning of 'Sit' has changed yet again. This time it is Salty who has enlarged the context, the arena of its use, by means of what we might as well go ahead and call the trope of projection. Sally and I are, for the moment at least, obedient to each other and to language. ('Fetch' 55–6)

This is lovely and striking. For now, note that even if we are not committed to a vigorous anthropomorphism, of the sort indicated by Hearne's injunction to 'respect the personhood' of a dog or by her attributing to the dog the use of a trope – which, if the phrase is intended seriously, indicates that Salty is able to distinguish between literal and metaphoric uses of 'language', and that the dog, communicating, installs, as the primary device in the symmetrical, intentional circuit of the language game that both dog and trainer employ and obey, the figure of projection – even if, as I say, we are not committed to this vigorously anthropomorphic description, we have at our disposal a weaker account of communicative disposition and a weaker version of this bidirectional 'flow of intention'. This version, which Hearne characterizes accurately as 'Skinnerite' but then dismisses too quickly, does the job even if we maintain that non-human animals can have no intention when they interact with human animals. We can fairly assert that Salty or Quigley or Koko is doing something, what we would call gesturing in American Sign Language, or sitting by the dogfood or pointing to an icon or baring its teeth, and that the ape or the dog is doing this because that gesture will have an effect on her trainer – the primate or the dog is making this sign in order to have that effect, which might be the effect of producing a treat, or a kitten, or panic, from the trainer. The word 'because' here means something weaker than or at least different from verbs like 'understands' or 'knows' – terms we would require in order to ascribe intention to the ape or the dog. The trainer has trained Salty or Koko or Quigley to respond in this or that way to one or another stimulus, and the ape or the dog has trained the trainer to respond in predictable ways to a counter-stimulus. (The animal does not have to intend to train the trainer for this to occur: a response to a stimulus or a counter-stimulus occurs 'because' training has happened, not because anything about the causal nature of the stimulus circle is understood or known.) Being 'in translation' in this sense means being within the closure of a stimulus circle, just as 'communicating' with my Japanese-speaking interlocutor means in the first place, before any specific translations begin, acknowledging that we share a common disposition towards a vacuous or horizon concept of translation, which may be inflected by different cultural or personal circumstances – by my economic interest in learning Japanese or by his interest in learning English for cultural purposes. In this restricted sense, whether what's at issue is my conversation with my Japanese interlocutor or Salty's attention-getting sitting or Koko's 'conversation' with her trainer, a fundamental but vacuous symmetry is installed. The common 'obedience to language' that Hearne offers axiomatically understands 'language' as a field of potentially translatable assertions, of assertions that all of us, the Japanese interlocutor, the trainer, the animal, myself, agree are or may be translated, are or may be understood by another about whom I can say, by means of the trope of projection precisely, that he or she or it could understand them. And when I say that 'we agree' to this, I am giving tongue to what Vicki Hearne designates when she uses terms like 'spontaneous' and phrases like 'unmistakably symmetrical, clean-edged way of formal work'. What gets our attention and brings us into recognition that we 'obey language' together, is 'unmistakable'; it occurs 'spontaneously'. Whatever this is, it lies behind the trope of projection; it might be said to be the tenor for the trope of projection, or its schematic condition of possibility. It is not language, but it founds the 'language' to which the animal and its trainer assent and to which interlocutors speaking recognizably different human languages also assent.

It is not language, but it furnishes the rules for thinking about the relation *to* a primary or primal language that human and non-human animals share. It is not language, but is this foundational point, this point on which the assent to language depends, this point from which depends our spontaneous recognition that we and the non-human animals we train are beings-in-language, translatable? Just what *are* these rules for thinking, and how are we to follow them?

In order to bring the question of rule-following into contact with the question of mediation in animal studies and in translation studies, let me designate two limits.

On the one side, obeying a rule, being named or naming or being trained or training are activities related *both* to the immediacy of the stimulus reaction *and* to the abstract translatability of concepts. It is, in fact, impossible to separate immediacy from abstraction on this point: the presumed immediacy of stimulus reactions *is* the condition on which concepts are understood across languages and idioms *and* vice versa: stimulus reactions are immediate to us *because* they are already abstract and fall for this reason outside of the domain of our particular interpretations. This reciprocal arrangement is logically shaky but wonderfully secure culturally and experientially. When Salty sits in her 'immediately and spontaneously recognizable way', I am 'on the ball' if I react to her stimulus. Under these circumstances, I am acting in a relation to my animality; I am well trained but I am also, inasmuch as I 'respect the dog's personhood', in a position in which my own 'personhood' is being 'respected' by the animal. We're both obedient to 'language', but my attending to Salty is not a rule that can be generalized. So what sort of a rule is it that cannot *be* generalized? All I can do is say, 'Be on the ball' to other human animals, and by this I mean something quite empty: I mean 'pay attention to the stimulus you will receive' or I mean, 'See, visualize', as Grandin would have it, or I mean, 'Don't mistake what is "immediately and spontaneously recognizable"; don't mistake what is unmistakable: make sure that a stimulus is a stimulus for you!'

The unity-and-emptiness-of-stimulus argument has any number of attractive and useful formulations, but probably the most explicit and the most famous one is to be found in W. V. Quine's account of the emergence of radical translation, as he tells it in *Word and Object*. Quine's famous story has a pleasantly jokey syntax: a field linguist meets a member of a 'hitherto untouched people', a speaker of a language that the field linguist cannot decipher.[3] A first occasion for establishing the point of contact, of translation, between these two languages presents itself when a rabbit 'scurries by'. Quine calls this a 'stimulus situation' and means by this that the field linguist and the native experience, roughly simultaneously, the stimulus of seeing the scurrying animal. 'Gavagai', says the native. Provisionally, Quine's field linguist notes down that 'Gavagai' may mean ' "rabbit" or "Lo, a rabbit!" ' Actually disambiguating the expression proves difficult, and impossible without 'supplying native sentences for [the native] informant's approval, despite the risk of slanting the data by suggestion'. 'For', says Quine,

> suppose the native language includes sentences S1, S2 and S3, really translatable respectively as 'Animal,' 'White,' and 'Rabbit.' . . . How then is the linguist to perceive that the native would have been willing to assent to S1 in all the situations where he happened to volunteer S3, and in some but perhaps not all of the situations where he happened to volunteer S2? Only by . . . querying combinations of native sentences. So we have the linguist asking 'Gavagai?' in each of various stimulatory situations, and noting each time whether the native assents, dissents, or neither. But how is he to recognize native assent and dissent when he sees or hears them? Gestures are not to be taken at face value; the Turks' are nearly the reverse of our own. (*Word and Object*, 26)

Faced with a palpable regressive paradox, Quine's conclusion, famously and controversially, is that in cases of radical translation, there is no way to establish definitively what 'Gavagai' refers to or what it means. The animal I name may be identified by means of a collection of descriptive attributes or predicates of identity, accidental or essential. In this situation, which goes beyond even what Wittgenstein calls 'aspect-seeing', 'Gavagai' could refer to an aspect, for instance, a temporal aspect, of the rabbit-in-motion; to a part of the rabbit, the tail say; to its colour; but 'Gavagai' could even refer to the finger pointing.[4] 'Gavagai' could mean 'I don't know what that is'. It could mean 'food'. Presumably the list of things the term could mean is not infinite, but it probably is not countable, either. I said that the animal I name may be identified by a collection of attributes that describe the animal, and the name 'Gavagai' refers to one or many of them; but this naming convention may not pertain in the discursive world of the native, who might be what Kripke might call a rigid designationist rather than a descriptivist, and of course 'Gavagai' might not be a noun at all.

Quine's philosophical fable has elicited a number of important glosses. Some of his readers – those interested in exacerbating the fable's regressiveness – have suggested that descriptive identity predicates are implied in the native's gesture of pointing and that these in turn are to be understood as collections of additional identity predicates requiring disambiguation, and so on. Neither do they share the word 'rabbit' or the word 'Gavagai' as a word; even the primitive ostensive function for language indicated by the native's pointing is suspect, since the native might be saying the word 'Finger!' or the phrase 'I am making an indexical sign!' Under the threat of regressions such as these, one solution is to stipulate that for there to be translation, indeed for there to be communication, a decision is called for: with sovereign assurance, one cuts through the thickening forest of predications and settles on one, the likeliest or the most motivated. The animal itself is manifestly not what the native and the non-native share when such decisions are called for, in the way that you might say that we share food, if we eat rabbit together. The analogy to a Schmittian scenario is useful: this is the sovereign in the bush. (He has emigrated from Sancho's protected island.) For the act of deciding (that 'Gavagai' means one or another thing, stimulated by the presence of the rabbit; or on a different, fundamental level, that 'Gavagai' is to be interpreted as a response to the stimulus of the question) is held privately by one side, on the field linguist's side, say, or on the side even of the analytic philosopher narrating the little fable. The native and the non-native do not decide together, according to criteria they share, or according to what Quine calls a 'manual'. (How would they arrive at these criteria or at a shared 'manual' without a primal moment in which each side designated for the other what the criterion is for deciding what 'Gavagai' means? Or what 'manual' they should share? And wouldn't that primal designation be subject to the same sceptical deflation as the moment when the native sees the rabbit, if that's what he sees, and says, to the incomprehension of the field linguist, 'Gavagai'? 'Gavagai' could, after all, be the name of 'concept' or of 'convention' or 'criterion' or 'object' in the native tongue: our little animal-and-forest fable could also be a fable concerning the designation of entities that appear, are observed, or are produced for thought and consideration.) Sovereign is one who decides whether there is, or is not, translation. Sovereign is one who stipulates the criteria according to which it is to be judged whether there is, or is not, translation. The sovereign designates the manual.

Or not quite. Yes, the native's perspective necessarily drops out of the field of decisions, but, on the other hand, for Quine's story-example to work, for the native's perspective *to* drop out, then alongside the perspective of the animal itself (whatever that might be), the native and the field linguist must share a notion of what a 'stimulus' is or, rather, they must both be obedient to the sovereign stimulus, as Vicki Hearne and Salty are obedient to language and to each other. The words we use to describe the rabbit may be conditioned, as the word 'red' is conditioned for me by my past, by my home's colour or by my political affiliation or as the colour 'white' and the noun 'snow' are said to be in the Inuit tongue by the circumstances of the Inuit's experience. 'Rabbit' may be translatable or radically untranslatable, but the fact that there is stimulus and that the stimulus is 'immediately and spontaneously recognized' as such is the condition on which there is a scene of pointing, the condition on which the question of translatability or untranslatability arises: it is the fable's ground. Even when we take the native to be saying, by 'Gavagai', 'this is my finger', or even if 'Gavagai' means nothing – it still stimulates. 'Gavagai' is a stimulus understood to arise in response to a stimulus, no matter what the first stimulus was or what the second stimulus, the enunciation of 'Gavagai', means. Even so, then, the conditions that Quine sets up are such that the native can only mean, 'This is my finger', or mean nothing, or simply set about stimulating us by uttering a word, 'Gavagai' that he knows to be utterly foreign to our lexicon – the native can mean or intend any of these only upon the stimulus reaction occasioned by the scurrying rabbit. 'Gavagai', he says, and whatever else might be at issue, we three, or four, the native, the field linguist, the narrating analytic philosopher and the readers of *Word and Object*, 'obey' the immediate and common agreed circumstance: there is a stimulus, and it is coincident or correlative with 'Gavagai'. For the question of translation, and for the question of decision, to be posed, Quine says, there has to have been stimulus in the first place, or rather there has to be agreement that there has been a stimulus in the first place. We recognize, 'immediately and spontane- ously', that we are, as Hearne puts it, obedient *to* language inasmuch as we agree that there *has been* stimulus. 'Agreement' does not mean something like 'the conscious or deliberate, common assent to a fact of some sort', but rather something like 'stipulation', or even – this is perhaps controversial – 'agreement' here means that we, the native, the field linguist, the narrating analytic philosopher and the readers of *Word and Object*, are all trained, have all been trained, to identify a stimulus in common. It is not required – indeed, it is excluded – that the field linguist and the native and the rest of us have an identical description of what 'stimulus' is (i.e., an identical collection of predicable attributes attached to the term 'stimulus') or of how a concept works, the concept of stimulus or of how a decision is reached. A stimulus, the change-of-state-of-affairs, is shared by the native and the field linguist and the rest of us and as a result we are obedient to language. A meadow with nothing happening in it is precisely not stimulating; it's the unmistakable and spontaneous change that's signalled by, that *is*, the animal's movement or that's signalled by or that *is* the stipulation 'There is stimulus' that gives rise to the question, 'Is it, the word for that which is producing the stimulus or for the stimulus itself, is it translatable or is it not translatable?'

'Stimulus' is neither translatable nor untranslatable between native and field-linguist-ese, nor *a fortiori* between natural languages, because, on Quine's account, 'stimulus' marks the as-yet-unpredicated spot, common to all languages, upon which all languages take the shape of syntactically orga- nized fields of differential predications, by means of the trope of projection. Not the rabbit but the *scurrying* rabbit is the functional term here, the term on which we can stand in order, by projection, to tell our story. I take Quine, Hearne and Temple Grandin to be raising a philosophical scaffolding on the ground of empirical but abstract immediacy and to require that both the native informant and the animal before us, the animal and the informant who bear attributes and are the subject and translator of definitional predicates, be sacrificed so as to produce the concept of the empty stimulus function on which natural language is built and on which decisions concerning the possibility of translating or not among natural languages are built. (I intend the range of senses associated with the word 'sacrificed': the native informant and the animal before us are taken in place of something else, more precious; they are offered up, propitiatory or apologetic, to a sovereign power; they are destroyed, as when we say that the stricken cattle had to be 'sacrificed'. Different approximations to translation, as we will see.)

I asked previously, regarding the foundational, void stimulus point on which empirical philosophies stand the assent to language and balance our spontaneous recognition that we and the non-human animals we train are beings-in-language and beings obedient-to-language, whether this non-linguistic point is *translatable*. This question cannot be understood in the lexicons that Hearne, and Quine, and Grandin, offer us. To approach it, allow me now to turn to the other limiting side to the question of how rule-following meets mediation.

Consider now a philosophy critical of the naked immediacy of empirical stimulus, and of the resilient correlation between the stimulus reaction and the *concept*. Does it too sacrifice the animal in translation?

Four animal scenes recur in Jacques Derrida's late writing. They are, first, the Adamic scene of the man who names the animal, who calls the animal by name ('I name you "Gavagai," my pet rabbit!'); second, the scene of the father who, required to sacrifice his son, finds, or is given, or produces, a substitute; third, the scene of the slaughterhouse, where the modern logic of industrial mass production brings about the phenomenon of the animal bred in great numbers in order to be slaughtered; fourth – last – is the scene of an encounter between a man, call him a philosopher, and a non-human animal whose presence offers the philosopher, or imposes upon the philosopher, what Derrida calls 'the certainty that what we have here is an existence that refuses to be conceptualized' [*qu'il s'agit là d'une existence rebelle à tout concept*].[5]

There are deep and exceptionally tricky relays among these four scenes, though they do not resolve themselves into a single scene, and they do not offer us a concept, or even a concept *of* concept, that would allow us to group them easily.[6] (One might say that they are, like the cat that presents itself to Derrida's gaze in *The Animal That Therefore I Am*, *rebellious to any concept*. Derrida's animal scenes are more like *animots*, animal words, in Derrida's splendidly strange usage, than like different animals of a single species, or different species of *animal*.) For Derrida, there is never a single encounter between the philosopher, or indeed between the human animal, and another animal, human or not. Instead, such encounters are always at least fourfold; they take place in and are always drawn from at least four at times incompatible registers and locations – the register of Adamic naming, Abrahamic sacrifice, industrial slaughter and the register in which the animal presents itself as, or impresses upon us that it *is*, irreplaceable life. Our singular ways of thought and of expression account in part for our need to think these scenes through systematically; in our little scenes, a philosopher is never a single philosopher, both in the ways that an animal is never just *an* animal and in other ways too; a philosophical scene – whether of writing or of encounter between a non-human animal and a human – is never one. (Remember Sancho: Solomon is never just *one thing*, one tradition, one sovereign standard of value.) In this manner at least the encounter between the philosopher or the philosophical human animal and the animal can never provide a 'stimulus', or indeed be a numerically discrete event like a *decision*. On this score, as on so many others, we would be hard-pressed to derive from Derrida's work rules based in agreed, translatable concepts, governing decisions taken in accord with classical, individualist ethics, or *regulae ad directionem ingenii*. Derrida's approach to Enlightenment is far from Habermas's.[7] The 'unshakable' certainty that this moment provides sits upon the shakiest of grounds: the 'certainty' that what stands there, the being that stands before the philosopher, is an existence 'rebellious to any concept' or, as David Wills translates it, 'an existence that refuses to be conceptualized' [*qu'il s'agit là d'une existence rebelle à tout concept*]. And how could I replace that irreplaceable living being with another, or think of it alongside another being; how could I gather both of them under the sheltering, sacrificial generality of the concept, translating them (in one version of the word 'translating') one into the other?

In Derrida's animal-human scenes, in each taken singly *and* taking the aggregate as a non-systematic collection, we come before something that rebels against any and every concept. But what does this mean? What *can* we then mean by 'thought'? By 'decision'? What sorts of rules can one build when one is unshakably certain that one faces, in the animal and in the scene and scenes in which the animal becomes present to thought, something – an existence, a word, a case – rebellious against any and every concept? Minimally, we would be exchanging the concept of *concept* for the mediated and discontinuous *circuit* – though this is not the language that Derrida will use. No Abrahamic sacrifice that does not pass through the slaughterhouse (and in this context the theologico-political value of the sacrifice acquires one order of significance in the post-industrial society); no presentation or intrusion of irreplaceable or unsubstitutable life without an Adamic exercise of mastery over it. The discipline of philosophy, even the project of thinking what the rebellion against the concept might look like, passes through the Edenic fantasy of primal naming rights. Adam's task is unthinkable outside of the shame of the abject, naked philosopher-namer. In the lexicon that we use to describe the relation among these scenes, or these classes of scenes, we lean heavily on the concepts of determination and overdetermination and underdetermination, that is, we lean heavily on the classic vocabulary of mediation. In this lexicon, the scenes of human-animal encounter are not single scenes, units to be coordinated or composed according to rules or syntaxes: there is always more than one scene, and this plurality is the abstract condition that they obey, the condition of their relationality – in contrast to the abstract visual unity of the stimulus that we find in Quine and in Hearne. Saying that each scene of this plural set 'passes through' all the others is my way of expressing what Derrida worries as the problem of a 'general singularity' or a 'singular that is general' [*un singulier générale*] or an 'indeterminate generality' [*une généralité indeterminée*]. The expressions 'an animal' and 'the I' or even the pronoun 'I' share this strange quality: they cannot be thought alone, and yet they are one, one scene, a singular scene, for instance the scene of the singular event of a naming or of an averted sacrifice or of the industrial slaughter of produce 'animals' or the scene of the philosopher's shame at the rebellious non-nudity of the animal. The scenes in which 'I' come before the 'animal' as its namer, as the father beholden to it inasmuch as it stands in for my son, as its executioner, as the man who cannot think his concept before this animal, are general singularities or indeterminate generalities.

So if we may not say that the scenes of human-animal encounter about which Derrida's late work turns resolve themselves into a concept; nor that there are systematic relays between them; nor that these scenes mediate each other; nor that they negate, determine, overdetermine, or underdetermine each other; then what is the rebellious, defective concept of discontinuous *circuit* that we *may* use to understand their relation? Derrida is entirely aware of the paradoxical nature of the structure he is furnishing, a structure at work not only in the philosopher's deployment of one or another of the human-animal scenes to this or that end – but at work also in the way that the scenes I've described come into relation with one another. The term that Derrida will use to describe this sort of relation is the term *translation*, though he is using it, as I'll suggest, in a way that's different from the more traditional, humanist ways in which I've been using it to this point. The scenes I have described translate each other, and they are untranslatable each into the other. Scenes in which radical translation and radical untranslatability are represented, they are radically translatable and radically untranslatable among each other. Everything is translatable between and among them; nothing is.

Let me show you what I mean. *Béliers: Le dialogue ininterrompu: entre deux infinis, le poème* is among Derrida's last works. It was delivered as a lecture in Hamburg in 2003, in memory of Hans-Georg Gadamer. It consists largely of an extended analysis of a poem by Paul Celan, which Derrida refers to in the English translation by Michael Hamburger. In this section, which I cite in Thomas Dutoit's and Philippe Romanski's English translation, *Rams*, from *Sovereignties in Question,* Derrida concentrates on the image of the ram:

> There is war, and the ram, the ram made of flesh or of wood, the ram on earth or in the sky, throws itself into the fray. . . . Against what does he not strike? . . . One imagines the anger of Abraham's and Aaron's ram, the infinite revolt of the ram of all holocausts. But also, figuratively, the violent rebellion of all scapegoats, all substitutes. Why me? . . . The ram would, finally, want to put an end to their common world. It would charge against everything and against whomever, in all directions, as if blinded by pain.
>
> That makes for many hypotheses, and for much indecision. That remains forever the very element of reading. Its 'infinite process.' Caesura, hiatus, ellipsis – all are interruptions that at once open and close. They keep access to the poem forever at the threshold of its crypts (one among them, only one, would refer to a singular and secret experience, wholly other, whose constellation is accessible only through the testimony of the poet and a few others). The interruptions also open, in a disseminal and non-saturable fashion, onto unforeseeable constellations, onto so many other stars, some of which would perhaps still resemble the seed that Yahweh told Abraham, after the interruption of the sacrifice, he would multiply like the stars: the abandon of traces left behind is also the gift of the poem to all readers and counter-signatories, who, always under the law of the trace at work, and of the trace as work, would lead to or get led along a wholly other reading or counter-reading. Such reading will also be, from one language to the other sometimes, through the abyssal risk of translation, an incommensurable writing.[8]

These lines repay very careful analysis. I would like to draw your attention to one thing only, because it allows me to imagine *Béliers* as a reflection of the ways in which Derrida's animal scenes come into relation with one another – that is, to read *Béliers* not just as a meditation on Gadamer's career but also as Derrida's meditation on the ways in which his own career organizes human-non-human animal scenes. On this reading, *Béliers* becomes an allegory of Derrida's human-non-human animal scenes: its constellations, the complex singular generality of Derrida's long visualization of the differentiated encounter between human and non-human animal; *Béliers* tells the story of the paradoxical sorts of representation these scenes turn on.

So note the complicated relation between numerability and dissemination in the scene I have excerpted. In Celan's poem and in Derrida's analysis of the poem, the stars' uncountability flows from two different sources. The first is the empirical difficulty that they might pose to the project of counting: one of the two infinities of the essay's title. (How do we count the stars without losing count? We capture the night sky at a moment, call it dawn, midnight or dusk, and we count the stars upon that spangled surface above us, hoping not to lose track, hoping to count all at once, before a star sets or rises, before one shoots across the vault: a star? A planet? An asteroid? A bit of technology orbiting above?) The other source of the stars' uncountability flows from their double function: they are units, single stars, astronomically observable elements like the morning star or like Hesperus (neither of which, of course, *is* a star – and both of which, though different in name and in cultural significance, are names for the same planet), but Celan's stars are also figures or placeholders making up a constellation, the constellation of the ram for instance. The animal these symbolic-literal stars form is then part of the firmament but also the means by which the sacrifice on earth is interrupted: a definitive, irreplaceable part of the world-down-here. Stars are and are not stars; their location is fixed, and yet they wander to earth on ram's hooves; they stand above, like the starry vault Kant so prized, reducing human animality to its contingent, material qualities and signalling perhaps the sublime domain of the moral law or the absolute violence of the sovereign concept; and they *also* form part of culturally defined constellations. The ram constellation *represents* or *is a translation of* the ram substitute in the Abrahamic tradition – and yet the poem, Derrida says, establishes each as a stand-in for the other, one ram for another, one irreplaceable form of life replacing another *par figure*, Derrida writes. And at the same time this act of figurative translation between mythologies, one irreplaceable ram replaced by another from an entirely different tradition, is or must be arrested because it is improper, sacrificial, sacrilegious, as Isaac's sacrifice is arrested by the ram who is, and cannot be, his figure.

Celan's stars, Derrida's stars, the animals in Derrida's stars and the animals in Celan's poem. Every animal in each of the scenes that Derrida sets before us, and every scene in which a non-human animal stands to hand, every animal and every scene stands in the place of the other and is sacrificed in its place. Each represents the others, *par figure*, but each is also held back from representing the other scenes or the other animals, ram for ram, a ram for a child, a cat for a philosopher, a ram for a cat. This is not, exactly, an exercise in contradiction – it is, rather, an exercise in *translation,* in what we would have to call *rebellious* translation.

Rebellious. The word crops up in *Béliers*, where it helps 'One' to 'imagine . . . figuratively, the violent rebellion of all scapegoats, all substitutes'. And of course it has been keeping us company all along, in the shape of the decisive modifier that Derrida's cat bears in *The Animal That Therefore I Am* – that existence that refuses every concept, that rebels against every concept. If Celan's poem is the 'figurative' image or imagination of this 'violent rebellion', then *Béliers* and *The Animal That Therefore I Am* are its philosophical 'figures'.

But what would a 'rebellious' translation then be? Let me now restate my original questions and show you how the philosophical figure of rebellion that Derrida provides rebels against the conventional accounts of translation, of animality, of rule-following, of conceptualization and of mediation. How, I asked, might the question of the animal and its relation to the human, and the question of the possibility or impossibility of translation, not only serve to limit each other but also serve to disclose, each about the other, matters that would otherwise remain obscure? My suggestion was that we should look at the point at which each of these fields of questions depends upon an account of mediation. I distinguished between translation and animal studies that depend upon the vacuous, visual immediacy of the notion of stimulus, under whose law translatability and untranslatability, training and person-hood, abstraction and concretion are marshalled. In contrast, non-empirical or anti-empirical accounts of human-animal/non-human-animal relations such as Derrida's offer a defective concept of the scene, numerically and semantically distinct, but also both singular and multiple.

Notice what is staked on calling this a *defective* concept rather than a non-concept.[9] That Derrida's cat, and Abraham or Isaac's ram, embody an existence rebellious to every concept does not mean that no concepts attach to the animal these animals are – rebellion and singularity, for instance, are also concepts. It means, however, that between the concept and the animal no immediate translation occurs. If this is so, though, then it would seem that the word, or the concept, of 'rebellion' occupies just the place that the terms 'scurrying' and 'stimulus' do in Quine's argument, and that 'rebellion' encodes, as the stimulus scene does in Quine's story and in Hearne's argument, an imperative, a ground rule. In Quine's case, the command sounded something like this: 'Recognize, see, in the world of the native and the field linguist but also in all possible worlds, recognize, see, rigidly, that a stimulus is a stimulus, and from that recognition, from that vision, may flow, in different, radically untranslatable or radically translatable languages, the analytically necessary notion that an animal is an animal, scurrying'. Upon this singular recognition, or vision, the field linguist, or Quine, or his readers, will then build their disposition towards non-human animals, and indeed towards human animals as well. To the extent that this disposition concerns how we will behave when faced with this or that non-human, or human, animal, we may call it *ethical*, or rather, we may call it the *ground* of ethics (which we understand, quite classically, to entail acting according to rules we give ourselves on intuited, axiomatic grounds: this is our autonomy, our sovereignty with regard to ourselves).

Derrida's ground rule, if indeed *Béliers* and the scenes I have been linking do provide one, is different, inasmuch as it does not simply place the faculty of *vision* or sense of *sight* at the heart of the scene; inasmuch as this imperative is addressed not only to the animal but also to his, Derrida's, reader; and inasmuch as it also serves both as a description of the cat-animal and of the addressed reader *and* as its or their concept. What results is not a version of autonomous ethics but a baldly political rule, that is, a rule that puts the axiomaticity of any ground rule, and of rule-following in general (my own rules to myself, those we appear to agree on), into conflict. 'Rebel!' – this seems to be Derrida's ground rule. 'Rebel', one might think, 'against allowing yourself and others to be translated into a concept'. 'Find a way of thinking or of "existing" that attends to this "rebellion"'. The mediated sacrifice, the substitution which is and is not one, rebels against making the other animal obey one's own concept, against translating the other's language even figuratively, *par figure*, into one's own.

But the ground rule of rebellion is indeed defective. At the end of the heroic, *soixante-huitardish* adventure we can glean from *Béliers* – where the call to *rebel* is sounded, as though on a ram's horn, for all to hear – still stand the still figures of the human and his sacrificed, because domesticated, because protected, animal, serviceably and companionably trained to each other's conduct, animals in translation each to each. The stakes are very high. 'Rebellion', as every classic manifesto hopes, travels; it is never just local. It travels by example; it travels on the wings of social media, of mediatized redistribution; 'rebellion' travels in translation, immediately. 'Rebellion' is what I undertake on the streets of Cairo and translate to Tripoli, or Madrid, or London, or Gaza, when I stand with others against constituted or usurping authority, in hopes of achieving a state of equity, domestic tranquillity, the restitution of my land or perpetual peace. But it is not only that. 'Rebellion', Derrida is reminding us, is *un*translatable on two poetic grounds. Rebellion, in his analysis of Celan's poem, is also the anagram for the name of the ram, *le belier* – and anagrammatical logic is at war with *any* translation. It is just what cannot be translated from one natural language to another. The rigid designators 'ram' or 'belier', rigid inasmuch as they have, like the word Hesperus or the word Phosphorus, the same real referent, inasmuch as they refer to the same real animal ('real' here meaning 'existing as the referent for a term', not 'really existing in the world'), these rigidly designating terms are translatable, always and universally translatable. More, though: the word *bélier* is the anagrammatical name for that animal's philosophico-political function as well: *Bélier* is an anagram for rebellion itself – and this anagrammaticality, lingering at the point of the letter, does not *refer* to 'rebellion', though it *produces* or *reveals* it; it has no relation, other than the circumstance that the word's letters can be scrambled in French to produce a rebel from a ram and a ram out of a rebel, to the concept to which 'rebellion' refers. Ana-grammatical effects are at war with standard semantics: they produce seman-tic effects accidentally; they submit reference to the rebellious wandering of letters. The war between and within 'ram', 'bélier' and 'rebellion' and within and between the noun 'bélier' and the verb 'revelle', is the re-enactment of, or return to, a state of war – a *re-bellum*. *Le bélier*'s rebellion against translation reveals without repeating, produces concepts without representing or figur-ing or referring to them, sacrifices without substituting or substitutes without sacrifice. *La rébellion révèle*: rebellion reveals an ancestral war waged not between 'animal' and 'human' or even within the languages we might use to number and negotiate their difference, but within the concept of their differ-ence and within the name that seems to secure the identity of each.

An empiricist account of the animal in translation, grounded in the single term 'stimulus' or in the rigid predication 'there is stimulus', permits the field linguist and the philosopher of language and their observers and readers to make practical assertions concerning descriptive predicates. This empiricist account permits us to make assertions regarding the substitutability of identi-ties organized in a concept that reveals or represents a generality to which their differences can be sacrificed. The visual, vacuous unity of the stimulus, however, is inadequate to the injunction we find in Derrida's account – the injunction not to 'respect the other animal's personhood' when that 'respect' amounts to the sacrifice of that other animal to its 'personhood'; to the sac-rifice of its rebellion to its proper name; the sacrifice of anagrammaticality to semantics; which is to say the sacrifice of that other animal's difference from ourselves or from the class or concept to which we say it belongs, to a difference we take to be constitutive of ourselves as 'animals' imbued with human 'personhood' and self-identity. The animal is never rigidly named, or immediately named, or named only with an eye to its domination in one field or under one aspect alone: the scene of naming is also the scene of the animal's sacrifice in a different, plausible world or in the same one. The scene of the animal's naming is also the scene of its mass production and of its mass execution. It is likewise the scene of its blank rebellion to the philosopher's name and against any and all concepts and the scene of its sacrifice.

I would rather not leave you with the unsatisfactory sense that my argu-ment stands on scrambling letters against the grain of one or another natural language, and then claiming that this old particularity – as old, indeed, as Lucretius's great poem – is definitive of rebellious translation as Derrida imagines it. I am not, and Derrida is not, looking for war and rebellion in the alphabetical seeds of things, as *De rerum natura* might have it. For Derrida, building out of Celan's poem a rebellion against translation does not entail asserting that there cannot *be* translation, that *nothing* can be translated: *Béliers* also shows its readers how to arrange, as one might arrange stars into a constellation, the defective concept of a rebellious translation. This rebellious translation, which is both the rebellion against conceptual translation and the practice of translation itself, does not stand or fall on what we can see literally about words: this is not a matter of finding hypograms, words under words or of finding the untranslatable unwording of words that attaches to the instance of letters alone. To show you what I mean, allow me to return to David Wills's exemplary translation of Derrida's *The Animal That Therefore I Am*. You will recall the passage I cited earlier. 'It is true', Wills' translation runs, 'that I identify [the animal before me] as a male or female cat'.

> But even before that identification, it comes to me [*il vient à moi*] as this irreplaceable living being that one day enters my space, into this place where it can encounter me, see me, even see me naked [*me voir, voire me voir nu*]. Nothing can ever rob me of the certainty that what we have here is an existence that refuses to be conceptualized [*qu'il s'agit là d'une existence rebelle à tout concept*].

I stressed the word 'rebellion' in these lines, which Wills renders as the 'refusal to be conceptualized'. The difference between 'rebellion' and 'refusal' is not trivial, because rebellion, as we have seen, returns us not to the heroic scene of an individual who asserts claims against a coercive constituted power – *non serviam!* – but to a state of war, to a sort of Hobbesian war of all against all. This is not trivial, but it is easily enough fixed, and changing 'rebellion' into 'refusal' or correcting 'refusal' with 'rebellion' tells us nothing about the concepts of translation, translatability or untranslatability that Derrida is setting before us. But note what happens just where the *visuality* or even better the *visualizability* of the scene of the animal is presented for translation. Here, Derrida's French marks the language's *internal* translation: the rearticulation of a French expression in French, which takes place *before* any identification occurs, an identification of the cat as a cat of one sort or another, even of it *as a cat*, but which seems also to be the condition on which French, the French language, can be identified, that is to say, *seen*, *as French*. 'Even before that identification', Derrida writes, 'it [the animal] comes to me [*il vient à moi*] as this irreplaceable living being that one day enters my space, into this place where it can encounter me, see me, even see me naked [*me voir, voire me voir nu*]'. Wills's phrase is 'see me, even see me naked'; Derrida, however, is stressing the homophony between the French verb 'to see', *voir*, and the syntactic marker of internal translation, *voire*, which is the equivalent, in a different sensory register, of *c'est à dire*. 'To see me, to see me see naked' would be one way to render Derrida's phrase; 'to see me, that is, to see me naked' would be another. This second marks the place where the animal is the mark of internal translation, the pause where French sees itself, sees itself for itself and as itself, sees itself naked. The first translation of *me voir, voire me voir nu* places the philosopher's vision on display, the vision of one particular human animal gazing at a non-human animal, seeing himself nakedly seeing. The two scenes may not be confused: everything cries out against confusing the scene of intra-linguistic mistranslation with the scene of viewing, and against confusing a scene granting primacy to the instant, the undifferentiated glimpse of the vision stimulus, with a scene in which the function of vision is disseminated, like a constellation whose stars fly from the figure they represent, from one another. Just here, where the animal comes to see and be seen before the philosophical animal, the scene's language places the difference between the two scenes in the reader's eye rather than his or her ear, in the silent letter 'e' that keeps *voir* from becoming *voire*. But this is no eye we have ever seen: it is, strangely, also the *language's* eye (for itself). The entrance of another sort of sight, another *voir*, right here, a *voir* meant to keep *voir* from becoming *voire* or vice versa, only exacerbates our difficulty, since it is not clear whether *this voir(e)* should come to us from the domain of the subjective phenomenology of reading or from the domain of the syntax of French. It is this, we conclude, that renders this scene of the animal in translation finally, and most radically, *translatable*, inasmuch as natural languages, the languages human animals write and read and speak, share the possibility of producing semantic effects, as an anagrammatical accident – including the effect of self-reference, or what might, for the human animal writing, speaking, reading, seeing itself in and by means of such language, be called self-consciousness, the attribute classically reserved for the human animal. It goes almost without saying that these effects of self-reference are also, inasmuch as they nest ineradicably in the particulars of one or another natural language, inasmuch as they are anagrammatical effects, quite *untranslatable* in content. To track, to account for, to guard and reproduce in thought and in act this war between translatability and untranslatability, this war of and within mediation and within naming, is the injunction that Derrida's late works lay upon us, lay beside the empiricist injunction that we derive from Quine, and Hearne and Grandin.

I will close this last chapter with three provocations.

The ethical ground comported by these two simultaneous injunctions, the empiricist, on one hand, and the rebellious, mediationist imperative, on the other, injunctions contradictory in ways we have yet to fathom, rule-generating and entailing, each distinctly, a practice of rule following – this divided ethical ground is the only one available to us when we seek to take account of those other animals, all those other animals, from which we draw sustenance and political life.

As for our *political* life, when we undertake to translate rebellion from the streets of Gaza to the streets of New York, from Madrid to Brussels, from Beijing to Cairo, we do so not only as human animals, bearers of natural or universal rights, dignities, languages, historical, biological or biopolitical qualities, but also according to accidental rules that dilapidate those concepts. Animals in translation – political rebellion is never just an attribute of *human* agents.

Finally – a question. Does the translation of rebellion across the cities I have named, within and across species borders, over the guarded edges that separate the sorts of entities that can, from those that cannot, be bearers of rights, languages and so on – does this translation on which I am closing *itself* survive the work of the axiom of untranslatability-that-is-not-one whose concept and genealogy this book has sought to lay out?

Afterword: Counter-*gift*

Only alienness is the antidote to alienation.

Nur Fremdheit ist das Gegengift gegen Entfremdung. (Adorno, *Minima Moralia*)

Every regulative 'limit' that capital poses to itself in this historical pursuit is the basis for the insurgence of new obstacles. This indefinite process encounters its blockage only in the class struggle. But the process of circulation has achieved such a broad and powerful expansion that it exposes the circulation of capital not only as an expression of its own collective potency but also as the privileged terrain for the emergence of the power antithetic to it. *The theme of the world market is the most mature exemplification of the revolutionary tendency of the capitalist development.* (Negri, *Marx beyond Marx*)

'To compare money with blood . . . is about as correct as Menenius Agrippa's comparison between the patricians and the stomach. To compare money with language is not less erroneous. Language', Marx writes in 'The Chapter on Money' in the first notebook to the *Grundrisse,* 'does not transform ideas, so that the peculiarity of ideas is dissolved and their social character runs alongside them as a separate entity, like prices alongside commodities. Ideas do not exist separately from language. Ideas which have first to be translated out of their mother tongue into a foreign language in order to circulate, in order to become exchangeable, offer a somewhat better analogy; but the analogy then lies not in language, but in the foreignness [*Fremdheit*] of language'.[1] These lines serve as the epigraph to *Untranslating Machines.* They are obscure and controversial: just what 'foreignness' means and even what it designates and modifies, *die Analogie liegt . . . nicht in der Sprache, sondern in ihrer Fremdheit*, are questions that worry scholars of Marx to a degree, and philosophers of translation extremely.

Let us not try to settle the debate.² Quite the contrary. In *Untranslating Machines* I have been trying to generalize the crisis that Marx's lines sketch for us; to provide a genealogy for that crisis, stretching at least to the moment Marx is recalling here, when he remembers Menenius Agrippa's fable of the belly, as translated and rewrought in Shakespeare's *Coriolanus*; and to indicate how deepening the crisis of translatability may help to provide limits, conceptual as well as institutional, to the paradigm of global thought – to hasten it to its ends and bring the era of the human animal to a close.³

What is the nature of that crisis, local here, generalized in my argument? 'Ideas', Marx writes, 'which have first to be translated out of their mother tongue into a foreign language in order to circulate, in order to become exchangeable, offer a somewhat better analogy; but the analogy then lies not in language, but in the foreignness [*Fremdheit*] of language'. Does Marx intend by *ihrer Fremdheit* the foreignness or strangeness of languages to each other? If so, the analogy is trivial. *Any* language is foreign to any other language, in just the way that a state bordering another state will be external to it or that one body stretches to the point where another encounters it: its outside. Of course the minute we draw analogies to this trivial scene, it becomes much less canny. A history of battles, scars, autoimmunities, invaginations and caresses will trouble it. But let's say we forget for a moment that complicating history. Here, where *ihrer Fremdheit* may mean for Marx just the foreignness or strangeness of languages to each other, translation among mutually foreign languages has its quotidian sense: Marx's German is foreign with regard to English – hence the need for translation, for instance, of the *Grundrisse* into English. Here the vast and differentiated machinery of globalizing capital moves along the channels we have seen – from the 'mother tongue' into 'foreign languages' in the way that a raw material might be converted or formed into a commodity.

Or does Marx mean the foreignness or strangeness to human animals of *all* languages, inasmuch as they are *languages*, and hence foreign to its users merely in the way that the hammer is foreign to the carpenter's hand? Here again an everyday sense of what is proper to bodies and to the use of different languages seems to be at work. Human animals, animal toolmakers, are different from the tools they make though they are defined reflexively by them, never more clearly than when the tool is the language the gregarious animal uses. Our philosophical genealogy – one of them, the European genealogy on which the modern University stands, on which the collective pronoun 'we' stands inasmuch as it is, as we are, products of the global University machine – will find its way this time among interpretations of Aristotle's lines, in the *Politics*, determining that 'man [ἄνθρωπος, *ánthrōpos*] is a political being more than any . . . [because] alone among the animals man has speech [logon dē monon anthrōpos ekhei ton zoon]'.⁴ Again things quickly get uncanny here too: the solitary and artisanal scene that paints *homo faber* at work with his handy tools is manifestly inadequate to Marx's technical, machinic description of industrial production. More so, differently so, to the scene of contemporary information capital, which might be called post-technical. Still, let's say we forget – for just a moment – that complicating history. Here, where *ihrer Fremdheit* may mean for Marx the foreignness or strangeness of languages to the human, political animal, inasmuch as they are tools or techniques that the political animal uses to build its world: external, prosthetic, technical, supplementary and so on. Here still translation among languages retains its quotidian sense, and from that fundamentally *external* domain, in which languages, equally foreign or strange to the human animals that use them, exchange properties and do each other's work, from the very strangeness of that fundamentally *external*, technical domain the human animal draws the likenesses for the dynamics of the money form.

'Ideas', Marx writes, 'which have first to be translated out of their mother tongue into a foreign language in order to circulate, in order to become exchangeable, offer a somewhat better analogy; but the analogy then lies not in language, but in the foreignness [*Fremdheit*] of language'. Marx is searching for an analogy that will translate for his reader, into a language familiar to him or to her, without loss or with a minimum of loss, the dynamic of money's circulation. His informal note doubly translates, as if a sense of urgency or incompleteness or dissatisfaction ate at the expression; as if a compensatory, surplus translation were required. The standard analogies, he says – 'money with blood . . . money with language' – are erroneous, the first about as erroneous as Menenius Agrippa's belly analogy, the second no less erroneous than the first, in a chain of analogies to analogies unfixed to any primal value, to any term literal and error-free.

Does Marx intend to act out thereby something still more foreign than the mutual foreignness of any language to any other, or of language or languages in general to the human animal that makes and uses them – does he want his reader to take account of a strangeness or foreignness of language, or of languages, that's constitutive *of* language, or of languages, as such? And which makes the as-such of language, or of languages, foreign and strange *to* language, or languages? Finally, would this constitutively strange, or foreign, aspect of the not-as-such of language, or languages, mark out a way of being that is other than political for the political animal in the age of global thought?

To this last question the answer would be clear, or clearer, *if* rather than that tool- or product-we-call-*language*, definitive for Aristotle of the human animal, we took as the literal *term* on which the chain of errant and erroneous analogies hangs, as the primal value from which these likenesses swerve, the quality definitive for Marx of the human animal, of the animal that produces surplus value: *labour*.[5] *If,* then, it were *labour* whose 'foreignness' Marx offered as the ground for the chain of translations and analogies that serve to describe, but also enact, the dynamics of the money form; *if* in place of the tool- or product-we-call-*language*, definitive for Aristotle of the human animal, we take the quality definitive for Marx of the human animal, the animal that produces surplus value: *labour*. If we accept this translation of the argument's primary term, then a labour *theory* of value follows; the noon-day clarity with which any reader understands her experience of work becomes the language into which money's dynamic can illuminatingly be translated. Labour, a universal and definitive condition of the human animal, would then serve as the raw stuff from which specific forms of labouring produce whatever-commodities for consumption: maternal, matricial. Labour would *also* serve as the machine translating values into equivalences; and as the guarantor of those equivalential chains. The term *Fremdheit*, strangeness or alien-ness, returns in Marx for use in just that complicated, multivalent context. A little farther along in the *Grundrisse* Marx proposes that 'the independent, for-itself existence [*Fürsichsein*] of value vis-à-vis living labor capacity – hence its existence as capital – the objective, self-sufficient indifference, the alien quality [*Fremdheit*] of the objective conditions of labor vis-à-vis living labor capacity . . . goes so far that these conditions confront the person of the worker in the person of the capitalist – as personification with its own will and interest' [daß diese Bedingungen der Person des Arbeiters in der Person des Kapitalisten – als Personifikationen mit eignem Willen und Interesse gegenübertreten]. So goes the standard translation of the *Grundrisse* into English, by Martin Nicolaus. A note by Ben Fowkes to the translation of the plural *Personifikationen mit eignem Willen und Interesse* by the singular 'as personification with its own will and interest' explains that 'the original text has "personifications", evidently referring back to "conditions"', *Bedingungen*.

Just here the translation between 'language' and 'labor' fails. The 'reference back' to 'the person of the capitalist' is hardly evident. By placing 'personification' on the side of the 'person of the capitalist' alone, Nicolaus and Fowkes stage for Marx's reader the confrontation, *gegenübertreten* is Marx's word, between a 'person', the labourer, and a 'personification' of the objective conditions under which the value of his or her labour is extracted and submitted to abstraction – the capitalist. In Nicolaus's translation the story that the *Grundrisse* tells, the story of the encounter of personifications, is translated into the humanist story of the confrontation between the bearer of personhood, the labourer, on whose *persona* eventually the historical role of motor of history will descend, and the capitalist, always only a personification, always only defined by his or her externality to, or foreignness or alienation from, the labour he or she works to extract. The symmetry in Marx's lines, which speaks of two 'persons' *both* having undergone 'personification' as a result of the 'alien quality [*Fremdheit*] of the objective conditions of labor', is lost. With it, we lose the drama of generalized alien-ness or strangeness that the *Grundrisse* is staging – a drama we can now characterize in two contradictory ways. Marx is staging at every level the generalized translation *from* constraint and contingency, from a condition almost thing-like [*be-dingung*, a term with its own long history], from allegory, from equivalence, from the work of abstraction *to* a person-hood never disengaged from personification. From the homely and self-identical idiotism of the mother tongue (of labour, of language) out into the strange, alien world that lies beyond its borders – the world of the market, of the market of markets, of universal translation, of the globe. But he is *also* and simultaneously hanging the defective, erroneous and partial chain of analogies, and translations of analogies, on a value or a sense that remains as untranslatable as a proper name: *labour, language*. The indices that support and organize the circulation of sense and value in the era of post-technical information capital are at once generally translatable and radically untranslatable. The logical form required to think or express this generalized condition, the institutions that support such thought and the drama of personifications it stages are strange, alien with respect to the alienating logic of global thought's human persona. 'Only alienness is the antidote to alienation', wrote Adorno, as the European states entered their crisis, in 1944–1945: *Nur Fremdheit ist das Gegengift gegen Entfremdung*. But 'antidote' is too tame a translation of Adorno's expression; even 'antivenin' is not quite right. *Gegengift*: poison against poison, a gift against the gift you and the world will offer me. The poisonous refusal of or rebellion against an equivalent exchange and the poisoned refusal to take this gift for that. This poison against that gift. Untranslating machines offer counter-*gifts* to the poison of global alienation: the genealogy of its general crisis; the defective critique of the logic of its thought; the ephemeral, democratic alternatives to its institutions; a drama of partial personifications against the tragedy of the late human animal.

Notes

Introduction

1. Karl Marx, *Grundrisse: Foundations of the Critique of Political Economy*, tr. Martin Nicolaus (London: Penguin, 1993), 163. The German, from Karl Marx, *Grundrisse der Kritik der Politischen Ökonomie*, in Karl Marx u. Friedrich Engels *Gesamtausgabe* (MEGA) 2. 1 (Institut für Marxismus-Leninismus beim ZK der SED/ Berlin: Dietz Verlag, 1976), 95.

2. My epigraph is from Karl Marx, *Grundrisse*. Tr. Martin Nicolaus (London: Penguin, 1973), 162–63. The German, from Karl Marx and Friedrich Engels, *Werke* (Berlin: Dietz Verlag, 1983), v. 42, 96: 'Die Vergleichung an der Stelle der wirklichen Gemeinschaftlichkeit und Allgemeinheit. (Das Geld mit dem Blute zu vergleichen – das Wort Zirkulation gab dazu Anlaß – ist ungefähr ebenso richtig wie das Gleichnis des Menenius Agrippa zwischen den Patriziern und dem Magen.) (Das Geld mit der Sprache zu vergleichen ist nicht minder falsch. Die Ideen werden nicht in die Sprache verwandelt, so daß ihre Eigentümlichkeit aufgelöst und ihr gesellschaftlicher Charakter neben ihnen in der Sprache existierte, wie die Preise neben den Waren. Die Ideen existieren nicht getrennt von der Sprache. Ideen, die aus ihrer Muttersprache erst in eine fremde Sprache übersetzt werden müssen, um zu kursieren, um austauschbar zu werden, bieten schon mehr Analogie; die Analogie liegt dann aber nicht in der Sprache, sondern in ihrer Fremdheit.) (Die Austauschbarkeit aller Produkte, Tätigkeiten, Verhältnisse gegen Drittes, *Sachliches*, was wieder gegen alles *ohne Unterschied* ausgetauscht werden kann – also die Entwicklung der Tauschwerte (und der Geldverhältnisse) ist identisch mit der allgemeinen Venalität, Korruption.)'

3. Barbara Cassin, 'Intraduisibles', in *L'archipel des idées de Barbara Cassin* (Paris: EMSH, 2014), 192. My translation. A recent review of definitions of untranslatability, and her own elaboration of the concept as it pertains to literary studies, in Emily Apter, 'Untranslatables: A World System', *New Literary History* 39:3 (2008), 581–98 and *Against World Literature: On the Politics of Untranslatability* (New York: Verso, 2013).

4. The American Academy of Arts and Sciences Commission on the Humanities and Social Sciences, 'The Heart of the Matter: The Humanities and Social Sciences

for a Vibrant, Competitive, and Secure Nation'. 19 June 2013, online at https://www. natcom.org/heartofthematter/.

5. Online at http://www.globaluniversitysystems.com/about-us.

6. Certain arguments in this chapter take up and revise previously published work, in my 'Translation', *Political Concepts: A Critical Lexicon* (New School for Social Research), v. 2, online at http://www.politicalconcepts.org/; and 'This Untranslatability Which Is Not One', *Paragraph* 38:2 (2015), 174–88.

7. For instance, Emily Apter, *Against World Literature: On the Politics of Untranslatability* (New York: Verso, 2013); Pascale Casanova, *La Langue Mondiale: Traduction Et Domination* (Paris: Seuil, 2015); David Damrosch, *How to Read World Literature* (Chichester, UK, Wiley-Blackwell, 2009); David Damrosch, ed. *World Literature in Theory* (Chichester, UK: 2014); Theo D'Haen, David Damrosch and Djelal Kadir, eds. *The Routledge Companion to World Literature* (Oxford and New York: Routledge, 2012); Mads Rosendahl Thomsen, Theo D' Haen and César Domínguez, eds. *World Literature: A Reader* (London and New York: Routledge, 2013).

8. Heidegger writes that *glossa* is language become 'mere hearsay.' *Glossa* is language become the mechanical organ of the tongue, language inasmuch as it represents the 'loosening' of 'truth', that is, language become, both gradually and catastrophically, the expression of a machine, 'the act of speaking, the activation of the organs of speech, mouth, lips, tongue'. See *Introduction to Metaphysics*. Tr. Gregory Fried and Richard Polt (New Haven, CT: Yale University Press, 2000), 198; see also Martin Heidegger, *On the Way to Language*. Tr. Peter D. Hertz (New York: Harper and Row, 1971; 1982), 96: 'If we take language directly in the sense of something that is present, we encounter it as the act of speaking, the activation of the organs of speech, mouth, lips, tongue. Language manifests itself in speaking, as a phenomenon that occurs in man. . . . Language is the tongue'.

9. See Wolfgang Pöckl, 'Apuntes para la historia de *traducere, I:* "Traducir,"' *Hieronymus Complutensis* 4/5 (1996–1997), 10ff. Online at http://cvc.cervantes.es/lengua/hieronymus/pdf/04_05/04_05_009.pdf. I take some of my examples here from Pöckl.

10. Thomas Hobbes, 'Philosophical Rudiments Concerning Government and Society', in *The English Works of Thomas Hobbes*, ed. William Molesworth (London: John Bohn, 1841), v. II, 17. Compare this recent translation: '*Certain rights must be transferred or abandoned*. For if each man held on to his *right to all things*, it necessarily follows that some men would be attacking and others defending themselves, and both by *right* (for each man strives by necessity of nature to defend his Body and whatever is necessary for its protection). *War* would ensue. Anyone, therefore, who does not give up his *right to all things* is acting contrary to the ways of peace, that is, contrary to the *law of nature'*. In Thomas Hobbes, *On the Citizen*. Ed. and Tr. Richard Tuck and Michael Silverthorne (Cambridge: Cambridge University Press, 1998), 34.

11. Thomas Hobbes, *Leviathan, or the Matter, Forme & Power of a Common-Wealth Ecclesiasticall and Civill* (London, 1651), 66.

12. Hobbes, Thomas, *Elementa philosophica de cive* (Amsterdam, 1647).

13. Thomas Hobbes, *Élémens philosophiques du bon citoyen*. Tr. Samuel Sorbière (Paris, 1651), 24–5.

14. Karl Marx, 'Introduction to the Critique of Political Economy,' in *A Contribution to the Critique of Political Economy*. Tr. S. W. Ryazanskaya and ed. *Karl Marx* (Moscow: Progress Publishers, 1970; London: Lawrence & Wishart, 1971; New York: International Publishers, 1971), 188–217. The German is from *Marx/Engels Werke* (Berlin: Dietz Vlg., 1971), B.13:7, 615.

15. 'Production is simultaneously consumption as well. [Die Produktion ist unmittelbar auch Konsumtion.] It is consumption in a dual form – subjective and objective consumption. [First] the individual, who develops his abilities producing expends them as well, using them up in the act of production, just as in natural procreation vital energy is consumed. Secondly, it is consumption of the means of production, which are used and used up and in part (as for instance fuel) are broken down into simpler components. It similarly involves consumption of raw material which is absorbed and does not retain its original shape and quality. The act of production itself is thus in all its phases also an act of consumption. The economists concede this. They call productive consumption both production that is simultaneously identical with consumption, and consumption which is directly concurrent with production. The identity of production and consumption amounts to Spinoza's proposition: *Determinatio est negatio*'. [Die Produktion als unmittelbar identisch mit der Konsumtion, die Konsumtion als unmittelbar zusammenfallend mit der Produktion, nennen sie *produktive Konsumtion*. Diese Identität von Produktion und Konsumtion kommt hinaus auf Spinozas Satz: *Determinatio est negatio*.] 'Introduction to the Critique of Political Economy', 188–217.

16. Ernesto Laclau, 'Identity and Hegemony', in *Contingency, Hegemony, Universality: Contemporary Dialogues on the Left*, eds. Judith Butler, Ernesto Laclau, and Slavoj Zizek (London: Verso, 2000), 58.

17. It is useful to contrast both Cassin's proposition regarding the plurality of untranslatabilities, and mine regarding the non-unity of untranslatability with Paul Ricoeur's account of the long 'battle' against untranslatability waged by forging 'equivalences' rather than 'identities' between natural languages in translation. For his suggestive if, to my mind, recuperative remarks, see Paul Ricoeur, *Sur la Traduction* (Paris: Bayard, 2004), especially 53–69.

18. 'FACT SHEET on the President's Plan to Make College More Affordable: A Better Bargain for the Middle Class', online at http://www.whitehouse.gov/the-press-office/2013/08/22/fact-sheet-president-s-plan-make-college-more-affordable-better-bargain-. Accessed 4 October 2014.

19. I've discussed the relation between globalization and translation, as a matter of the political economy of literary phrases, in a number of spots. The most recent is Jacques Lezra, 'Translation', in *Political Concepts: A Critical Lexicon* (New School for Social Research), v. 2, online at http://www.politicalconcepts.org/.

20. Jacques Derrida, *Monolingualism of the Other*. Tr. Patrick Mensah (Palo Alto, CA: Stanford University Press 1998), 56–67.

21. Jacques Derrida, *Monolinguisme de l'autre* (Paris: Galilee, 1996), 100.

22. Jacques Derrida, *El monolingüismo del otro, o la prótesis de origen* (Buenos Aires: Manantial, 1997), 80.

23. It is useful to contrast both Cassin's proposition regarding the plurality of untranslatabilities, and mine regarding the non-unity of untranslatability with Paul Ricoeur's account of the long 'battle' against untranslatability waged by forging 'equivalences' rather than 'identities' between natural languages in translation. For his suggestive if, to my mind, recuperative remarks, see Paul Ricoeur, *Sur la Traduction* (Paris: Bayard, 2004), especially 53–69.

Chapter 1

1. I wish to acknowledge the generous support of the University of Wisconsin-Madison Graduate School Research Fund, which made much of the work on this chapter possible. A first version of 'The Indecisive Muse' was presented in September 2003 at The English Institute, Harvard University. I have profited immensely from conversations about translation in general, and about this chapter in particular, with Patricia López, who read a draft carefully, intelligently and most generously.

Where no translator is named, the translation is my own.

2. I say 'nameless translator', but this is not true of recent editions of the 'Asterix' series. The Salvat and Bruguera editions – from the early 1970s forward – shear the appealing, asterisked note to the untranslatable quality of Spanish, regularize the print (they move from hand lettering to print) and attribute the translations to Víctor Mora Pujadas, Jaime Perich and Mireia Porta. The earliest editions, from Editorial Molino – *Asterix el Galo* (1965), *La Hoz de Oro* (1966), *Asterix y los Godos* (1966) – carry no translator's name. These are the texts with my asterisked note. Finally, note the droll redoubling of the eponymous Gaulish character in the diacritical: an asterisk note to the text of 'Asterix'. It is as though Asterix himself were drawing our attention to the insufficiencies of the translation (or as though we were to see the asterisk under the Asterix from these points on: the indexical function inhabiting the nominal one).

3. And not only this notional 'tired Spaniard': the English 'Dogmatix' is exceptional among translations of the dog's name, which mostly remains 'Idefix'. Esperanto ('Snufiks') and Welsh ('Bitabix'), along with Slovenian and Breton, are also unusual. On the translations (primarily into English) of Goscinny and Uderzo, see Sheila Embleton, 'Names and Their Substitutes: Onomastic Observations on Astérix and Its Translations', *Target* 3:2 (1991), 175–206 and Keith Harvey, 'A Descriptive Framework for Compensation', *The Translator* 1:1 (1995), 65–86. Ignacio Villena Álvarez's unpublished PhD dissertation, *Problemática teórico-practica de la traducción subordinada de cómics (Análisis de un caso práctico: La colección de historietas de Astérix en francés y en español)* (Universidad de Málaga: Facultad de Filosofía y Letras, May 2000) is a systematic treatment of the translation of the Asterix series into Spanish. Villena's project is primarily practical and descriptive: he seeks to locate 'dynamic equivalents' of the French terms and expressions in Spanish, evaluate the existing translations and propose alternatives that come closer to fulfilling the semantic and other functions of the French terms in the field of Spanish.

4. Villena considers the translation of 'Idéfix' as 'Idefix' to be a case of 'adaptación ortográfica del español' (214). He says about 'Idefix': 'En español, alternan las traducciones de IDEFIX e IDEAFIX. Nos parece que el efecto que se consigue

con esta adaptación ortográfica es bastante bueno, aunque se podría haber optado por ser aún más explícito y buscar la equivalencia dinámica adoptando el nombre de IDEAFIJIX' (216) [In Spanish, the translations IDEFIX and IDEAFIX alternate. We believe the effect achieved by this orthographic adaptation is fairly good, although it would have been possible to be even more explicit, and seek dynamic equivalence adopting the name IDEAFIJA.]

5. The European 'invention' of modern 'transnational humanism' in the years from 1933 to 1948, and then its revival by Edward Said in the last decade of his life, are the subject of Emily Apter's crucial *The Translation Zone* (Princeton: Princeton University Press, 2006). For Apter, the modern 'translation zone' is both a war zone and, in its production of the possibility of comparativism, an image of what comes *after* war.

6. Sebastián de Covarrubias, *Tesoro de la lengua castellana, o española*, edición de Martín de Riquer (Barcelona: Editorial Alta Fulla, 1998), 972: 'Traduzir: Del verbo latino *traduco, is,* por llevar de un lugar a otro alguna cosa o encaminarla. . . . En lenga latina tiene algunas significaciones analógicas, pero en la española sinifica el bolver la sentencia de una lengua en otra' [From the Latin word *traduco,- is,* meaning to take something from one place to another, or to set it on a path. . . . In the Latin tongue it has some analogical senses, but in Spanish it means to change the phrase from one language into another].

7. 'Kenne ich etwa die Bedeutung eines englischen und eines gleichbedeutenden deutschen Wortes, so is es unmöglich, daß ich nicht weiß, daß die beiden gleichbedeutend sing; es ist unmöglich, daß ich sie niche ineinander übersetzen kann'. Ludwig Wittgenstein, *Tractatus Logico-Philosophicus*. Tr. C. K. Ogden (London: Kegan Paul, 1922), 91. The translation by D. F. Pears and B. F. McGuinness (London: Routledge, 1961) is not significantly different.

8. A variant of this example crops up in Wittgenstein's *Lectures on the Foundations of Mathematics: Cambridge 1939*, ed. Cora Diamond (Chicago: University of Chicago, 1975), 275–76: 'If a man didn't understand these symbols [the logical notation of a proposition], you could read them off in English; and this would be an explanation of a sort. Or you could say it means: "*il pleut*"; if he can already apply the French sentence but not the English sentence'. The French, one should say in passing, are among Wittgenstein's primary examples when he treats specifically the question of translation. He remarks famously, both in the *Philosophical Investigations* and in his remarks on anthropology, on the puzzle posed for speakers of German by the French language's unhappy propensity to add a gender to predicate adjectives. Here Wittgenstein is speaking of the 'interpretation' or the 'reading' of the expression upon a person's face and draws this analogy: '[W]e [Anscombe interpolates: Germans] are surprised that in French the predicate adjective agrees with the substantive in gender, and when we explain it to ourselves by saying: they mean: "the man is *a good one*"'. Ludwig Wittgenstein, *Philosophical Investigations*, 2nd ed. Tr. G. E. M. Anscombe (London: Blackwell, 1953; 1997), ¶538. (Unless indicated otherwise, references to the *Philosophical Investigations* [PI], by paragraph number, are to this edition and translation.)

9. We know – or we believe that we know – that the later Wittgenstein abandoned this atomic principle, as well as the requirement that grammatical rules that *precede*

and *determine* usage be analytically, rather than perspicuously available (the general rule that 'in communicative speech-situations certain rules must be followed' is not understood to be a *necessary* rule, but rather to be based on local *need*). Recent work – by James Conant and Cora Diamond, among others – suggests that the *tractarian* Wittgenstein was considerably less committed to an analytic determination of grammaticality than has conventionally been assumed. For Conant's best-known treatment of the topic, see his 'Throwing Away the Top of the Ladder', *The Yale Review* 79:3 (1990), 328–64.

10. Lawrence Venuti, *The Scandals of Translation: Towards an ethics of difference* (London and New York: Routledge, 1998), 81–7. Venuti rightly notes that 'canons of accuracy [for judging the merits of translations] are articulated and applied in the domestic culture and therefore are basically ethnocentric' (82).

11. Jorge Luis Borges, 'Tlön, Uqbar, *Orbis Tertius*', *Sur (Buenos Aires)* 68:3 (1940), 30–46. Borges's mention of the *Antología de la literatura fantástica* in which the article on 'Tlön' was supposed to appear is a not-so-masked reference to the collection that he, along with Bioy and Silvina Ocampo, the editor of *Sur*, published that same year: *Antología de la literatura fantástica*. Buenos Aires: Editorial Sudamericana (Colección Laberinto, 1), 1940.

12. Christopher Johnson, in his 'Intertextuality and Translation: Borges, Browne, and Quevedo', *Translation and Literature* 11:2 (2002), 174–94, argues for the importance of the term 'quevediana' and provides valuable background on Borges's (and Bioy's) translation of Browne and fascination with Quevedo. Johnson tends to place the stress on Borges's intertextuality (hence Johnson's interest in the 'quevedian' reference), where I lay it rather on the problematic of decision in Borges's account of translation. For Borges's interest in Browne, see also Cynthia Stephens, 'Borges, Sir Thomas Browne and the Theme of Metempsychosis', *Forum for Modern Language Studies* 28:3 (1992), 268–79.

13. A useful review of Borges's own theories of translation, with an analysis of the ethics of translation in Borges, may be found in Sergio Waisman's *Borges and Translation: The Irreverence of the Periphery* (Lewisburg, PA: Bucknell University Press, 2005). Waisman arranges his analysis of Borges's practice and theory of translation cartographically, with important results for our understanding of Borges's geopolitical engagement. Some loss of precision in the treatment of the texts themselves is the result. Waisman is especially astute in discussing 'Writing as Translation' in Borges: 'Borges's irreverent moves are so innovative that questions such as "is the translation faithful to the original?" can be restated as "is the original faithful to the translation?" His texts consistently challenge the "supersticiosa ética del lector" [superstitious ethics of the reader] and reveal the prejudices behind the privileging of the original. . . . Borges shows that the traditional demand for fidelity is merely another way to express the power and determinacy assigned to the original over the translation – and, by implication, to the canons of the center over the simulacra of the margins' (122).

14. Thomas Browne, *Hydriotaphia, Urne-Buriall, or, a Discourse of the Sepulchral Urns Lately Found in Norfolk* (London: Printed for Hen. Brome at the Signe of the Gun in Ivy-Lane, 1658), A1–2.

15. Borges has more than a little to say elsewhere about Francisco de Quevedo; indeed, his enthusiasm for Quevedo has led more than one critic to compare

Quevedo's eccentric stoicism with Borges's own, equally exorbitant political and aesthetic stances. See Christopher Maurer, 'The Poet's Poets: Borges and Quevedo', in *Borges the Poet*, ed. Carlos Cortínez (Fayetteville: University of Arkansas Press, 1986), 191 and 193. Efraín Kristal's discussion of Borges's interest in Quevedo bears particularly on 'Tlön, Uqbar, *Orbis Tertius*'. See his *Invisible Work: Borges and Translation* (Nashville, TN: Vanderbilt University Press, 2002), 89–98. Borges rather intriguingly concludes a 1948 'Prólogo' to a selection of Quevedo's prose and verse with this lapidary comment: 'Como Joyce, como Goethe, como Shakespeare, como ningún otro escritor, Francisco de Quevedo es menos un hombre que una dilatada y compleja literatura' – ['Like Joyce, Goethe, Shakespeare, but also like no other, Quevedo is less a man than an extended and complex literature'.] Borges, 'Francisco de Quevedo: Prosa y verso', in *Obras Completas* (Barcelona: Emecé, 1996), v. IV, 117.

16. Jacques Derrida, 'Des Tours de Babel', in his *Psyche: inventions de l'autre* (Paris: Galilée, 1987), 208–09. English version in 'Des Tours de Babel', *Difference in Translation*, Tr. and ed. Joseph F. Graham (Ithaca, NY: Cornell University Press, 1985); reprinted in Rainer Schulte and John Biguenet, eds. *Theories of Translation: An Anthology of Essays from Dryden to Derrida* (Chicago: University of Chicago Press, 1992), 224–25.

17. The example of the French *Pierre-pierre* is not accidental – the foundational story of the building of the Church, typologically twinned with the Pentecost as the inverse or the completion of the Babelic dispersal, is based upon the Vulgate's pun on the Latin *petrus-Petrus*: 'et ego dico tibi quia tu es Petrus et super hanc petram aedificabo ecclesiam meam' (Matthew 16:19: ['And I also say to you that you are Peter, and upon this rock I will build My church']).

18. By the time of 'The Art of Memoires' (1984) Derrida's thought on the status of this notion of history – and of what it would mean to be 'outside of history' in this sense – has been sharpened, passing through de Man's work: 'What constrains us to think (without ever believing in it) a "true mourning" (if such there be) is the essence of the proper name. . . . At the moment of death the proper name remains; through it we can name, call, invoke, designate, but we know, we can think (and this thought cannot be reduced to mere memory, though it comes from a memory) that. . . the bearer of the name and the unique pole of all these acts, these references, will never again answer to it, never himself answer, except through what we mysteriously call our memory'. Derrida, *Memoires for Paul de Man*. Tr. Cecile Lindsay, Jonathan Culler and Eduardo Cadava (New York: Columbia University Press, 1986), 48. Needless to say, the so-called de Man affair led Derrida and many others to refine quite considerably this still-inchoate description of the relation between 'mourning' and the proper name.

19. For instance, by Derrida himself, and by Gayatri Spivak, in 'The Setting to Work of Deconstruction', her 'Appendix' to *A Critique of Postcolonial Reason* (Cambridge: Harvard University Press, 1999), 426.

20. Ludwig Wittgenstein, *The Blue and Brown Books* (New York: Harper and Row, 1958), viii.

21. See PI ¶ 19:

But how do you do this: how do you mean that while you say 'Slab!'? Do you say the unshortened sentence to yourself? And why should I translate the call

'Slab!' into a different expression in order to say what someone means by it? And if they mean the same thing – why should I not say: 'When he says "Slab!"' he means 'Slab!'? Again, if you can mean 'Bring me the slab', why should you not be able to mean 'Slab!'? – But when I call 'Slab!', then what I want is, that he should bring me a slab! – Certainly, but does 'wanting this' consist in thinking in some form or other a different sentence from the one you utter?

[[Der], der 'Platte!' ruft, eigentlich meint: 'Bring mir eine Platte!' – Aber wie machst du das, dies meinen, während du 'Platte' sagst? Sprichst du dir inwendig den unverkürtzen Satz vor? Und warum soll ich, um zu sagen, was Einer mit dem Ruf 'Platte!' meint, diesen Ausdruck in einen andern übersetzen? Und wenn sie das Gleiche bedeuten,—warum soll ich nicht sagen: 'wenn er "Platte!" sagt, meint er "Platte!"?' Oder: warum sollst du nicht 'Platte!' meinen können, wenn du 'Bring mir die Platte' meinen kannst? – Aber wenn ich 'Platte!' rufe, so will ich doch, er soll mir eine Platte bringen! – Gewiß, aber besteht, 'dies wollen' darin, daß du in irgend einer Form einen andern Satz denkst, als den, den du sagst?]

For an account of Wittgenstein's 'horrified' reaction to Rush Rhees's first translation of the PI, see Ray Monk, *Wittgenstein: The Duty of Genius* (New York: Penguin Books, 1990), 414. Venuti is particularly astute in discussing Anscombe's translation of PI, especially the key German words *seltsam* [Anscombe: 'queer'], *feiern* [Anscombe: 'to go on holiday'] and *hinweisende* [Anscombe: 'ostensive']. He concludes that 'the remainder in a translation demonstrates. . . that the philosophical project of concept formation is fundamentally determined by its linguistic and cultural conditions. Translation remains the dark secret of philosophy precisely because the remainder shatters the bedrock assumption of this project in its modern academic form: the stability and authority of the philosophical subject as the autonomous agent of reflection'. (*Scandals of Translation*, 115) Marjorie Perloff makes a rather similar point, and goes some distance in identifying the nature of this 'dark secret'. In her *Wittgenstein's Ladder: Poetic Language and the Strangeness of the Ordinary* (Chicago: University of Chicago Press, 1996), she comments that '[n]ational identity is a defining feature of the Wittgensteinian text. And so is ethnicity'.

22. Anscombe acknowledges the help of Rhees, among others, in making the translation. In fact two other drafts of this paragraph exist, though squabbles over the publication of Wittgenstein's papers have made them rather hard to obtain. Rhees's own translation survives, as does a holograph with Wittgenstein's manuscript corrections of Rhees's translation. It is in that corrected manuscript that 'Nothung' is changed to 'Excalibur' by Wittgenstein, though only the first time that the sword's name occurs. Here are the two, 'primitive' versions. The first is Rush Rhees's:

But what gives people the idea of wanting to make just this word a name, when it so obviously isn't a name? – just that; they are inclined to make an objection to what is generally called 'name'; and the objection can be put in this way: that the name really ought to indicate something simple. And for this one might give the following reasons: A proper name in the ordinary sense would be, for instance, the word 'Nothung.' The sword Nothung consists of parts put together in a particular way. If they are put together differently, then Nothung doesn't exist. Now the sentence 'Nothung has a sharp edge' obviously has meaning, whether 'Nothung' is still whole or has been smashed to bits. Yet if 'Nothung' is the name of an object, then this object doesn't exist any more when Nothung has been smashed; and since the name couldn't have any object corresponding to it then, it wouldn't have any meaning. But then in the sentence 'Nothung has a sharp edge', there would be a word that has no meaning, and so the sentence would be nonsense. But the sentence does have meaning, and so the words of which it consists must always correspond to something. So that in an analysis of the meaning of the word 'Nothung' must disappear, and in its place must come words that name something simple. And these words we may reasonably call the real names.

This is Wittgenstein's version (Rhees's version, with Wittgenstein's corrections incorporated):

But why should one wish to regard just this word as a name, when it so obviously isn't a name? For this very reason; for we are inclined to raise an objection to calling 'a name' what is generally called so, and this objection can be expressed by saying: that the name really ought to stand for something simple. And this can be defended as follows:—A proper name in the ordinary sense is, e.g., the word 'Excalibur.' The sword Nothung consists of various parts put together in a certain way. If they are not put together in this way, Nothung doesn't exist. Now the sentence 'Nothung has a sharp edge' obviously has sense, whether 'Nothung' is still whole or has been smashed. Yet if 'Nothung' is the name of an object, then this object doesn't exist any more when Nothung has been smashed; and since the name then has no object corresponding to it, it hasn't any meaning. But then in the sentence 'Nothung has a sharp edge', there is a word without a meaning, and therefore 'Nothung has a sharp edge' would be nonsense. But to say this does have meaning, and so the words of which it consists something must always correspond. Therefore in an analysis of the sense the word 'Nothung' must disappear, and instead of it words must appear which denote simple objects. These words we may reasonably call the real names.

From *The Wittgenstein Papers* (Papers, photocopy of manuscript notebooks) (microform), Cornell University (Reel 6). See also G. P. Baker and P. M. S. Hacker, *An Analytical Commentary on the 'Philosophical Investigations'* (Chicago: University of Chicago Press, 1980), v. 1, 247 and Eike von Savigny, *Wittgensteins 'Philosophische Untersuchungen': Ein Kommentar fur Leser* (Frankfurt A. M.: Klostermann, 1994), v. 1, 85–6. E. F. Thompkins gives a brief criticism of Wittgenstein's sword example in '"Sachverhalt" and "Gegenstand" Are Dead', *Philosophy*, 66:256 (April 1991), 217–34, especially 230–31.

23. In an early work on naming in the PI, Robert Fogelin analyses PI ¶ 79 (on the proper name 'Moses') and discusses Saul Kripke's suggestion 'that the relation between a name and the thing named is actually *causal or historical*. [A] name becomes the name of a thing through a historical act of dubbing. The use of the name to name just this object is then preserved as it is passed along from language

user to language user'. In Robert J. Fogelin, *Wittgenstein*, 2nd ed., revised (London and New York: Routledge, 1995), 139. More recently, Fogelin turns to PI ¶ 39 for a useful account of Wittgenstein's alternative to the referential model of naming – an alternative that Fogelin calls a 'use of proper names. . . governed by a loose set of descriptions'. This 'looseness' sets Wittgenstein's later positions on naming apart from strongly descriptivist accounts based on Russell's work on denoting and from causal or 'historical' accounts of naming (those based on Kripke's work). See Robert J. Fogelin, 'Wittgenstein's Critique of Philosophy', in *The Cambridge Companion to Wittgenstein*, eds. Hans Sluga and David G. Stern (Cambridge: Cambridge University Press, 1996), 34–58, especially 40–1.

24. Alfred Tennyson, 'Idylls of the King: The Passing of Arthur', in *The Poems and Plays of Tennyson* (London: Oxford University Press, 1963), 436–37.

25. For a wealth of companion material on the uses of Arthuriana during the War, see Roger Simpson, 'King Arthur in World War Two Poetry: His Finest Hour?' *Arthuriana* 13:1 (2003), 66–91. I am borrowing from Simpson's pages 68–77.

26. Fritz Lang's *Siegfrids Tod* (1922) calls Siegfried's sword 'Balmung'. Siegfried is led to it by the dwarf Alberich and uses it to kill the marvelous (mechanical) dragon, Fafnir.

27. In Ludwig Wittgenstein, *Denkbewegungen: Tagebücher 1930–1932, 1936–1937 (MS 183)*, Herausgegeben von Ilse Somaville (Innsbruck: Haymon, 1997), 52. The translation is mine.

28. Wittgenstein's notebooks generally mention Wagner in the context of fairly technical discussions of musical points – where Wittgenstein considers the status of melody in a piece, or comments on the *motif*. In 1941, Wittgenstein remarks of Wagnerian drama in general that it 'is not drama so much as an assemblage of situations strung together as though on a thread which, for its part, is merely *cleverly* spun and not inspired as the motifs and situations are'. In Ludwig Wittgenstein, *Culture and Value*. Ed. G. H. von Wright (Chicago: University of Chicago Press, 1980), 41. Perhaps the most interesting of these observations is a brief, later remark (from 1949) in which Wittgenstein contrasts Beethoven's 'irony' to Wagner's: 'With [Beethoven], it's a terrible irony, the irony of fate perhaps.— Irony reappears with Wagner, but this time transposed into the civic mode' [*ins Bürgerliche gewendet*] (*Culture and Value* 81–2). For a fuller view of Wittgenstein's important training and interest in music, see *Wittgenstein und die Musik*. Ed. Martin Alber (Innsbruck: Haymon-Verlag, 2000). M. Costis comments on Wittgenstein's apparent reliance on Wagner (and on 'Nothung') when, in discussing Frazer's *Golden Bough*, he should instead be citing the *Nibelungenlieder*. In 'Wittgenstein on Frazer's Golden Bough', *Philosophy* 65:254 (October, 1990), 518–21, especially 520.

29. Monk, *Wittgenstein: The Duty of Genius*, 389. See also Perloff's comments about the circumstances in which the *Philosophical Investigations* are composed: 'The writing of the *Investigations* took place in precisely the years when Wittgenstein was forced to recognize that, despite the baptism and Catholic upbringing that generations of Wittgensteins had undergone, from the perspective of the Nazi regime, they were simply Jews. In this context, even the "mastery" of his chosen "country's language"

cannot eradicate the sense of difference Wittgenstein speaks of. . . . Indeed, it may be the very *distance* from others that makes this philosopher-poet so determined to live *inside* the *ordinary* language field of his adopted nation, and yet to be so aware of its vagaries' (76).

30. Monk, *Wittgenstein: The Duty of Genius*, 394–95. See also M. O'C. Drury, 'Conversations with Wittgenstein', in *Ludwig Wittgenstein: Personal Recollections*, ed. Rush Rhees (Totowa, NJ: Rowman and Littlefield, 1981), 152–54.

31. Richard Wagner, *Der Ring des Nibelungen: Die Walküre/The Nibelung's Ring: The Valkyrie*, vocal score by Karl Klindworth. Tr. Frederick Jameson (Mainz: B. Schott's Söhne, 1904), 37–9. I have lightly modified Jameson's translation.

32. The standard Grimm brothers' *Wörterbuch* stresses the connection of 'Noth' to 'rubbing', 'grating', 'braying', 'galling' or 'pushing', 'passing (as in fencing)', 'pressing' and 'afflicting', 'cramping' and 'constraining'. Jakob Grimm und Wilhelm Grimm, *Deutsches Wörterbuch*. Siebenter Band. Bearbeitet von Dr. Matthias von Lexer (Leipzig: Verlag von S. Hirzel, 1889), 905–21.

33. It is not to my mind an especially *good* poem, but it is worth citing a couple of verses. The poem opens like this. (The unpublished translation is by Matthias Rudolf): 'Jetzt kenn' ich nur noch Einen Gott,/ der Gott, er heißt – die Noth'. ['Now I know only One God,/ The God, he is called – Necessity,' or 'need,' or 'want,' or 'constraint,' or 'affliction']. In Richard Wagner, *Gedichte*. Ed. Carl Friedrich Glasenapp (Berlin: G. Grote'sche Verlagsbuchhandlung, 1905), 16–22. The largely materialist tenor of the poem involves a droll, glancing critique of Idealism (in the shape of a stanza that runs, in a prosaic translation, something like this, 'Philosophy after Kant and Hegel, It educates their spirit, For he who knows it, Now sleeps and drinks and eats according to a higher rule: With a hundred-thousand Spirit-whistles every earthly dung is here scraped [or polished] from their being: They know you not, Necessity!'), before coming to a ringing conclusion:

> Natur und Mensch – Ein Elemente!
>   vernichtet ist, was je sie trennte!
> Der Freiheit Morgenroth—,
> Entzündet hat's – DIE NOTH!
> For over all the ruins/ Life's fortune blossoms: There stayed behind humankind free from chains, And nature. Nature and Man – One Element! What had ever divided them has been destroyed! The dawn of freedom –, It was kindled by –, Necessity!

34. Freud himself has almost nothing to say about the *Nibelungenlieder*, though there are comments here and there in his works concerning the symbolism of swords. The most famous is the analysis of the two 'Japanese swords', 'marriage' and 'copulation', in the 'Rat-Man' case. See *The Standard Edition of the Works of Sigmund Freud*. Tr. James Strachey (London: The Hogarth Press, 1955), v. X, 267–68: 'The lady was under some kind of restraint. He took his two Japanese swords and set her free. Clutching them, he hurried to the place where he suspected she was. He knew that they meant "marriage" and "copulation". Both things now came true'.

Chapter 2

1. This chapter was first delivered as a lecture at 'Early Modern Translation: Theory, History, Practice', a conference held at the Folger Shakespeare Library in March 2011, and then at the invitation of the Department of English at the University of Maryland. A revised version was read in May 2011 at the Facultad de Traducción e Interpretación at the Universidad de Granada. I am delighted to acknowledge the insightful questions and comments I received on all three occasions, which helped me to focus and shift the argument. Except where indicated, the translations are my own.

2. Fernando de Rojas, *The Spanish Bavvd, Represented in Celestina: or, The Tragicke-Comedy of Calisto and Melibea.* Tr. James Mabbe (London: Printed by I[ohn] B[eale], 1631), 14.

3. Fernando de Rojas, *La Celestina: Comedia o tragicomedia de Calisto y Melibea.* Ed. Peter E. Russell (Madrid: Castalia, 2001), 256–57; a useful companion edition is *Tragi/Comedia de Calisto y Melibea.* Ed. Fernando Caltalapiedra Erostarbe (Kassel: Reichenberger, 2000). The translations are mine, except where indicated.

4. This is Mabbe's translation of the passage: 'Sir why doe you vexe your selfe? why grieue you? Doe you thinke, that in the eares of this woman, the name, by which I now call her doth any way sound reproachfully? Beleeue it not. Assure your selfe, she glories as much in this name, as oft as shee heares it, as you do, when you heare some voyce, Calisto to be a gallant Gen|tleman. Besides, by this is she commonly called, and by this Title is shee of all men generally knowne. If she passe along the streetes among a hundred women, and some one perhaps blurts out, See, where's the old Bawd; without any impatiency, or any the least distemper, shee presently turnes her selfe about, nods the head, and answers them with a smiling countenance, and cheerefull looke. At your solemne banquets, your great feasts, your weddings, your gossippings, your merry meetings, your funeralls, and all other assemblies what-soeuer, where there is any resort of people, thither doth shee repaire, and there they make pastime with her. And if shee passe by where there be any dogs, they straight-way barke out this name; If shee come amongst birds, they haue no other note but this; If she sight vpon a flocke of sheepe, their bleatings proclaime no lesse; If she meet with beasts, they bellow forth the same: The frogges that lie in ditches, croake no other tune; Come shee amongst your Smithes, your Carpenters, your Armourers, your Ferriers, your Brasiers, your Ioyners: why, their hammers beate all vpon this word. In a word, all sorts of tooles and instruments returne no other Eccho in the ayre; your Shoomakers sing this song; your Combe-makers joyne with them, your Gardeners, your Plough-men, your Reapers, your Vine-keepers passe away the painefulnesse of their labours, in making her the subject of their discourse; your Table-players, and all other Gamesters neuer lose, but they peale foorth her prayses: To be short, be she wheresoeuer she be, all things whatsoeuer are in this world, repeate no other name but this: O what a deuourer of rosted egges was her husband? What would you more? Not one stone that strikes against another, but presently noyseth out, Old whore' (14–15). Stephen Gilman, *The Art of 'La Celestina'* (Westport, CT: Greenwood Press, 1956) argued that in these lines Rojas is borrowing from Petrarch's Preface to *De Remediis utriusque Fortunae* II. Alan D. Deyermond acknowledges the Petrarchan influence

in his *The Petrarchan Sources of 'La Celestina'* (Westport, CT: Greenwood Press, 1961; 1975, 64–6) but points out that these sorts of lists are conventional in late antiquity and early modernity, and argues against a direct borrowing here.

5. Antonio de Nebrija, *Gramática de la lengua castellana*. Ed. I. González-Llubera (London: Oxford University Press, 1926), 3.

6. For a view of the ideology of historiography under the Hapsburgs, see Richard L. Kagan, *Clio and the Crown: The Politics of History in Medieval and Early Modern Spain* (Baltimore, MD: The Johns Hopkins University Press, 2009).

7. Sebastián de Covarrubias, *Tesoro de la lengua castellana española* (Madrid: Luis Sánchez, 1611).

8. Ambrosius Calepinus, *Ambrosii Calepini Dictionarii Octolingvis Altera Pars* (Lugduni: Prost, 1647), online at http://diglib.hab.de/wdb.php?dir=drucke/kb-40-2f-2&pointer=259.

9. Miguel de Cervantes Saavedra, *The Second Part of the History of the Valorous and Witty Knight Errant Don Quixote of the Mancha*. Tr. Thomas Shelton? (but see below, n. 16) (London: Ed. Blount, 1620).

10. Miguel de Cervantes Saavedra, *Don Quijote de la Mancha*. Ed. Francisco Rico (Barcelona: Crítica—Biblioteca Clásica, 1998).

11. Antonio Medina Molera, *Cervantes y el Islam: El Quijote a cielo abierto*. (Barcelona: Ediciones Carena, 2005), 84.

12. Maria Rosa Menocal, *The Ornament of the World: How Muslims, Jews and Christians Created a Culture of Tolerance in Medieval Spain* (Boston, MA: Little, Brown, 2002). A more nuanced review of the place of *aljamiado* literature in Spain was already available in Luce López Baralt, 'Crónica de la destrucción de un mundo: La literatura aljamiado-morisca', *Bulletin Hispanique* 82:1–2 (1980), 16–58. Treatments of Cervantes's reference to this *morisco aljamiado* include Monika Walter, 'La imaginación de moro historiador y morisco traductor : algunos aspectos de la ficticia autoría en el Don Quijote', in *'Bon compaño jura di!'?: el encuentro de moros, judíos y cristianos en la obra cervantina*, eds. Caroline Schmauser and Monika Walter (Vervuert: Frankfurt A. M. Main; Iberoamericana: Madrid, 1998), 35–49. More recently, Nuria Martínez de Castilla, 'Anduve mirando si parecía por allí algún morisco aljamiado', in *De Cervantes y el islam*, eds. Martínez de Castilla, Nuria, Ma. Soledad Carrasco Urgoiti and Rodolfo Gil (Madrid: Ministerio de Cultura: Sociedad Estatal de Conmemoraciones Culturales, 2006), 235–46, as well as Carroll Johnson, *Transliterating a Culture: Cervantes and the Moriscos* (Newark, DE: Juan de la Cuesta, 2010).

13. Eric C. Graf, 'When an Arab Laughs in Toledo: Cervantes's Interpellation of Early Modern Spanish Orientalism', *Diacritics* 29:2 (1999), 80.

14. Michel Moner's useful 'Cervantes y la traducción', *Nueva Revista de Filología Hispánica* 38:2 (1990), 513–24, is updated and recast in Carlos Moreno's 'Multiculturalismo y traducción en el Quijote', *Hispanic Review* 71:2 (2003), 205–28.

15. Edwin B. Knowles, Jr. 'The First and Second Editions of Shelton's Don Quixote Part I: A Collation and Dating', *Hispanic Review* 9:2 (1941), 262.

16. The differences between the 1612 and 1620 editions are indeed so numerous, the 'mannerisms' so different in the later translation, as to have given rise to speculation that much of the second edition and the translation of the second half

are not Shelton's at all. See Anthony G. Lo Ré, 'The Second Edition of Thomas Shelton's *Don Quixote*, Part I: A Reassessment of the Dating Problem', *Cervantes: Bulletin of the Cervantes Society of America* 11:1 (1991), 99–118 and, more recently, James H. Montgomery, 'Was Thomas Shelton the Translator of the "Second Part" (1620) of *Don Quixote?' Cervantes: Bulletin of the Cervantes Society of America* 26:1–2 (2006), 209–17.

17. In *Covert Gestures: Crypto-Islamic Literature as Culture Practice in Early Modern Spain* (Minneapolis: University of Minnesota Press, 2005), xvii, Vincent Barletta provides this rather limited definition of 'aljamiado': 'A system of handwritten textual production that made use of an idiosyncratic form of Arabic script to copy out Castilian and Aragonese texts'. His thesis is more arresting, though his concern remains with the lexical component of aljamiado: '[T]he use of aljamiado by Castilian and Aragonese Moriscos has an extraordinarily important cross-temporal as well as cross-cultural function. It is a mistake, in other words, to view the use of Arabic script in the production of Romance texts simply as a means of connecting the Moriscos to the larger Islamic *umma* situated around the Mediterranean during the sixteenth and seventeenth centuries. This synchronic view of aljamiado-morisco textuality ignores the powerful manner in which the use of Arabic script situated Morisco scribes and readers within a thousand-year tradition of God's relationship with Muslims. It also ignores the tremendous promises for the future' (137). Mary Elizabeth Perry's *The Handless Maiden: Moriscos and the Politics of Religion in Early Modern Spain* (Princeton: Princeton University Press, 2005) provides a much more nuanced account of the 'function' of *aljamía*.

18. Miguel de Cervantes Saavedra, *The History and Adventures of the Renowned Don Quixote*. Tr. Tobias Smollett (London: A. Millar, 1755).

19. Richard Perceval and John Minsheu, *A Dictionarie in Spanish and English* (London: Bollifant, 1599).

Chapter 3

1. My epigraphs are from John Florio, *A Worlde of Wordes* (better known, in its second, 1611 edition, as *Queen Anna's New Worlde of Wordes*), printed at London, by Arnold Hatfield for Edw. Blount, 1598 (n.p.); and from Jacques Derrida, *Specters of Marx: The State of the Debt, the Work of Mourning, & the New International*. Tr. Peggy Kamuf (London: Routledge, 1994), 104. Derrida is citing from Marx's *Contribution to the Critique of Political Economy*. Tr. S. W. Ryazanskaya, ed. Maurice Dobb (New York: International Publishers, 1970), 107.

Except where indicated, the translations throughout this chapter are mine.

2. Michael Hardt and Antonio Negri, *Empire* (Cambridge, MA: Harvard University Press, 2000), 57.

3. The same is achieved, to some extent, by Ernesto Laclau's call for a 'constructed universal'. See Ernesto Laclau, 'Constructing Universality', in *Contingency, Hegemony, Universality: Contemporary Dialogues on the Left*, eds. Judith Butler, Ernesto Laclau and Slavoj Žižek (London and New York: Verso, 2000).

4. Much of the recent, fine work discussing the formation of 'national' identity in early English modernity draws from Richard Helgerson's careful and searching *Forms of Nationhood: The Elizabethan Writing of England* (Chicago: University of Chicago Press, 1992). I have also found especially intriguing Peter Sahlins's studies of border communities, especially his *Boundaries: The Making of France and Spain in the Pyrenees* (Berkeley: University of California Press, 1989). I hope that my debt to the work of Ben Anderson, Homi Bhabha and others will be clear throughout.

5. Renan, *Qu'est-ce qu'une nation? (Conférence faite en Sorbonne 11 Mars, 1882)*. In Ernest Renan, *Œuvres complètes*. Ed. Henriette Psichari (Paris: Corbeil Press, Calmann-Levy, 1947), v. 1, 903.

6. Renan, *Qu'est-ce qu'une nation?* 899.

7. Renan, 'Des services rendus aux sciences historiques par la philologie', in *Œuvres complètes*, ed. Henriette Psichari (Paris: Corbeil Press, Calmann-Levy, 1947), v. 8, 1231–32.

8. Renan, *Qu'est-ce Qu'une nation?* 899–900.

9. One might also list the dictionaries of Estienne (in the 1530s), Plantin (beginning in the 1560s), Florio (1598 and 1611), Perceval, Cawdrey (1604) and Covarrubias (1611 and 1613).

10. Jürgen Schäfer has written of the 'insecurity of many speakers' at this time, and of the 'socio-linguistic' problem posed in England 'at the beginning of the seventeenth century [by] the influx of new words derived from Latin and the Romance languages'. He maintains that '[a]t this critical juncture in the development of the English language a new genre of books . . . began to appear, the lists of hard words' (in his 'The Hard Word Dictionaries: A Re-Assessment', *Leeds Studies in English* n.s. 4, 1970, 31). This assessment of the lexical 'insecurity' prevalent in early modern Europe, and in England in particular, has a different valence in Noel Osselton's *Branded Words in English Dictionaries before Johnson*: 'To the purist's protest that the ale-wife cannot know Latin, the dictionary provides the answer: she need not – she need only have access to a dictionary, and then she may understand and speak as finely powdered a language as any' (9). And, 'In the early dictionaries . . . this intention is clearly an educational one first and foremost. The object was to instruct those who did not understand. . . . Up to 1656 the dictionary was undoubtedly intended for the guidance of those people who were in difficulties among the host of new words; and these included – notably – foreigners, the ladies and the young'. In Noel E. Osselton, *Branded Words in English Dictionaries before Johnson* (Groningen: J. B. Wolters, 1958), 11–13.

11. In the mid-to-late sixteenth century, the study of the 'antiquities' of England – Saxon customs, artefacts and language – was used to assert that the English Reformation was nothing less than a return to earlier forms of Christian worship, a triple articulation of linguistic, 'nationalist' and religious idioms that effectively delegitimates the importation of 'foreign' or 'Popish' translations of the Gospel. In an early article Rosemond Tuve linked this well-known historical thesis to contemporary, twentieth-century protocols of research and critical professionalization, briefly opening a fascinating line of inquiry that circumstances – mobilization for a European and American war – soon closed down. See her 'Ancients, Moderns, and Saxons', *ELH*

6:3 (1939), 165–90. Tuve remembers that William L'Isle calls '"the Saxons a people most devout" who have left us not only all these monasteries and churches but also "in our Libraries so goodly monuments of reverend antiquitie, divine handwritings"' (169–70), and she dates the articulation of 'nationalist', religious and lexical idioms to John Bale's and John Leland's *The Laboryouse Journey & Serche of John Leylande, for Englands Antiquitees . . . with Declaracyons Enlarged, by Iohan Bale* (London, 1549). She cites these remarkable lines from the *Laboryouse Journey*. Addressing the 'cyties of Englande', Bale-Leland cries: 'Steppe you fourth . . . and shewe your naturall noble hartes to your nacyon. As ye fynde a notable Antyquyte . . . lete them anon be imprented . . . both to their and your owne perpetuall fame'. (Cv-C2r)

12. Sebastián de Covarrubias Horozco, *Tesoro de la lengua castellana, o española* (Madrid: Luis Sánchez, 1611). I have lightly modernized the text.

13. This 'increasing differentiation' refers not only to increased technical specialization (on the manufacturing side) or to progressively more specific demands (on the side of consumption) but also to the waning of what Marx calls (but only 'approximatively!') the mythic, early modern 'co-operative form' of the capitalist mode of production, the 'handicraft-like beginnings of manufacture' [*handwerksmäßigen Anfängen der Manufaktur*]; see *Capital* I, 4, chapters 13 and 14. Tr. Samuel Moore and Edward Aveling (New York: International Publishers, 1967), 317–18. For the tradition associating *translation* with economic value, see Doug Robinson's 'Translation and the Repayment of Debt', *Delos* 7:1–2 (April 1997), 10–22 and Anthony Pym's work, especially 'Translation as a Transaction Cost', *Meta* 40:4 (1995), 594–605.

14. A *seeming* translator, or perhaps better, a translator barely *manqué*: at the end of his life Covarrubias was completing a translation into Spanish of Horace's *Odes*; the Royal licence to print 'un libro intitulado *Las Sátiras, Epístolas y Arte poético de Quinto Oracio Flaco*' was granted a month after the lexicographer's death.

15. Covarrubias is remembering these lines attributed to Horace:

> Publica materies privati iuris erit, si
> 　non circa vilem patulumque moraberis orbem;
> 　nec verbum verbo curabis reddere fidus
> 　interpres, nec desilies imitator in artum,
> 　unde pedem proferre pudor vetet aut operis lex.

Ben Jonson's 1640 translation, in *Q. Horatius Flaccus: His Art of poetry. Englished by Ben: Jonson. With Other Workes of the Author, Never Printed before* (London: Printed by I. Okes, for Iohn Benson, 1640), 10; reprinted in Edward Blakeney, ed. *Horace on the Art of Poetry* (Freeport, NY: Books for Libraries Press, 1970), 114), reads as follows: 'For, being a Poet, thou maist feigne, create,/ Not care, as thou wouldst faithfully translate, / To render word for word'.

16. Roger Ascham, *The Schole-Master* (London: John Daye, 1570 [–71]), n.p.

17. Richard Verstegan (a.k.a Verstegen), *A Restitution of Decayed Intelligence: In antiquities. Concerning the Most Noble and Renowmed English Nation. By the Studie and Travaile of R.V. Dedicated unto the Kings Most Excellent Maiestie*. Printed at Antwerp by Robert Bruney, 1605 and to be sold at London in Paules-Churchyard, by Iohn Norton and Iohn Bull.

18. For a recent account of Verstegan's role in the pamphlet débacle that followed the 1591 edict, see Victor Houliston, 'The Lord Treasurer and the Jesuit: Robert Person's Satirical *Responsio* to the 1591 Proclamation', *Sixteenth Century Journal* 32:2 (2001), 383–401, especially 384–93. Anthony G. Petti's 'Richard Verstegan and Catholic Martyrologies of the Later Elizabethan Period', *Recusant History* 5:2 (1959–1960), 64–90, has a fuller account of Verstegan's role in publicizing the persecution of Catholic dissenters under Elizabeth, in works like Verstegan's *Briefve Description des diverses Cruautez que les Catholiques endurent en Angleterre pour la foy* (Paris, 1584) and most importantly in the *Theatrum crudelitatum haereticorum nostri temporis* (Anvers, 1587). A full account of the impact of Verstegan's *Theater of Cruelties* may be found in Frank Lestringant's edition of the work's first French translation, *Le Théâtre des cruautés des heretiques de nostre temps* ([Anvers, 1588] Paris: Éditions Chandeigne, 1995).

19. And to his *linguistic* policies as well: note that Randall Cotgrave, like Ascham before him, dedicates his 1611 *Dictionarie of the French and English Tongues* (London: Adam Islip, 1611) to Cecil; clearly Cecil's circle perceived that the wars of 'sedition' were carried out in the domain of the lexical as well. Cotgrave's *Dictionarie* addresses to Cecil the following, rather heavily veiled complaint: 'My desires have aimed at more substantial markes [than "so meane a Peece" as the *Dictionarie*]; but mine eyes failed them, and forced me to spend much of their vigour on this Bundle of words; which though it may be unworthie of your Lordships great patience, and perhaps ill sorted to the expectation of others, yet is it the best I can at this time make it, and were, how perfect soever, no more then due to your Lordship, to whom I owe, for what I have beene many yeres, whatsoever I am now, or looke to be hereafter'.

20. This is how Hobbes puts it: 'But all this language gotten, and augmented by *Adam* and his posterity, was again lost at the Tower of *Babel*, when by the hand of God, every man was stricken for his Rebellion with an oblivion of his former Language. And being hereby forced to disperse themselves into several parts of the world, it must needs be, that the diversity of Tongues that now is, proceeded by degrees from them, in such manner, as need (the mother of all inventions) taught them; in tract of time grew everywhere more copious'. In Thomas Hobbes, *Leviathan, or, the Matter, Form, and Power of a Common-Wealth Ecclesiastical and Civil* (London: Printed for Andrew Crooke, 1651), Book I, chapter 4, 12.

21. See Houliston, 'The Lord Treasurer and the Jesuit', 399–401.

22. Accusations of plagiarism were not uncommon in the small world of writers of dictionaries, for obvious reasons. John Rider, author of what comes to be known as *Riders Dictionarie* (1589), was also accused of plagiarism; Thomas Thomas's heirs brought charges against him for filching material from Thomas's own dictionary.

23. Edward Phillips, *The New World of English Words, or a Generall Dictionary* (London: Printed for Nath Brooke at the Angell in Cornhill, 1658), n.p.

24. The *Ductor in linguas* is explicitly intended for the use of 'merchants'. John Minsheu, *Ductor in Linguas and Vocabularium Hispanicolatinum (A Most Copious Spanish Dictionary)* (London: John Brown's shop, 1617. Facsimile edition, with an introduction by Jürgen Schäfer. Scholar's Facsimiles & Reprints: Delmar, NY, 1978). Schäfer's introduction helpfully distinguishes Minsheu's project from that of scholars

interested in 'elucidating Latin texts for an international audience'. *Ductor in Linguas* is instead 'a practical guide for merchants', a work that aims to help 'the native speaker of English to express himself in a foreign language' (vii). This is consistent with the practice at the time. Compare these prefatory words by John Rider [Ryder] to his *Bibliotheca Scholastica. A Double Dictionarie*, printed by Joseph Barnes, Printer to the Universitie of Oxford, 1589. The 'double dictionary', Rider writes, is '[p]enned for all those that would have within short space the use of the Latin tongue, either to speake, or write. Verie profitable and necessarie for Scholers, Courtiers, Lawyers and their Clarkes, Apprentices of London, Traveliers, Factors for Marchants, and briefly for all Discontinuers within her Maiesties Realmes of England and Ireland'. Cited in DeWitt T. Starnes, *Renaissance Dictionaries: English-Latin and Latin-English* (Austin: University of Texas Press, 1954).

25. For an account of Minsheu's sources and of his lavish use of Percyvall's *A Dictionarie in Spanish, English, and Latine* (bound as part II in the *Bibliotheca hispanica* of 1591) (London: John Jackson for Richard Watkins), see the description of Minsheu's 1599 *Dictionarie in Spanish and English* (as well as its 1623 edition, and a description of the 1617 *Ductor in Linguas*) in Roger J. Steiner, *Two Centuries of Spanish and English Lexicography* (The Hague: Mouton, 1970), 38–57. Steiner's 'Appendix C' (113–14) enlarges his discussion on pages 40–2 of Minsheu's 'difficulties as far as borrowing and copyright were concerned'. Titled 'Intrigue in the 16th-Century English Book Trade', the appendix imagines Percyvall and his co-author Thomas Doyley (or D'Oylie) 'swinging into action in an effort to stop Minsheu's edition of their work' (113). More recently, see Daniel W. Noland, 'The Sources and Methods of John Minsheu's *A Dictionary of Spanish and English (1599)*', in *Dictionaries: Journal of the Dictionary Society of North America* 11 (1989), 41–52; Daniel M. Sáez Rivera, 'Vida y obra de Francisco Sobrino', *Introducción a Francisco Sobrino. Anexos Revista LEMIR*, 18–21. Sáez reviews much of the biographical material on Minsheu, mentioning his Jewish roots, nodding also to the controversy over the authorship of the 'Pleasant and delightfull dialogues' (attributed by Steven Ungerer to Alonso de Baeza, and by José Antonio Cid to the Erasmist scholar Antonio del Corro). Consult as well the edition of Minsheu's *A Dictionarie in Spanish and English* prepared by Gloria Guerrero Ramos and Fernando Pérez Lagos (Málaga: Servicio de Publicaciones de la Universidad de Málaga, 2000), 5–22.

26. The title of Barlement's work varies almost as much as his own name does: *Vocabulaer*, *Vocabulaire* and so on. For a vivid sense of his influence in England, see the '[c]hronological list of the relevant works' that Gabriele Stein provides in *The English Dictionary before Cawdrey* (Tübingen: Max Niemeyer Verlag, 1985), 410–31: Stein lists thirty-three editions of the *Dictionariolo* between 1567 and 1623. Minsheu may also have had access to *The Spanishe Schoolemaster conteyninge 7 Dialogues, according to everie daie in the weeke . . .* by William Stepney (London, 1591). For the tradition of didactic dialogues, see Werner Hüllen, *English Dictionaries 800–1700: The Topical Tradition* (Oxford: Clarendon Press, 1999), 104–32.

27. William Camden's *Rerum Anglicarum et Hibernicarum Annales, regnante Elizabetha* mentions that Edward Hobby was the ensign-bearer for the 1596 incursion

against Spain, at which Lord Thomas Howard, Sir Wiliam Paget, Sir Walter Raleigh, Sir Robert Southwell, Richard Levison, Philip Woodhouse and Robert Mansfield also fought; by 1603, Hobby is mentioned as a member of parliament, and in March 1603 is being considered for the position of Speaker. See *The Historie of the Life and Reigne of the Most Renowmed [sic] and Victorious Princesse Elizabeth, Late Queene of England . . . Composed by Way of Annals, by the Most Learned Mr. William Camden; and Faithfully Translated into English* (London: Printed for Benjamin Fisher, 1630), Book 4, 92–3, a translation of Camden's *Annales Rerum Gestarum Angliae et Hiberniae Regnante Elizabetha* of 1615–1625. For Hobby's role in Parliament, see Great Britain. Parliament. House of Commons. *Journals* 1 (1547–1628), 140–41.

28. In Pliny, according to Holland's 1601 translation:

His [Apelles's] order was when he had finished a peece of worke or painted table, and laid it out of his hand, to set it forth in some open gallerie or thorow fare to be seene of folke that passed by, and himselfe would lie close behind it to hearken what faults were found therewith; preferring the judgment of the common people before his owne, and imagining they would spie more narrowly and ensure his doings sooner than himselfe: and ass the tale is told, it fell out upon a time, that a shoemaker as he went by seemed to controule his workemanship about the shoe or pantophle that he had made to a picture, and namely, that there was one latchet fewer than there should bee: *Apelles* acknowledging that the man said true indeed, mended that fault by the next morning, and set forth his table as his manner was. The same shomaker coming again the morrow after, and finding the want supplied which he noted the day before, tooke some pride unto himselfe, that his former admonition had sped so well, and was so bold as to cavil at somewhat about the legs: *Apelles* could not endure that, but putting forth his head from behind the painted table, and scorning thus to be checked and reproved, Sirrha (quoth he) remember you are but a shoemaker, and therefore meddle no higher I advise you, than with shoes: which word also of his came afterwards to bee a common proverbe, *Ne sutor supra crepidam.*

In *Historie of the World, Pliny the Elder.* Tr. Philemon Holland (London: Printed by Adam Islip, 1601).

[Apelli fuit alioqui perpetua consuetudo numquam tam occupatum diem agendi, ut non lineam ducendo exerceret artem, quod ab eo in proverbium venit. idem perfecta opera proponebat in pergula transeuntibus atque, ipse post tabulam latens, vitia quae notarentur auscultabat, vulgum diligentiorem iudicem quam se praeferens; feruntque reprehensum a sutore, quod in crepidis una pauciores intus fecisset ansas, eodem postero die superbo emendatione pristinae admonitionis cavillante circa crus, indignatum prospexisse denuntiantem, ne supra crepidam sutor iudicaret, quod et ipsum in proverbium abiit.]

29. This is *Leviathan*, Book I, chapter 14, 64: 'THE Right of Nature, which Writers commonly call *Jus Naturale*, is the Liberty each man hath to use his own power as he will himself for the preservation of his own Nature; that is to say, of his own Life; and consequently, of doing anything which, in his own Judgement and Reason, he shall conceive to be the aptest means thereunto. By LIBERTY is understood, according to the proper signification of the word, the absence of external Impediments; which Impediments may oft take away part of a man's power to do what he would,

but cannot hinder him from using the power left him according as his judgement and reason shall dictate to him'.

Chapter 4

1. *The Testament of Solomon*. Tr. F. C. Conybeare, *The Jewish Quarterly Review* (London and New York: Macmillan, 1899), 45.
2. Salvador de Madariaga, 'Our Don Quijote', *Hispania* 11:2 (1928), 92.
3. Miguel de Cervantes, *Don Quijote de la Mancha*. Ed. Francisco Rico, ed. Real Academia Española: Asociación de Academias de la Lengua Española (Madrid: Alfaguara, 2004), 934.
4. In recent work I have approached the relation between translation, cultural and economic mobility and commodity trade.
5. Louise George Clubb, *Italian Drama in Shakespeare's Time* (New Haven, CT: Yale University Press, 1989), 5.
6. Sebastián de Covarrubias, *Tesoro de la lengua Castellana, o española* (Madrid: Luis Sánchez, 1611).
7. The bibliography on the episodes in Barataria is ample. Among the most important recent works on the chapters – Anthony J. Cascardi's *Cervantes, Literature, and the Discourse of Politics* (Madrid: Vervuert, 2006) (especially for Don Quijote's advice to Sancho). A more recent review of work on Sancho's governance, in Guillermo Fernández Rodríguez-Escalona, 'Pensamiento político y concepción del mundo en Cervantes: El gobierno de la ínsula Barataria', *Cervantes* 31:2 (2011), 125–52. An argument relating the ínsula to America, and thus the governance of one with the governance of the other, in Daniel Nemser, 'Governor Sancho and the Politics of Insularity', *Hispanic Review* 78:1 (Winter 2010), 1–23. I have found of particular use Verónica Ázcue Castillón, 'Cervantes, Don Quijote y Sancho Panza en el teatro del exilio', *Cervantes* 35:2 (2015), 161–92 (for republican adaptations of the episodes making Sancho out to be a figure of good popular government);
8. Tito Livio, *Historias de Roma* I. 56. Tr. José Antonio Villar Vidal (Madrid: Gredos, 1990), 259–60: 'Tito y Arrunte partieron; les fue adsprito como acompañante Lucio Junio Bruto, hijo de Tarquinia, hermana del rey, un joven de carácter muy distinto al que aparentaba. Éste, cuando supo que los ciudadanos principales, y entre ellos su hermano, habían sido muertos por su tío materno, resolvió no dar al rey motivo de temor por su manera de ser, ni motivo de ambición por su fortuna, y basar su seguridad en ser despreciable, dado que la justicia no suponía una gran protección. Con toda intención, por consiguiente, se dedicó a parecer tonto, dejó que el rey dispusiera de su persona y de sus bienes, ni siquiera rechazó el sobrenombre de Bruto: encubierto bajo tal apelativo aquel libertador del pueblo romano, aquel valiente desconocido, aguardaba su hora. Fue a él a quien los Tarquinios llevaron a Delfos en aquella ocasión, más como diversión que como compañero; dicen que llevó como ofrenda a Apolo un bastón de oro envainado en un bastón de cornejo vaciado con este objeto, como símbolo con rodeos de su propia personalidad'. The Latin is from *Livy: Book I*. Ed. H. J. Edwards (Cambridge: Cambridge University Press, 1968),

71–2: '[H]aec agenti portentum terribile visum: anguis ex columna lignea elapsus cum terrorem fugamque in regia fecisset, ipsius regis non tam subito pavore perculit pectus quam anxii implevit curis. Itaque cum ad publica prodigia Etrusci tantum vates adhiberentur, hoc velut domestico exterritus visu Delphos ad maxime inclitum in terris oraculum mittere statuit; neque responsa sortium ulli alii committere ausus duos filios per ignotas ea tempestate terras, ignotiora maria in Graeciam misit. Titus et Arruns profecti. comes iis additus L. Iunius Brutus, Tarquinia, sorore regis, natus, iuvenis longe alius ingenio, quam cuius simulationem induerat. is cum primores civitatis in quibus fratrem suum ab avunculo interfectum audisset, neque in animo suo quicquam regi timendum neque in fortuna, concupiscendum relinquere statuit, contemptuque tutus esse, ubi in iure parum praesidii esset. ergo ex industria factus ad imitationem stultitiae, cum se suaque praedae esse regi sineret, Bruti quoque haud abnuit cognomen, ut sub eius obtentu cognominis liberator ille populi Romani animus latens opperiretur tempora sua. is tum ab Tarquiniis ductus Delphos, ludibrium verius quam comes, aureum baculum inclusum corneo cavato ad id baculo tulisse donum Apollini dicitur, per ambages effigiem ingenii sui. quo postquam ventum est, perfectis patris mandatis cupido incessit animos iuvenum sciscitandi, ad quem eorum regnum Romanum esset venturum. ex infimo specu vocem redditam ferunt, "imperium summum Romae habebit qui vestrum primus, o iuvenes, osculum matri tulerit." Tarquinius Sextus, qui Romae relictus fuerat, ignarus responsi expersque imperii esset, rem summa ope taceri iubent; ipsi inter se uter prior, cum Romam redisset, matri osculum daret, sorti permittunt. Brutus alio ratus spectare Pythicam vocem, velut si prolapsus cecidisset, terram osculo contigit, scilicet quod ea communis mater omnium mortalium esset. reditum inde Romam, ubi adversus Rutulos bellum summa vi parabatur'. Cervantes seldom uses the term 'bruto' for human animals, in the pejorative, more or less metaphorical sense that Covarrubias (*Tesoro . . .*) gives us after his first, literal definition – 'BRVTO, comunmente se toma por el animal irracional, quadrupede, tardo, grossero, cruel, indisciplinable. . . . De do vino llamar brutos a los hombres de poco discurso y grosseros, qual se fingio Iunio Bruto: de donde tuuo el nombre. Brutal, cosa de brutos, no le doy otra etymologia, que la Latina'.

9. Some of the source material for Cervantes's depiction of Sancho's decisions, in Camille Pitollet, 'Un jugement rendu par Sancho Panza dans son île', *Bulletin Hispanique* 39:2 (1937), 105–19. Here is the analogue in Iacobus De Voragine, *Historia Sancti Nicolai:* 'Vir quidam ab uno Iudaeo quandam summam pecuniae mutuo accepit iurans super altare sancti Nicolai, cum alium fideiussorem habere nequiret, quod, quam citius posset, sibi redderet. Tenente autem illo diu pecuniam Iudaeus eam expostulavit, sed eam sibi reddidisse affirmat. Trahit ergo eum ad iudicium, et iuramentum indicitur debitori. Ille baculum cavatum, quem auro minuto impleverat, secum detulerat, ac si eius adminiculo indigeret. Volens igitur facere iuramentum Iudaeo baculum tradidit reservandum. Iuravit ille, quod plus igitur reddiderit etiam, quam deberet. Facto iuramento baculum suum repetiit, et Iudaeus ignarus astutiae eum sibi reddidit. Rediens autem, qui fraudem fecerat, in quodam bivio oppressus corruit somno currusque cum impetu veniens eum necavit et plenum baculum auro fregit et aurum effudit. Audiens hoc Iudaeus concitus illico venit cumque dolum

vidisset et a multis ei suggereretur, ut aurum reciperet, omnino renuit, nisi, qui defunctus fuerat, ad vitam beati Nicolai meritis redderetur, asserens se, si hoc fieret, baptismum suscepturum et Christianum futurum. Continuo qui defunctus fuerat, suscitatur et Iudaeus in Christi nomine baptizatur'. In *El espéculo de los legos*, in *EL cuento medieval español: Revisión crítica y antología*, ed. Carmen Hernández Valcárcel (Murcia: Universidad de Murcia, 1997), 248–49, Capítulo LXXI, Del Perjurio, Enxemplo 459: 'E aún en la Vida de Sant Nicolás se lee que un judío prestó a un christiano çierta cantidad de moneda e tomó a Sant Nicolás por fiador. E desque vino el día de la paga, el christiano fizo fazer un bordón hueco de dentro e puso en él el oro que le avíe enprestado el judío, e diógelo para que lo levase algund espacio e tornólo a tomar después. E el judío demandó al christiano lo que le avía enprestado, e el christiano afirmó que gelo avía pagado e fizo dello juramento delante el juez. E tornándose el christiano para su casa con el bordón en el que levava el oro, fue apremiado gravemente de suenno e acostóse a dormir en la encruzijada de dos carreras e vino un carro cargado e pasó por encima dél e matólo e quebrantó el blao e derramóse el oro. E oyendo esto el judío vino a lo veer e conosçió el enganno, e dixo que non reçebiría el oro si non resuçitase el muerto por los meresçimientos de Sant Nicolás. E resuçitó el muerto e confesó manifiestamente el enganno que avía fecho e batizóse el judío e reçebió la fe de Ihesu Christo. E de aquí es lo que dize Salomón en el nono capítulo del Eclesiastés: "Así es el que jura verdad con enganno commo el que jura falso"'. In *Libro de los enxiemplos por A. B. C.* (2a. parte), ed. María del Mar Gutiérrez Martínez, *Memorabilia* 13 (2011), 331, 234 (165), *Jurans per fraudem mendacium graviter pugnietur*: ' "Quien por engaño ha jurado / Por mala muerte es penado". Un cristiano tomó cierta quantía de dineros emprestados de un judío, e non podiendo aver fviador, juró sobre el altar de Sant Nicolás que lo más aína que podiesse se lo pagaría. E pasando muchos días que le non pagava, el judío demndava sus dineros. El cristiano dezía que ge los avía pagado, e assí óvolo de llamar a juizio, e non lo podiendo provar, ovo de echar el juramento al cristiano. E este debdor tenía un bordón cavado de dentro e lleno de oro, e levávalo consigo para si alguna cosa oviese menester. E queriendo fazer el juramento, dio el bordó al judío. E él, non sabiendo del enganno, diógelo. E tornándosse, el cristiano que avía fecho el juramento e el engaño, tomole el sueño en el camino, e acostósse a dormir. E passó un carro sobre él, e matólo e quebrantó el bordón e espazió el oro. E desque esto oyó el judío, fue allá luego, e veyendo este engaño muchos le dezían que tomasse el oro. E él dixo que non lo tomaría, salvo si por ruego de Sant Nicolás el que moriera tornasse a vida, prometiendo si esto fuesse, de recebir baptismo e ser cristiano. E luego el que moriera resuçitó e el judío recebió el sacramento del baptismo'.

10. I am not in entire agreement, then, with Hernán Vidal, who argues in '*Don Quijote*: Una lectura militar y gnóstica' (*Lemir* 2010) that: 'Desde sus comienzos el episodio del gobierno de la ínsula de Barataria escapa a la lógica estática del poder establecido. Con los consejos a Sancho a su partida a la gobernación, don Quijote expone el espíritu de ascenso social de la caballería que encarna, dando por sentado que el buen gobierno es cuestión de sentido común, ecuanimidad y anhelo de justicia de cualquier ser humano éticamente sano, aun de un loco, no un monopolio de la

gran nobleza. Para sorpresa de los Duques, las sabias decisiones de Sancho en las consultas legales que se le hacen en la ínsula lo comprueban. Sus decisiones, por lo demás hacen tabula rasa del sistema legal ya que Sancho no necesitó echar mano de los códigos existentes ni de asesores' (80). Sancho does not face his decisions from a *tabula rasa*; his 'table' is, rather, cluttered with existent, contradictory codes, interacting dynamically, unpredictably adding and subtracting legitimacy to one another, making it impossible for us, as well as for his subjects, to decide, according to any code or group of codes, just *which* standard or principle underlies the sovereign's decisions.

11. A useful interpretation of the novel's allusions to figures from Hebrew scripture, forming what the author calls a 'series of intertextual echoes of Hebrew legends . . . [that] "culminat[es in] this allusion to the figure of Salomon"', in Francisco Peña Fernández, 'Medieval Traditions of Jewish Origin in the Episode of Sancho Panza and the Island of Barataria', *South Atlantic Review* 72:1 (Winter 2007), 212–29, 212. Peña makes the case for a much broader identification of Sancho with Salomon throughout the novel.

12. Max Weber, *Economy and Society*. Ed. Guenther Roth and Claus Wittich (Berkeley: University of California Press, 1978), 845 and 1115. A useful reading of the Barataria episode in the context of Weber and Maravall, in Belén A. Barbosa Muñiz, *El 'Quijote', Sancho y la Sociología del Derecho* (online). For a much more nuanced account of Weber's use of the Baratarian episode, and of the lines I cite, in David Kettler and Volker Meja, 'Legal Formalism and Disillusioned Realism in Max Weber', *Polity* 28:3 (Spring, 1996), 307–31, especially 316ff, where the authors make a case for understanding that Sancho's *failure* as both a formal or rational sovereign, and as a 'Cadi' or charismatic sovereign, are the expression of his 'freedom from the passive injustice of his social betters', a 'freedom' that 'qualifies him as model citizen even if it makes him a failed judge' (331). See also their ' "Sancho Pansa als Statthalter": Max Weber und das Problem der materialen Gerechtigkeit', in *Max Webers Wissenschaftslehre. Interpretation und Kritik*, eds. Heinz Zipprian and Gerhard Wagner (Frankfurt: Suhrkamp, 1994), 713–54.

13. Thomas d'Urfey, *The Comical History of Don Quixote* (London: Printed for Samuel Briscoe, 1694).

14. D'Urfey's rather loose way with Cervantes's text caused Frederick Pilon, the author of an adaptation *Barataria: Or, Sancho Turn'd Governor, A Farce in Two acts* (London: J. Almon, 1785), to explain that '[t]hree scenes only of the original have been retained; and even these it was found necessary to materially alter, and enrich with additions to give them a modern, a novel complexion. – Impressed with veneration for the genius of Cervantes, the present writer has adhered to him as closely as the nature of dramatic writing would admit' (3). The 'modern, novel' complexion involves some drastic changes. The scenes from the court of justice are quite marvelously transformed, for instance: Sancho's Salomonic decisions become in Pilon's farce the means for the hungry governor to procure himself pheasant and wine, and to appropriate the bribes a smuggler used to pay one of the constables.

15. Tony Aston, 'The Drama: A Brief Supplement to Colley Cibber: Sandford – Cave Underhill – and Doggett', in *The Cabinet, or, Monthly Report of Polite Literature* (London: Matthew and Leigh, 1808), 193–94: '[Underhill's] face very like the *Homo Sylvestris* or *Champanza;* for his nose was flattish and short, and his upper lip very long and thick, with a wide mouth and short chin, a churlish voice, and awkward action, (leaping often up with both legs at a time, when he conceved anything waggish, and afterward hugging himself at the thought). He could not enter into any serious character . . . and was the most confined actor I ever saw: and could scarce be brought to speak a short *Latin* speech in Don Quixot, when *Sancho* is made to say, *Sit bonus Populus, bonus ero Gubernator;* which he pronounced thus: *Sh[it] bones and bobble ar[se] / Bones, and ears gobble nature'*.

Chapter 5

1. For a review of recent theories of translation in an historical context, see Susan Bassnett-McGuire, *Translation Studies* (New York: Routledge, 2002). The most forceful articulation of the 'domesticating-foreignizing' distinction is to be found in Lawrence Venuti's *The Translator's Invisibility: A History of Translation* (London: Routledge, 1995). Lydia He Liu's edited volume *Tokens of Exchange: The Problem of Translation in Global Circulations* (Durham, NC: Duke University Press, 2000), along with Emily Apter's *The Translation Zone: A New Comparative Literature* (Princeton: Princeton University Press, 2005), provides the most comprehensive contemporary approaches to the relation between globalization and translation – from a conceptual rather than a practical perspective. See particularly Liu's 'The Question of Meaning-Value in the Political Economy of the Sign', in *Tokens of Exchange: The Problem of Translation in Global Circulations*, 13–41, for a very clear reconsideration of the rather muddy analogy between meaning and value to be found in weak readings of Baudrillard's early works. My own earlier work on the philosophy of translation seems to me to settle too quickly on a polar or focal structure I would now like to distress – the distinction between 'idealist' and 'materialist' philosophies of translation. See Jacques Lezra, 'The Indecisive Muse: Ethics in Translation and the Idea of History', *Comparative Literature* 60:4 (2008), 301–30.

2. On the structuring of the 'pure expenditure of time and money' in post-Fordist economies, see Maurizio Lazzarato, *Lavoro immateriale. Forme di vita e produzione di soggettivita* (Verona: Ombre Corte, 1997) and *Videofilosofia. Percezione e lavoro nel postfordismo* (Rome: Manifestolibri, 1996).

3. Saul Kripke, *Naming and Necessity* (Cambridge, MA: Harvard University Press, 1980), 48. The bibliography regarding possible worlds, including possible worlds semantics, modal semantics and the so-called Kripke semantics, is vast. A milestone, and among the most controversial works in the field, remains David Lewis's *On the Plurality of Worlds* (Oxford: Blackwell, 1986). I take Lewis's necessarily guarded allowance for the operation, 'perhaps', of 'immanent universals exercising their characteristic privilege of repeated occurrence' (2) to be a way of

securing the principle of translatability across possible worlds that I describe here. The bibliography on possible world semantics includes important contributions not only from the perspective of the philosophy of language but also from psychoanalysts and political philosophers (see Slavoj Zizek, *The Sublime Object of Ideology* [London: Verso, 1989]; Judith Butler, *Bodies that Matter* [New York: Routledge, 1993], 187–223; Ernesto Laclau, *On Populist Reason* [London: Verso, 2005], 101–17) and critical theologians (Hent de Vries, *Philosophy and the Turn to Religion* [Baltimore, MD: Johns Hopkins University Press, 1999], 147–58). Only two aspects of the argument need to concern us here: the bare indexicality of the scenario (the eventual, and necessary, *description* to another, my translator and then my partner, of the 'widget's' uses, qualities, value and so on stands on an act of ostension understood as such) and the universalizability of this primary act of ostension (it is the ground on which the possibility of translation stands). In the meta-world of possible worlds, a world is only a world when acts of ostension secure the designation of things in that world, whether they are subsisting or non-subsisting things.

4. Plato, *Ion* 533d. In *The Dialogues of Plato*, vol. 3: *Ion; Hippias minor; Laches; Protagoras*. Tr. Reginald E. Allen (New Haven, CT: Yale University Press, 1996), 13. The Greek is from the online edition provided by Project Perseus, online at http://www.perseus.tufts.edu/hopper/text?doc=plat.+ion+530a. Accessed 9 March 2012. See Adriana Cavarero, *For More than One Voice: Toward a Philosophy of Vocal Expression* (Stanford, CA: Stanford University Press, 2005), 85–9, who reads Socrates's story as an allegory of the loss of particular voice from *logos*.

5. The values of the term 'real' in this sort of claim, as in Lewis's early arguments for 'modal realism', are rather hard to parse. Securing the ontological priority of objects is not the same, exactly, as granting them the quality of 'reality'. Here – though not at all elsewhere – I am in agreement with the work of Graham Harman, for instance, his *Tool-Being: Heidegger and the Metaphysics of Objects* (Peru, IL: Open Court Publishing, 2002).

6. I am drawing my example of the 'present king of France' from Russell's 'On Denoting', where it is used to show that phrases denote formally rather than according to the existence or non-existence of what it is they are supposed to denote. Bertrand Russell, 'On Denoting', *Mind* (New Series) 14:56. (October 1905), 479–93.

7. OED, 'Widget, n.' Second edition, 1989; online version December 2011. Online at http://www.oed.com/view/Entry/228908. Accessed 13 March 2012. First published in *A Supplement to the OED* IV (1986). The updated (post-2003) entry adds: '*(a)* A visual component of a graphical user interface (and the code associated with it), which allows a user to perform a particular function (e.g. a scroll bar, dialogue box, menu, etc.). *(b)* A small software application'.

8. Heidegger not infrequently cites Aristotle's definition or description, in Greek, of man as *zoon logon ekhon*, in order *then* to translate that into Latin as *animale rationale*, and to argue that this translation from *logos* to *ratio* is the mark of a characteristic and definitive metaphysical forgetting. The phrase *zoon logon ekhon* occurs nowhere, exactly thus, in Aristotle – so Heidegger's seeming citation is in fact already something more like a gloss or a translation. To cite the phrase, then, and to attribute it

to Aristotle is to obscure a specific sort of work – a sort of thought. *Zoon logon ekhon* may not figure as such in Aristotle, but its constituent terms and their relations do appear, in different spots. We may say that Heidegger assembles the definition from other places in Aristotle's corpus where nearly synonymous expressions do occur: he gathers them together from the point of view of what lay before him, recognizing the kinships of the terms from the point of view of what the definition will come to be. Heidegger 'translates' Aristotle when appearing to cite him, and this 'translating' expresses Heidegger's gleaning of the traces of man's disposition towards the word from within the word, from a corpus in which the expression of that disposition lay scattered. Elsewhere Heidegger will call this assembling-gathering by the name of 'thought'. Here, as in Heidegger's treatment of the translation of Aristotle's term *energeia*, it is only slightly more modestly called 'translation'. See Martin Heidegger, 'The Anaximander Fragment', in *Early Greek Thinking*. Tr. David Farrell Krell and Frank A. Capuzzi (San Francisco, CA: Harper and Row, 1975; 1984).

   9. The history of the development of MT is a complicated and rich one; the term is the most recent of a series and is not guaranteed to last. An excellent review of the history of MT – and a useful definition – 'The term [MT] is the now traditional and standard name for computerised systems responsible for the production of translations from one natural language into another, with or without human assistance' – may be found in W. John Hutchins and Harold L. Somers, *An Introduction to Machine Translation* (London: Academic Press, 1992). Calling it a Cold War phenomenon does not seem to me controversial. The first major studies of MT in the United States were all funded by the U.S. Department of Defense and the CIA, who were interested among other things in finding ways of translating, quickly and accurately, documents in Russian.

   10. In Martin Heidegger, 'Logos', we find this famous concluding thought-image: 'Once, however, in the beginning of Western thinking, the essence of language flashed in the light of Being – once, when Heraclitus thought the *logos* as his guiding word, so as to think in this word the Being of beings'. In *Early Greek Thinking*, 78.

   11. Heidegger, *Introduction to Metaphysics*. Tr. Gregory Fried and Richard Polt (New Haven, CT: Yale University Press, 2000), 198; see also Martin Heidegger, *On the Way to Language*. Tr. Peter D. Hertz (New York: Harper and Row, 1971; 1982), 96: 'If we take language directly in the sense of something that is present, we encounter it as the act of speaking, the activation of the organs of speech, mouth, lips, tongue. Language manifests itself in speaking, as a phenomenon that occurs in man. . . . Language is the tongue'.

   12. Among the most promising developments of this line of thought are to be found in treatments of the so-called immaterial labour by the Italian sociological and philosophical school since Negri's *Marx beyond Marx* (Italian Edition 1979, *Marx oltre Marx: quaderno di lavoro sui Grundrisse*; French and English translations, 1984). See Negri's remarks about Marx's 'Machine Fragments', in *Marx beyond Marx*, ed. Jim Fleming, tr. Harry Cleaver et al. (New York: Autonomedia, 1991), 139–50 and Paolo Virno, 'The Ambivalence of Disenchantment', in *Radical Thought in Italy: A Potential Politics*, eds. Michael Hardt and Paolo Virno (Minneapolis: University of Minnesota Press, 1996), 21–4, especially his comments regarding the

'general intellect' in Marx, the 'epistemic models that structure social communication [and] incorporates the intellectual activity of mass culture, no longer reducible to "simple labor," to the pure expenditure of time and money. There converge in the productive power of the general intellect artificial languages, theorems of formal logic . . . and images of the world'.

13. David Sarno, 'Franz Josef Och, Google's Translation Über-Scientist, Talks about Google Translate', by, *Los Angeles Times* 11 March 2010, online at http://latimesblogs.latimes.com/technology/2010/03/the-web-site-translategooglecom-was-done-in-2001-we-were-just—licensing-3rd-party-machine-translation-technologies-tha.html. Accessed 3 March 2012.

14. Online at http://latimesblogs.latimes.com/technology/2010/03/the-web-site-translategooglecom-was-done-in-2001-we-were-just—licensing-3rd-party-machine-translation-technologies-tha.html. Accessed 3 March 2012.

15. William Shakespeare, *A Midsummer Night's Dream*, in *The Riverside Shakespeare: The Complete works*, 2nd ed., eds. G. Blakemore Evans et al. (Boston, MA: Houghton Mifflin, 1997), by act, scene and line in the text. The reading of this famous scene that most closely resembles mine is in John Sallis's *On Translation* (Bloomington: Indiana University Press, 2002), 25–31, see also page 94. Sallis's excellent, brief analysis of Schlegel's translation of the scene stresses the paradoxical need to translate proper names, which might be considered, strictly speaking, untranslatable. He is concerned, as are most critics who write about the encounter between Schlegel and Shakespeare, with ways in which Schlegel 'compensates' for the necessary 'losses' (94) in his translation – and to this extent Sallis is very much at work within the economic register that organizes conventional theories of translation. A helpful review of the scene's intertexts, in Madeleine Forey's '"Bless Thee, Bottom, Bless Thee! Thou Art Translated!": Ovid, Golding, and *A Midsummer Night's Dream*', *The Modern Language Review* 93:2 [April 1998], 321–29). More pertinent in a sense is Margaret Tudeau-Clayton's 'Scenes of Translation in Jonson and Shakespeare: "Poetaster, Hamlet," and "A Midsummer Night's Dream"', *Translation and Literature* 11:1 (Spring 2002), 1–23. Tudeau-Clayton uses Shakespeare's play to suggest the limits of Lawrence Venuti's notion that translations can be 'domesticating' or 'foreignizing'.

16. Marcus Tullius Cicero, 'De optimo genere oratorum', in *De inventione. De optimo genere oratorum. Topica. With an English translation by H.M. Hubbell* (Cambridge, MA: Harvard University Press, 1960), 364.

17. August Wilhelm von Schlegel, *A Course of Lectures on Dramatic Art and Literature*. Tr. John Black and A. J. W. Morrisonn (London: George Bell and Sons, 1815), 329; the German is from A. W. v. Schegel, *Kritische Schriften und Briefe*, Ed. Edgar Lohner (Stuttgart: Kohlhammer, 1962), v. 6, 159.

18. *Deutsches Wörterbuch von Jacob und Wilhelm Grimm*, 16 Bde., in 32 Teilbänden. Leipzig 1854–1961, online at http://woerterbuchnetz.de/DWB/. Accessed 9 March 2012.

19. Anston Bosman notes the problem of Bottom's translation into German as well, though he does not work through the oddities of the moment. Note the persistence, in even so astute a critic, of Venuti's 'domesticating' and 'foreignizing' lexicon: 'An obvious problem is how to translate the name "Bottom", which

evokes the character's profession by denoting a weaver's implement – the spool on which yarn was wound – but also has bawdy connotations, even if different in the Renaissance from those picked up by modern ears. No translation could capture this *double-entendre*. Günther's word *Zettel* designates the warp in a woven fabric, but lacks bodily resonance. . . . Both choices [German and French translations of Bottom] yield losses and gains. They exemplify opposing strategies of translation: the German option domesticates the source in the target culture while the French marks the source as foreign. Most choices in translation fall between these extremes, and the diffusion of Shakespeare's texts depends on innumerable compromises made by editors and translators between the poles of alienation and acculturation'. In 'Shakespeare and Globalization', in *The New Cambridge Companion to Shakespeare*, eds. Stanley Wells and Margareta de Grazia (Cambridge: Cambridge University Press, 2010), 293.

Chapter 6

1. Temple Grandin and Catherine Johnson, *Animals in Translation: Using the Mysteries of Autism to Decode Animal Behavior* (New York: Harcourt, Brace, Jovanovich, 2005).

2. Vicki Hearne, 'How to Say "Fetch!"', in *Adam's Task: Calling Animals by Name* (New York: Knopf, 1986), 55–6

3. W. V. Quine, 'Translation and Meaning', in *Word and Object* (Cambridge, MA: MIT Press, 1960; 2013), 25.

4. The bibliography on this extraordinary passage is immense. Quine's own review of early criticism of the *gavagai* example is most useful. See his 'On the Reasons for Indeterminacy of Translation', *The Journal of Philosophy* 67:6 (1970), 178–83. An early, critical piece of value still is Steven Davis, 'Translational Indeterminacy and Private Worlds', *Philosophical Studies: An International Journal for Philosophy in the Analytic Tradition* 18:3 (April 1967), 38–45. Christopher S. Hill's early 'gavagai', *Analysis* 32 (1972), 68–75, reprinted with an important 'Postscript' in his 2014 *Meaning, Mind, and Knowledge* (Oxford: Oxford University Press, 2014), and his recent 'How Concepts Hook onto the World', also in *Meaning, Mind, and Knowledge* (66–87), seem to me the most serious and consequential arguments retaining both Quine's deflationary position with respect to translation, and a strong affirmation of the determinability of meaning, where 'meaning' is understood to pertain to what Hill calls the 'reference of concepts' (4). Narrowing the definition of 'meaning' in this way succeeds only partly in limiting the argument to the ways in which concepts in 'possession' of qualities refer to objects which are in 'possession' of those concepts, a chain of 'possessions' which may then be said to make reference determinable strictly. The hint of tautology on which Hill verges should prove disconcerting (an object determinably possesses a concept, and that concept's possession of a quality entails that that quality necessarily 'hooks onto' the concept; that 'hooked-onto concept' then 'hooks onto' the object and this chain stands in for reference). Hill leaves open the question whether statements regarding the 'possession of a quality' 'really do have determinate answers' (4), which seems to open a further, if different, domain for indeterminacy. Lieven Decock provides a helpful overview

of Quine's developing position with regard to indeterminacy (as it pertains to reference, to phrases in a language, to 'manuals' for decoding statements) in 'Domestic Ontology and Ideology', in *Quine: Naturalized Epistemology, Perceptual Knowledge and Ontology*, eds. Lieven Decock and Leon Horsten (Amsterdam: Rodopi, 2000), 189–207. For further accounts of Quine's position, see among others Patricia Hanna and Bernard Harrison, *Word and World: Practice and the Foundations of Language* (Cambridge: Cambridge University Press, 2004), 203–07 and 291–309.

5. 'And a mortal existence, for from the moment that it has a name, its name survives it. It signs its potential disappearance. Mine also, and that disappearance, from this moment to that, fort/da [here/there, present/absent], is announced each time that, with or without nakedness, one of us leaves the room'. (9) Jacques Derrida. *The Animal That Therefore I Am*. Ed. Marie-Louise Mallet, Tr. David Wills (New York: Fordham University Press, 2008). First published in English as 'The Animal That Therefore I Am (More to Follow)', tr. David Wills, *Critical Inquiry* 28:2 (Winter 2002), 369–418. The French is from Jacques Derrida, *L'animal que donc je suis* (Paris: de Galilée, 2006), 26. Other, important, work by Derrida on animality: ' "Eating Well," or The Calculation of the Subject: An Interview with Jacques Derrida', in *Who Comes after the Subject?* eds. Eduardo Cadava, Peter Connor and Jean-Luc Nancy (New York: Routledge, 1991), 96–119; 'Force of Law: The "Mystical Foundation of Authority" ', in *Deconstruction and the Possibility of Justice,* tr. Mary Quaintance, eds. Drucilla Cornell, Michel Rosenfeld and David Gray Carlson (London: Routledge, 1992), 3–67; 'Geschlecht II: Heidegger's Hand', in *Deconstruction and Philosophy, tr. John P. Leavey, Jr.*, ed. John Sallis (Chicago: University of Chicago Press, 1986), 161–196 and 'Violence against Animals', in *For What Tomorrow. . . : A Dialogue*, eds. Jacques Derrida and Elisabeth Roudinesco, tr. Jeff Fort (Stanford: Stanford University Press, 2004), 62–76.

6. See Leonard Lawlor, ' "Animals Have No Hand": An Essay on Animality in Derrida', *CR: The New Centennial Review* 7:2 (2007), 43–69.

7. And from Martha Nussbaum's as well. See Cary Wolfe's careful positioning of Derrida's thought, in contrast to Nussbaum's and Cora Diamond's, in this passage in particular. Wolfe notes the way the animal/*animot* poses a limit to philosophical humanism. In Wolfe's 'Flesh and Finitude: Thinking Animals in (Post)Humanist Philosophy', *SubStance* 37:3 (2008), 8–36.

8. Jacques Derrida, *Béliers: Le dialogue ininterrompu: entre deux infinis, le poème* (Paris: Galilée, 2003). The French reads in full:

Il y a la guerre et le bélier, le bélier de chair ou de bois, le bélier sur terre ou dans le ciel s'élance dans une course. Il fonce pour enfoncer l'adversaire. C'est une charge ('In- / to what does he not charge?' pour citer ici la judicieuse traduction de Michael Hamburger). Cette charge – l'équivoque entre les langues donne ici plus d'une chance –, n'est-ce pas aussi une accusation ou un prix à payer ('charge' en anglais), donc l'acquittement d'une dette ou l'expiation d'un péché? Le bélier ne charge-t-il pas l'adversaire, un sacrificateur comme un mur, de tous les crimes? Car la question, nous le notions plus haut, est de forme interro-négative: contre quoi ne court-il pas? Ne charge-t-il pas? Il peut le faire pour attaquer ou pour se venger, il peut déclarer la guerre ou répondre au sacrifice en y opposant sa protestation. Le sursaut de son incompréhension indignée n'épargnerait rien ni personne au monde. Nul au monde n'est innocent, ni le monde même. On imagine la colère du bélier d'Abraham et d'Aaron, la révolte infinie du bélier de tous les holocaustes. Mais aussi, par figure, la rébellion violente de tous les boucs émissaires, de tous les substituts. Pourquoi moi? Leur adversité, leur adversaire serait partout. Le front de sa protestation jetterait le bélier contre le sacrifice même, contre les hommes et contre Dieu. Il voudrait enfin mettre fin à leur monde commun. Le bélier chargerait contre tout et contre quiconque, dans toutes les directions, comme si la douleur l'aveuglait. Le rythme de cette strophe, Wo- /gegen / rennt er nicht an?, scande bien le mouvement saccadé de ces coups. Quand on se rappelle que Aaron associait de jeunes taureaux au sacrifice du bélier, on pense à la dernière ruée de l'animal avant sa mise à mort. Le toréador ressemble aussi à un prêtre sacrificateur.

Autant d'hypothèses, bien sûr, et d'indécisions. Cela reste à jamais l'élément même de la lecture. Son 'processus infini'. La césure, le hiatus, l'ellipse, autant d'interruptions qui à la fois ouvrent et ferment. Elles retiennent à jamais l'accès du poème sur le seuil de ses cryptes (l'une d'entre elles, l'une seulement, ferait référence à une expérience singulière et secrète, toute autre, dont la constellation n'est accessible qu'au témoignage du poète ou de quelques-uns). Les interruptions ouvrent aussi, de façon disséminale et non saturable, sur des constellations imprévisibles, sur tant d'autres étoiles, dont certaines ressembleront peut-être encore à cette semence dont Iahvé dit à Abraham, après l'interruption du sacrifice, qu'il la multiplierait comme des étoiles: l'abandon de la trace laissée, c'est aussi le don du poème à tous les lecteurs et contre-signataires qui, toujours sous sa loi, celle de la trace à l'œuvre, de la trace comme œuvre, entraîneront ou se laisseront entraîner vers une tout autre lecture ou contre-lecture. Celle-ci sera aussi, d'une langue à l'autre parfois, dans le risque abyssal de la traduction, une incommensurable écriture.

9. I have tried to spell out at some length the notion of a 'defective concept', in *Wild Materialism: The Ethic of Terror and the Modern Republic* (New York: Fordham University Press, 2010), especially 110–50.

Afterword: Counter-*gift*

1. My first epigraph is from Theodor W. Adorno, *Minima Moralia* § 58, 'Die Wahrheit über Hedda Gabler', ed. Georg A. Mathéy (Berlin: Suhrkamp, 1951), 166. The English translation is by Dennis Redmond, available online at http://www.efn. org/~dredmond/MinimaMoralia.html. Compare E. F. N. Jephcott's version: 'Retention of Strangeness Is the Only Antidote to Estrangement', in *Minima Moralia*, eds. T.W.A. Adorno, tr. E. F. N. Jephcott (London and New York: Verso, 2005), 94. My second epigraph, from Antonio Negri, *Marx beyond Marx*. Tr. Harry Cleaver, Michael Ryan and Maurizio Viano (New York: Autonomedia, 1991), 121.

The citation from Karl Marx, *Grundrisse*. Tr. Martin Nicolaus (London: Penguin, 1973), 162–63. The German, from Karl Marx and Friedrich Engels, *Werke* (Berlin: Dietz Verlag, 1983), v. 42, 96.

2. Influential treatments of the analogy between the circulation of money and that of language include Negri's meticulous *Marx beyond Marx*; Jacques Derrida, *Given-Time* (Chicago: University of Chicago Press, 1994) and Sp*ecters of Marx* (New York: Routledge, 1994). Derrida's different, complementary arguments regarding the human animal's disposition towards language are well known; see in particular his comments on Aristotle's determination of human animality as both political and linguistic, in *The Beast and the Sovereign*. Tr. Geoffrey Bennington (Chicago: University of Chicago Press, 2009). Further on the analogy between money and language, Jean-Joseph Goux, *Symbolic Economies* (Ithaca, NY: Cornell University Press, 1990) and *The Coiners of Language* (Norman: University of Oklahoma Press, 1994); Marc Shell, *The Economy of Literature* (Baltimore, MD: Johns Hopkins University Press, 1993); Kojin Karatani, *Architecture as Metaphor: Language, Number, Money* (Cambridge: MIT Press, 1994). More recently, see Anna Kornbluh's important 'On Marx's Victorian Novel', *Mediations* 25:1 (Fall 2010), 15–37. As the analogy pertains to the philosophy of translation, see Lydia Liu, *Tokens of Exchange: The Problem of Translation in Global Circulation* (Stanford, CA: Stanford University Press, 1999) and the extended analysis and critique of her reading of the passage from Marx that I cite, in Douglas Robinson, *Critical Translation Studies* (Oxford and New York: Routledge, 2017), especially 33–66.

3. The bibliography concerning money in Shakespeare more generally is rich and deep; so is the bibliography regarding Marx's readings of Shakespeare. On Shakespeare's references to Agrippa's fable in *Coriolanus*, I've found useful Bryan Reynolds's *Performing Transversally: Reimagining Shakespeare and the Critical Future* (New York: Palgrave Macmillan, 2003); David McNally's recent *Monsters of the Market: Zombies, Vampires and Global Capitalism* (Chicago: Haymarket, 2012); Michael C. Schoenfeldt, *Bodies and Selves in Early Modern England* (Cambridge: Cambridge University Press, 1999), 28–31; Derek Stanovsky, 'Organizing Marx's Multitude: A Composition on Decomposition', *Rethinking Marxism* 21:2 (2009), 216–27 and Zvi Jagendorf, '*Coriolanus*: Body Politic and Private Parts', in *Coriolanus: Critical Essays*, ed. David Wheeler (New York: Garland, 1995), 229–51.

4. Aristotle, *Politics* 1253a, in *Aristotle in 23 Volumes*. Tr. H. Rackham (Cambridge, MA: Harvard University Press, 1944), v. 21.

5. Among many other places, here: 'Das selbständige Fürsichsein des Werts gegenüber dem lebendigen Arbeitsvermögen – daher sein Dasein als Kapital – die objektive, an sich haltende Gleichgültigkeit, die *Fremdheit* der objektiven Arbeitsbedingungen gegen das lebendige Arbeitsvermögen, die bis zu dem Punkt fortgeht, daß diese Bedingungen der Person des Arbeiters in der Person des Kapitalisten – als Personifikationen mit eignem Willen und Interesse gegenübertreten – diese absolute *Scheidung, Trennung* des Eigentums, d.h. der sachlichen Arbeitsbedingungen vom lebendigen Arbeitsvermögen – daß sie ihm als *fremdes Eigentum,* als die Realität einer andren juristischen Person, das absolute Gebiet *ihres* Willens gegenübertreten – und daß daher andrerseits die Arbeit als *fremde Arbeit* gegenüber dem im Kapitalisten personifizierten Wert oder den Arbeitsbedingungen erscheint – diese absolute Trennung zwischen Eigentum und Arbeit, zwischen dem lebendigen Arbeitsvermögen und den Bedingungen seiner Realisierung, zwischen vergegenständlichter und lebendiger

Arbeit, zwischen dem Wert und der wertschaffenden Tätigkeit – daher auch die Fremdheit des Inhalts der Arbeit gegen den Arbeiter selbst – diese Scheidung erscheint jetzt ebenfalls als Produkt der Arbeit selbst, als Vergegenständlichung, Objektivierung ihrer eignen Momente'. Karl Marx, *Grundrisse der Kritik der politischen Ökonomie*, in *Karl Marx/Friedrich Engles: Werke* (Berlin: Dietz Verlag, 1983), v. 42, 365; 'The independent, for-itself existence [*Fürsichsein*] of value *vis-à-vis* living labour capacity – hence its existence as capital – the objective, self-sufficient indifference, the *alien quality* [*Fremdheit*] of the objective conditions of labour *vis-à-vis* living labour capacity, which goes so far that these conditions confront the person of the worker in the person of the capitalist – as personification with its own will and interest – this absolute *divorce, separation* of property, i.e. of the objective conditions of labour from living labour capacity – that they confront him as *alien property,* as the reality of other juridical persons, as the absolute realm of *their* will – and that labour therefore, on the other side, appears as *alien labour* opposed to the value personified in the capitalist, or the conditions of labour – this absolute separation between property and labour, between living labour capacity and the conditions of its realization, between objectified and living labour, between value and value-creating activity – hence also the alien quality of the content of labour for the worker himself – this divorce now likewise appears as a product of labour itself, as objectification of its own moments. For, in the new act of production itself – which merely confirmed the exchange between capital and living labour which preceded it – surplus labour, and hence the surplus product, the total product of labour in general (of surplus labour as well as necessary labour), has now been posited as capital, as independent and indifferent towards living labour capacity, or as exchange value which confronts its mere use value'. Karl Marx, *Grundrisse: Foundations of the Critique of Political Economy*. Tr. Martin Nicolaus (London and New York: Penguin Books, 1993), 52–3.

Works Cited

Adorno, Theodor W. *Minima Moralia*. Ed. Georg A. Mathéy. Berlin: Suhrkamp, 1951.

Adorno, Theodor W. *Minima Moralia*. Tr. Dennis Redmond, online at http://www. efn.org/~dredmond/MinimaMoralia.html.

Adorno, Theodor W. *Minima Moralia*. Tr. E. F. N. Jephcott. London and New York: Verso, 2005.

Anon, *The Testament of Solomon*. Tr. F. C. Conybeare, *The Jewish Quarterly Review* (London and New York: MacMillan, 1899).

Apter, Emily. *Against World Literature: On the Politics of Untranslatability*. New York: Verso, 2013.

Apter, Emily. *The Translation Zone: A New Comparative Literature*. Princeton: Princeton University Press, 2005.

Apter, Emily. 'Untranslatables: A World System'. *New Literary History* 39: 3 (2008), 581–98.

Aristotle, *Politics*, in *Aristotle in 23 Volumes*. Tr. H. Rackham. Cambridge, MA: Harvard University Press, 1944, v. 21.

Ascham, Roger. *The Schole-Master*. London, printed by John Daye, 1570 [–71], n.p.

Assmann, Jan. *Politische Theologie zwischen Ägypten und Israel*. Bonn: VG Bild-Kunst, 1992.

Aston, Tony. 'The Drama: A Brief Supplement to Colley Cibber: Sandford – Cave Underhill – and Doggett'. In *The Cabinet, or, Monthly Report of Polite Literature*. London: Matthew and Leigh, 1808, 193–94.

Automatic Language Processing Advisory Committee Division of Behavioral Sciences. 'Language and Machines: Computers in Translation and Linguistics', a Report by the Automatic Language Processing Advisory Committee Division of Behavioral Sciences (ALPAC Report), National Academy of Sciences (1966).

Ázcue Castillón, Verónica. 'Cervantes, Don Quijote y Sancho Panza en el teatro del exilio'. *Cervantes* 35: 2 (2015), 161–92.

Baker, George P. and Peter M. S. Hacker. *An Analytical Commentary on the 'Philosophical Investigations'*. Chicago: University of Chicago Press, 1980.

Bale, John and John Leland. *The Laboryouse Journey & Serche of John Leylande, for Englands Antiquitees . . . with Declaracyons Enlarged, by Iohan Bale*. London, 1549.

Barbosa Muñiz, Belén A. *El 'Quijote', Sancho y la Sociología del Derecho*, online at http://www.lulu.com/shop/bel%C3%A9n-a-barbosa-mu%C3%B1iz/el-quijote-sancho-y-la-sociolog%C3%ADa-del-derecho/ebook/product-17557216.html.

Bassnett-McGuire, Susan. *Translation Studies*. New York: Routledge, 2002.

Benjamin, Andrew. *Translation and the Nature of Philosophy: A New Theory of Words*. London: Routledge, 1989.

Berman, Antoine. *The Experience of the Foreign: Culture and Translation in Romantic Germany*. Tr. S. Heyvaert. Albany: State University of New York Press, 1992.

The Blackwell Companion to Political Theology. Ed. Peter Scott and William T. Cavanaugh. London: Wiley-Blackwell, 2004.

Blumenberg, Hans. *The Legitimacy of the Modern Age*. Tr. Robert M. Wallace. Cambridge, MA: MIT Press, 1985.

Borges, Jorge Luis. 'Francisco de Quevedo: Prosa y verso'. In *Obras Completas de Jorge Luis Borges*. Barcelona: Emecé, 1996.

Borges, Jorge Luis. 'Tlön, Uqbar, *Orbis Tertius*'. *Sur* 68: 3 (1940), 30–46.

Borges, Jorge Luis, *Adolfo Bioy Casares and Silvina Ocampo*, eds. *Antología de la literatura fantástica*. Buenos Aires: Editorial Sudamericana (Colección Laberinto, 1), 1940.

Bosman, Anston. 'Shakespeare and Globalization'. In *The New Cambridge Companion to Shakespeare*. Ed. Stanley Wells and Margareta de Grazia. Cambridge: Cambridge University Press, 2010.

Browne, Thomas. *Hydriotaphia, Urne-Buriall, or, a Discourse of the Sepulchral Urns Lately Found in Norfolk*. London: Printed for Hen. Brome at the Signe of the Gun in Ivy-Lane, 1658.

Butler, Judith. *Bodies that Matter*. New York: Routledge, 1993.

Camden, William. *Rerum Anglicarum et Hibernicarum Annales, Regnante Elizabetha The Historie of the Life and Reigne of the Most Renowmed [sic] and Victorious Princesse Elizabeth, Late Queene of England . . . Composed by Way of Annals, by the Most Learned Mr. William Camden; and Faithfully Translated into English*. London: Printed for Benjamin Fisher (1630). A translation of Camden's *Annales Rerum Gestarum Angliae et Hiberniae Regnante Elizabetha* of 1615–1625.

Casanova, Pascale. *La Langue Mondiale: Traduction Et Domination*. Paris: Seuil, 2015.

Cascardi, Anthony J. *Cervantes, Literature, and the Discourse of Politics*. Madrid: Vervuert, 2006.

Cassin, Barbara. 'Intraduisibles'. In *L'archipel des idées de Barbara Cassin*. Paris: EMSH, 2014.

Cavarero, Adriana. *For More than One Voice: Toward a Philosophy of Vocal Expression*. Tr. Paul A. Kottman. Stanford, CA: Stanford University Press, 2005.

Cervantes, Miguel de. *Don Quijote de la Mancha*. Ed. Francisco Rico. Real Academia Española: Asociación de Academias de la Lengua Española. Madrid: Alfaguara, 2004.

Cicero, Marcus Tullius. 'De optimo genere oratorum'. In *De inventione. De optimo genere oratorum. Topica. With an English Translation by H. M. Hubbell*. Cambridge, MA: Harvard University Press, 1960.

Clubb, Louise George. *Italian Drama in Shakespeare's Time*. New Haven, CT: Yale University Press, 1989.

Conant, James. 'Throwing away the Top of the Ladder'. *The Yale Review* 79: 3 (1990), 328–64.

Cotgrave, Randall. *A Dictionarie of the French and English Tongues*. London: Printed by Adam Islip, 1611.

Covarrubias Horozco, Sebastián de. *Tesoro de la lengua castellana, o española*. Edición de Martín de Riquer. Barcelona: Editorial Alta Fulla, 1998.

Covarrubias Horozco, Sebastián de. *Tesoro de la lengua castellana, o española*. Madrid: Luis Sánchez, 1611.

Coveos, Costis M. 'Wittgenstein on Frazer's Golden Bough'. *Philosophy* 65: 254 (1990), 518–21.

Damrosch, David. *How to Read World Literature*. Chichester, UK: Wiley-Blackwell, 2009.

Damrosch, David, ed. *World Literature in Theory*. Chichester, UK: Wiley-Blackwell, 2014.

Davis, Creston, John Milbank, and Slavoj Žižek, eds. *Theology and the Political: The New Debate*. Durham, NC: Duke University Press, 2005.

Davis, Steven. 'Translational Indeterminacy and Private Worlds'. *Philosophical Studies: An International Journal for Philosophy in the Analytic Tradition* 18: 3 (April 1967), 38–45.

Decock, Lieven. 'Domestic Ontology and Ideology'. In *Quine: Naturalized Epistemology, Perceptual Knowledge and Ontology*. Ed. Lieven Decock and Leon Horsten. Amsterdam: Rodopi, 2000, 189–207.

Derrida, Jacques. *The Animal That Therefore I Am*. Ed. Marie-Louise Mallet, tr. David Wills. New York: Fordham University Press, 2008.

Derrida, Jacques. *The Beast and the Sovereign*. Tr. Geoffrey Bennington. Chicago: University of Chicago Press, 2009.

Derrida, Jacques. *Béliers: Le dialogue ininterrompu: entre deux infinis, le poème*. Paris: Galilée, 2003.

Derrida, Jacques. 'Des Tours de Babel'. In *Psyche: inventions de l'autre*. Ed. Jacques Derrida. Paris: Galilée, 1987. English tr. Joseph F. Graham. From Joseph P. Graham, ed. *Difference in Translation*. Ithaca, NY: Cornell University Press, 1985. Reprinted in Rainer Schulte and John Biguenet, eds. *Theories of Translation: An Anthology of Essays from Dryden to Derrida*. Chicago: University of Chicago Press, 1992.

Derrida, Jacques. '"Eating Well," or the Calculation of the Subject: An Interview with Jacques Derrida'. In *Who Comes after the Subject?* Ed. Eduardo Cadava, Peter Connor, and Jean-Luc Nancy. New York: Routledge, 1991.

Derrida, Jacques. *El monolingüismo del otro, o la prótesis de origen*. Buenos Aires: Manantial, 1997.

Derrida, Jacques. 'Force of Law: The "Mystical Foundation of Authority".' In *Deconstruction and the Possibility of Justice*. Ed. Drucilla Cornell, Michel Rosenfeld, and David Gray Carlson, tr. Mary Quaintance. London: Routledge, 1992.

Derrida, Jacques. 'Geschlecht II: Heidegger's Hand'. In *Deconstruction and Philosophy*. Ed. John Sallis, tr. John P. Leavey, Jr. Chicago: University of Chicago Press, 1986.

Derrida, Jacques. *Given-Time*. Chicago: University of Chicago Press, 1994.

Derrida, Jacques. *L'animal que donc je suis*. Paris: Galilée, 2006.

Derrida, Jacques. *Le monolinguisme de l'autre, ou la prothèse d'origine*. Paris: Galilée, 1996.

Derrida, Jacques. *Memoires for Paul de Man*. Tr. Cecile Lindsay, Jonathan Culler, and Eduardo Cadava. New York: Columbia University Press, 1986.

Derrida, Jacques. *Monolingualism of the Other*. Tr. Patrick Mensah. Palo Alto, CA: Stanford University Press, 1998.

Derrida, Jacques. 'Qu'est-ce qu'une traduction "relevante"?' In *Jacques Derrida*. Ed. M. L. Mallet and Ginette Michaud, and Cahier de l'Herne. Paris: L'Herne, 2004, 561–76. First published as 'Qu'est-ce qu'une traduction "relevante"'. In *Quinzième assises de la traduction littéraire, 1998*. Arles: Actes Sud, 1999.

Derrida, Jacques. *Specters of Marx: The State of the Debt, the Work of Mourning, & the New International*. Tr. Peggy Kamuf. London: Routledge, 1994.

Derrida, Jacques. 'Violence against Animals'. In *For What Tomorrow . . .: A Dialogue*. Ed. Jacques Derrida and Elisabeth Roudinesco, tr. Jeff Fort. Stanford: Stanford University Press, 2004.

Derrida, Jacques. 'What Is a "Relevant" Translation?' Tr. Lawrence Venuti. *Critical Inquiry* 27: 2 (2001), 174–200.

De Vries, Hent. *Philosophy and the Turn to Religion*. Baltimore: Johns Hopkins University Press, 1999.

D'Haen, Theo, David Damrosch, and Djelal Kadir, eds. *The Routledge Companion to World Literature*. Oxford and New York: Routledge, 2012.

d'Urfey, Thomas. *The Comical History of Don Quixote*. London: Printed for Samuel Briscoe, 1694.

Eagle, Morris N. *Recent Developments in Psychoanalysis: A Critical Evaluation*. New York: McGraw-Hill, 1984.

Embleton, Sheila. 'Names and Their Substitutes: Onomastic Observations on *Astérix* and Its Translations'. *Target* 3: 2 (1991), 175–206.

'FACT SHEET on the President's Plan to Make College More Affordable: A Better Bargain for the Middle Class', online at http://www.whitehouse.gov/the-press-office/2013/08/22/fact-sheet-president-s-plan-make-college-more-affordable-better-bargain-.

Fernández Rodríguez-Escalona, Guillermo. 'Pensamiento político y concepción del mundo en Cervantes: El gobierno de la ínsula Barataria'. *Cervantes* 31: 2 (2011), 125–52.

Florio, John. *A Worlde of Wordes*. Printed at London, by Arnold Hatfield for Edw. Blount, 1598.

Fogelin, Robert J. 'Wittgenstein's Critique of Philosophy'. In *The Cambridge Companion to Wittgenstein*. Ed. Hans Sluga and David G. Stern. Cambridge: Cambridge University Press, 1996, 34–58.

Fogelin, Robert J. *Wittgenstein*. London and New York: Routledge, 1995 (2nd ed., revised).

Forey, Madeleine. '"Bless Thee, Bottom, Bless Thee! Thou Art Translated!": Ovid, Golding, and *A Midsummer Night's Dream*'. *The Modern Language Review* 93: 2 (1998), 321–29.

Goux, Jean-Joseph. *The Coiners of Language.* Norman: University of Oklahoma Press, 1994.

Goux, Jean-Joseph. *Symbolic Economies.* Ithaca, NY: Cornell University Press, 1990.

Grandin, Temple and Catherine Johnson. *Animals in Translation: Using the Mysteries of Autism to Decode Animal Behavior.* New York: Harcourt, Brace, Jovanovich, 2005.

Great Britain. Parliament. House of Commons. *Journals 1* (1547–1628), 140–41.

Grimm, Jakob und Wilhelm Grimm. *Deutsches Wörterbuch.* Siebenter Band. Bearbeitet von Dr. Matthias von Lexer. Leipzig: Verlag von S. Hirzel, 1889.

Grimm, Jakob und Wilhelm Grimm. *Deutsches Wörterbuch von Jacob und Wilhelm Grimm,* 16 Bde. in 32 Teilbänden. Leipzig 1854–1961, online at http://woerterbuchnetz.de/DWB/. Accessed 9 March 2012.

Gutiérrez Martínez, María del Mar, ed. *Libro de los enxiemplos por A. B. C.* (2a. parte). *Memorabilia* 13 (2011).

Hanna, Patricia and Bernard Harrison. *Word and World: Practice and the Foundations of Language.* Cambridge: Cambridge University Press, 2004.

Hardt, Michael and Antonio Negri. *Empire.* Cambridge, MA: Harvard University Press, 2000.

Harman, Graham. *Tool-Being: Heidegger and the Metaphysics of Objects.* Peru, IL: Open Court Publishing, 2002.

Harvey, Keith. 'A Descriptive Framework for Compensation'. *The Translator* 1: 1 (1995), 65–86.

Hearne, Vicki. *Adam's Task: Calling Animals by Name.* New York: Knopf, 1986.

Heidegger, Martin. *Early Greek Thinking.* Tr. David Farrell Krell and Frank A. Capuzzi. San Francisco, CA, and New York: Harper and Row, 1975; 1984.

Heidegger, Martin. 'Logos'. In *Festschrift für Hans Jantzen.* Ed. Kurt Bauch. Berlin: Verlag Gebr. Mann, 1951, 7–18.

Heidegger, Martin. 'Logos'. Tr. Jacques Lacan. *La psychanalyse* 3 (1957), 47–81.

Heidegger, Martin. *Introduction to Metaphysics.* Tr. Gregory Fried and Richard Polt. New Haven, CT: Yale University Press, 2000.

Heidegger, Martin. *On the Way to Language.* Tr. Peter D. Hertz. New York: Harper and Row, 1971; 1982.

Helgerson, Richard. *Forms of Nationhood: The Elizabethan Writing of England.* Chicago: University of Chicago Press, 1992.

Hernández Valcárcel, Carmen. *El cuento medieval español: Revisión crítica y antología.* Murcia: Universidad de Murcia, 1997.

Hill, Christopher S. 'Gavagai'. *Analysis* 32 (1972), 68–75.

Hill, Christopher S. *Meaning, Mind, and Knowledge.* Oxford: Oxford University Press, 2014.

Hobbes, Thomas. *Élémens philosophiques du bon citoyen.* Tr. Samuel Sorbière. Paris, 1651.

Hobbes, Thomas. *Elementa philosophica de cive.* Amsterdam, 1647.

Hobbes, Thomas. *Leviathan, or, the matter, Form, and Power of a Common-Wealth Ecclesiastical and Civil.* London: Printed for Andrew Crooke, 1651.

Hobbes, Thomas. *On the Citizen.* Ed. and tr. Richard Tuck and Michael Silverthorne. Cambridge: Cambridge University Press, 1998.

Hobbes, Thomas. *Philosophical Rudiments Concerning Government and Society, in the English Works of Thomas Hobbes.* Ed. William Molesworth. London: John Bohn, 1841.

Horace, Q. *Horatius Flaccus: His Art of Poetry. Englished by Ben: Jonson. With Other Workes of the Author, Never Printed before.* Tr. Ben Jonson. London: Printed by I. Okes, for Iohn Benson, 1640, 10; reprinted in Edward Blakeney, ed. *Horace on the Art of Poetry.* Freeport, NY: Books for Libraries Press, 1970.

Houliston, Victor. 'The Lord Treasurer and the Jesuit: Robert Person's Satirical *Responsio* to the 1591 Proclamation'. *Sixteenth Century Journal* 32: 2 (2001), 383–401.

Hüllen, Werner. *English Dictionaries 800–1700: The Topical Tradition.* Oxford: Clarendon Press, 1999.

Hutchins, W. John and Harold L. Somers. *An Introduction to Machine Translation.* London: Academic Press, 1992.

Jagendorf, Zvi. '*Coriolanus:* Body Politic and Private Parts'. In *Coriolanus: Critical Essays.* Ed. David Wheeler. New York: Garland, 1995, 229–51.

Johnson, Christopher. 'Intertextuality and Translation: Borges, Browne, and Quevedo'. *Translation and Literature* 11: 2 (2002), 174–94.

Karatani, Kojin. *Architecture as Metaphor: Language, Number, Money.* Cambridge, MA: MIT Press, 1994.

Kettler, David and Volker Meja. 'Legal Formalism and Disillusioned Realism in Max Weber'. *Polity* 28: 3 (Spring 1996), 307–31.

Kettler, David and Volker Meja. '"Sancho Pansa als Statthalter": Max Weber und das Problem der materialen Gerechtigkeit'. In *Max Webers Wissenschaftslehre. Interpretation und Kritik.* Ed. Heinz Zipprian and Gerhard Wagner. Frankfurt: Suhrkamp, 1994, 713–54.

Kornbluh, Anna. 'On Marx's Victorian Novel'. *Mediations* 25: 1 (Fall 2010), 15–37.

Kreuzer, Gundula. 'Voices from beyond: Verdi's *Don Carlos* and the Modern Stage'. *Cambridge Opera Journal* 18: 2 (2006), 151–79.

Kripke, Saul. *Naming and Necessity.* Cambridge, MA: Harvard University Press, 1980.

Kristal, Efraín. *Invisible Work: Borges and Translation.* Nashville, TN: Vanderbilt University Press, 2002.

Lacan, Jacques. *Écrits: A Selection.* Tr. Alan Sheridan. New York: W. W. Norton & Co., 2002, 138–69.

Lacan, Jacques. 'The Instance of the Letter in the Unconscious or Reason since Freud'. In *Écrits: The First Complete Edition in English.* Tr. Bruce Fink. New York: W. W. Norton & Co., 2006.

Lacan, Jacques. 'L'instance de la lettre dans l'inconscient'. In *Écrits.* Paris: Seuil, 1966.

Laclau, Ernesto. 'Constructing Universality'. In *Contingency, Hegemony, Universality: Contemporary Dialogues on the Left.* Ed. Judith Butler, Ernesto Laclau and Slavoj Žižek. London: Verso, 2000.

Laclau, Ernesto. 'Identity and Hegemony'. In *Contingency, Hegemony, Universality: Contemporary Dialogues on the Left*. Ed. Judith Butler, Ernesto Laclau, and Slavoj Zizek. London: Verso, 2000.

Laclau, Ernesto. *On Populist Reason*. London: Verso, 2005.

Lawlor, Leonard. '"Animals Have No Hand": An Essay on Animality in Derrida'. *CR: The New Centennial Review* 7: 2 (2007), 43–69.

Lazzarato, Maurizio. *Lavoro immateriale. Forme di vita e produzione di soggettivita*. Verona: Ombre Corte, 1997.

Lazzarato, Maurizio. *Videofilosofia. Percezione e lavoro nel postfordismo*. Rome: Manifestolibri, 1996.

Lewis, David. *On the Plurality of Worlds*. Oxford: Blackwell, 1986.

Lezra, Jacques. 'The Animal in Translation'. *Postmodern Culture* 24: 1 (September 2013) (March 2015), online at https://muse.jhu.edu/journals/postmodern_culture/v024/24.2.lezra.html.

Lezra, Jacques. 'Nationum Origo'. In *Nation, Language and the Ethics of Translation*. Ed. Sandra Bermann and Michael Wood. Princeton: Princeton University Press, 2005, 203–29.

Lezra, Jacques. 'On Contingency in Translation'. In *Early Modern Cultures of Translation*. Ed. Karen Newman and Jane Tylus. Philadelphia: University of Pennsylvania Press, 2015, 153–74.

Lezra, Jacques. 'Soberanía o traducción: las decisiones de Sancho'. In *El lugar de la literatura en el siglo XXI*. Ed. Juan Pablo Hormazábal, Josefina Rodríguez and Nicolás Vicente. Valparaíso: Ediciones Universitarias de Valparaíso, 2016, 133–61.

Lezra, Jacques. 'This Untranslatability Which Is Not One'. *Paragraph* 38: 2 (2015), 174–88.

Lezra, Jacques. 'Translation'. In *Political Concepts: A Critical Lexicon*. Tr. Liron Mor (New School for Social Research), v. 2, online at http://www.politicalconcepts.org/ Full version in Hebrew translation, at Mafte'akh (University of Tel Aviv), http://mafteakh.tau.ac.il/en/.

Lezra, Jacques. *Wild Materialism: The Ethic of Terror and the Modern Republic*. New York: Fordham University Press, 2010.

Liu, Lydia He, ed. *Tokens of Exchange: The Problem of Translation in Global Circulations*. Durham, NC: Duke University Press, 1999.

Livius, Titus. *Historias de Roma*. Tr. José Antonio Villar Vidal. Madrid: Gredos, 1990.

Livius, Titus. *Livy: Book I*. Ed. H. J. Edwards. Cambridge: Cambridge University Press, 1968.

Madariaga, Salvador de. 'Our Don Quijote'. *Hispania* 11: 2 (1928), 91–118.

Mansau, Andrée. *Saint-Réal et l'humanisme cosmopolite*. Lille – Paris: Université de Lille III, 1976.

Marx, Karl. *Capital*. Tr. Samuel Moore and Edward Aveling. New York: International Publishers, 1967.

Marx, Karl. *Grundrisse Werke*. Karl Marx and Friedrich Engels. Berlin: Dietz Verlag, 1983, v. 42.

Marx, Karl. *Grundrisse: Foundations of the Critique of Political Economy*. Tr. Martin Nicolaus. London and New York: Penguin Books, 1973; 1993.

Marx, Karl. 'Introduction to the Critique of Political Economy'. In *A Contribution to the Critique of Political Economy*. Ed. Karl Marx. Tr. S. W. Ryazanskaya. Moscow: Progress Publishers, 1970; London: Lawrence & Wishart, 1971; New York: International Publishers, 1971, 188–217.

Maurer, Christopher. 'The Poet's Poets: Borges and Quevedo'. In *Borges the Poet*. Ed. Carlos Cortínez. Fayetteville: University of Arkansas Press, 1986.

McNally, David. *Monsters of the Market: Zombies, Vampires and Global Capitalism*. Chicago: Haymarket, 2012.

Meier, Heinrich. *Carl Schmitt and Leo Strauss: The Hidden Dialogue*. Tr. J. Harvey Lomax. Chicago: University of Chicago Press, 1995.

Minsheu, John. *A Dictionarie in Spanish and English*. Ed. Gloria Guerrero Ramos and Fernando Pérez Lagos. Málaga: Servicio de Publicaciones de la Universidad de Málaga, 2000.

Minsheu, John. *Ductor in linguas and Vocabularium hispanicolatinum (A Most Copious Spanish Dictionary)*. London: at John Brown's shop, 1617. Facsimile edition, with an introduction by Jürgen Schäfer. Scholar's Facsimiles & Reprints: Delmar, NY, 1978.

Monk, Ray. *Wittgenstein: The Duty of Genius*. New York: Penguin Books, 1990.

Negri, Antonio. *Marx Beyond Marx*. Tr. Harry Cleaver, Michael Ryan, and Maurizio Viano. New York: Autonomedia, 1991.

Nemser, Daniel. 'Governor Sancho and the Politics of Insularity'. *Hispanic Review* 78: 1 (Winter 2010), 1–23.

Noland, Daniel W. 'The Sources and Methods of John Minsheu's *A Dictionary of Spanish and English (1599)*'. *Dictionaries: Journal of the Dictionary Society of North America* 11 (1989), 41–52

Osborne, Peter. *The Politics of Time: Modernity and the Avant-Garde*. London and New York: Verso, 1995.

Osselton, Noel E. *Branded Words in English Dictionaries before Johnson*. Groningen: J. B. Wolters, 1958.

Oxford English Dictionary. 'Widget'. n. Second edition, 1989; online version December 2011, online at http://www.oed.com/view/Entry/228908. Accessed 13 March 2012. First published in *A Supplement to the OED* IV, 1986.

Patterson, Annabel. *Reading between the Lines*. Madison: University of Wisconsin Press, 1993.

Peña Fernández, Francisco. 'Medieval Traditions of Jewish Origin in the Episode of Sancho Panza and the Island of Barataria'. *South Atlantic Review* 72: 1 (Winter 2007), 212–29.

Percyvall, Richard. *A Dictionarie in Spanish, English, and Latine*. Bound as part II in the *Bibliotheca hispanica*. London: John Jackson for Richard Watkins, 1591.

Perloff, Marjorie. *Wittgenstein's Ladder: Poetic Language and the Strangeness of the Ordinary*. Chicago: University of Chicago Press, 1996.

Petti, Anthony G. 'Richard Verstegan and Catholic Martyrologies of the Later Elizabethan Period'. *Recusant History* 5: 2 (1959–1960), 64–90.

Phillips, Edward. *The New World of English Words, or a Generall Dictionary*. London: Printed for Nath Brooke at the Angell in Cornhill, 1658.

Pilon, Frederick. *Barataria: Or, Sancho Turn'd Governor, A Farce in Two Acts*. London: J. Almon, 1785.

Pitollet, Camille. 'Un jugement rendu par Sancho Panza dans son île'. *Bulletin Hispanique* 39: 2 (1937), 105–19.

Plato, *Ion*. In *The Dialogues of Plato*, vol. 3: *Ion; Hippias minor; Laches; Protagoras*. Tr. Reginald E. Allen. New Haven, CT: Yale University Press, 1996.

Plato, *Ion*. Online Greek edition provided by Project Perseus, online at http://www.perseus.tufts.edu/hopper/text?doc=plat.+ion+530a. Accessed 9 March 2012.

Pliny. *Historie of the World, Pliny the Elder*. Tr. Philemon Holland. London: Printed by Adam Islip, 1601.

Pöckl, Wolfgang. 'Apuntes para la historia de *traducere*, I: "Traducir"'. *Hieronymus Complutensis* 4: 5 (1996–1997), online at http://cvc.cervantes.es/lengua/hieronymus/pdf/04_05/04_05_009.pdf.

Pym, Anthony. 'Translation as a Transaction Cost'. *Meta* 40: 4 (1995), 594–605.

Quine, Willard V. 'On the Reasons for Indeterminacy of Translation'. *The Journal of Philosophy* 67: 68 (1970), 178–83.

Quine, Willard V. *Word and Object*. Cambridge, MA: MIT Press, 1960; 2013.

Rand, Nicholas. 'The Political Truth of Heidegger's "Logos": Hiding in Translation'. *PMLA* 105: 3 (May 1990), 436–47.

Reik, Theodor. 'The Compulsion to Confess'. In *The Compulsion to Confess and the Need for Punishment*. Ed. J. Farrar. New York: Farrar, Straus, and Cudahy, 1959, 176–356.

Reik, Theodor. *Geständniszwang und Strafbedürfnis: Probleme der Psychoanalyse und der Kriminologie*. Vienna: Internationale Psychoanalytisch Verlag, 1925; In *Psychoanalyse und Justiz*. Ed. Alexander Mitscherlich. Frankfurt A. M.: Suhrkamp, 1974, 9–201 (2nd ed.).

Renan, Ernest. 'Des services rendus aux sciences historiques par la philologie'. In *Œuvres Complètes*. Ed. Henriette Psichari. Paris: Corbeil Press, Calmann-Levy, 1947, v. 8, 1231–32.

Renan, Ernest. *Qu'est-ce qu'une nation? (Conference faite en Sorbonne 11 Mars, 1882)*. In *Œuvres Complètes*. Ed. Henriette Psichari. Paris: Corbeil Press, Calmann-Levy, 1947, v. 1.

Reynolds, Bryan. *Performing Transversally: Reimagining Shakespeare and the Critical Future*. New York: Palgrave MacMillan, 2003.

Rhees, Rush, ed. *Ludwig Wittgenstein: Personal Recollections*. Totowa, NJ: Rowman and Littlefield, 1981.

Richens, R. H. 'Preprogramming for Mechanical Translation'. *Mechanical Translation* 3: 1 (1956), 20–27.

Ricoeur, Paul. *On Translation*. Tr. Eileen Brennan. London: Routledge, 2006.

Ricoeur, Paul. *Sur la Traduction*. Paris: Bayard, 2000.

Rider [Ryder], John. *Bibliotheca Scholastica. A Double Dictionarie*, printed by Joseph Barnes, Printer to the Universitie of Oxford, 1589.

Robinson, Doug. 'Translation and the Repayment of Debt'. *Delos* 7: 1–2 (April 1997), 10–22.

Robinson, Douglas. *Critical Translation Studies*. Oxford and New York: Routledge, 2017.

Rosendahl Thomsen, Mads, Theo D' Haen, and César Domínguez, eds. *World Literature: A Reader*. London and New York: Routledge, 2013.

Russell, Bertrand. 'On Denoting'. *Mind*, New Series, 14: 56 (October 1905), 479–93.

Sáez Rivera, Daniel M. 'Vida y obra de Francisco Sobrino'. *Introducción a Francisco Sobrino. Anexos Revista LEMIR*, 18–21.

Sahlins, Peter. *Boundaries: The Making of France and Spain in the Pyrenees*. Berkeley: University of California Press, 1989.

Sallis, John. *On Translation*. Bloomington: Indiana University Press, 2002.

Sarno, David. 'Franz Josef Och, Google's Translation Über-Scientist, Talks about Google Translate'. *Los Angeles Times*, 11 March 2010, online at http://latimesblogs. latimes.com/technology/2010/03/the-web-site-translategooglecom-was-done-in-2001-we-were-just--licensing-3rd-party-machine-translation-technologies-tha. html. Accessed 3 March 2012.

Schäfer, Jürgen. 'The Hard Word Dictionaries: A Re-Assessment'. *Leeds Studies in English* n.s. 4 (1970).

Schaub, Jean-Frédéric, *La France espagnole: Les racines hispaniques de l'absolutisme français*. Paris: Seuil, 2003.

Schlegel, August Wilhelm von. *A Course of Lectures on Dramatic Art and Literature*. Tr. John Black and A. J. W. Morrison. London: George Bell and Sons, 1815 (reprinted 1846).

Schlegel, August Wilhelm von. *Kritische Schriften und Briefe*. Ed. Edgar Lohner. Stuttgart: Kohlhammer, 1962, v. 6.

Schmitt, Carl. *Political Theology: Four Chapters on the Concept of Sovereignty*. Tr. Gorge Schwab. Chicago: University of Chicago Press, 2005.

Schoenfeldt, Michael C. *Bodies and Selves in Early Modern England*. Cambridge: Cambridge University Press, 1999.

Shakespeare, William. *A Midsummer Night's Dream*. In *The Riverside Shakespeare: The Complete Works*. Ed. G. Blakemore Evans and J J. M. Tobin. Boston, MA: Houghton Mifflin, 1997 (2nd ed.).

Shell, Marc. *The Economy of Literature*. Baltimore, MD: Johns Hopkins University Press, 1993.

Simpson, Roger. 'King Arthur in World War Two Poetry: His Finest Hour?' *Arthuriana* 13: 1 (2003), 66–91.

Spivak, Gayatri. *A Critique of Postcolonial Reason*. Cambridge, MA: Harvard University Press, 1999.

Stanovsky, Derek. 'Organizing Marx's Multitude: A Composition on Decomposition'. *Rethinking Marxism* 21: 2 (2009), 216–27.

Starnes, DeWitt T. *Renaissance Dictionaries: English-Latin and Latin-English*. Austin: University of Texas Press, 1954.

Stein, Gabriele. *The English Dictionary before Cawdrey*. Tübingen: Max Niemeyer Verlag, 1985.

Steiner, Roger J. *Two Centuries of Spanish and English Lexicography*. Mouton: The Hague, 1970.

Stephens, Cynthia. 'Borges, Sir Thomas Browne and the Theme of Metempsychosis'. *Forum for Modern Language Studies* 28: 3 (1992), 268–79.

Stepney, William. *The Spanishe Schoolemaster conteyninge 7 Dialogues, according to everie daie in the weeke*. London, 1591.

Tennyson, Alfred. 'Idylls of the King: The Passing of Arthur'. In *The Poems and Plays of Tennyson*. London: Oxford University Press, 1963.

Thompkins, E. F. '*"Sachverhalt"* and *"Gegenstand"* Are Dead'. *Philosophy* 66: 256 (1991), 217–34.

Tudeau-Clayton, Margaret. 'Scenes of Translation in Jonson and Shakespeare: "Poetaster, Hamlet," and "A Midsummer Night's Dream"'. *Translation and Literature* 11: 1 (2002), 1–23.

Tuve, Rosemond. 'Ancients, Moderns, and Saxons'. *ELH* 6: 3 (1939), 165–90.

Venuti, Lawrence. *The Scandals of Translation: Towards an ethics of difference*. London and New York: Routledge, 1998.

Venuti, Lawrence. *The Translator's Invisibility: A History of Translation*. London: Routledge, 1995.

Verstegan [a.k.a Verstegen], Richard. *Briefve Description des diverses Cruautez que les Catholiques endurent en Angleterre pour la foy*. Paris, 1584.

Verstegan [a.k.a Verstegen], Richard. *Le Théâtre des cruautés des heretiques de nostre temps* [Anvers, 1588]. Ed. Frank Lestringant. Paris: Éditions Chandeigne, 1995.

Verstegan [a.k.a Verstegen], Richard. *A Restitution of Decayed Intelligence: In Antiquities. Concerning the Most Noble and Renowned English Nation. By the studie and travaile of R.V. Dedicated unto the Kings most excellent Maiestie*. Printed at Antwerp by Robert Bruney, 1605 and to be sold at London in Paules-Churchyard, by Iohn Norton and Iohn Bull.

Verstegan [a.k.a Verstegen], Richard. *Theatrum crudelitatum haereticorum nostri temporis*. Anvers, 1587.

Vidal, Hernán. '*Don Quijote*: Una lectura militar y gnóstica'. *Lemir-Estudios* 104 (2010), 1–104.

Villena Álvarez, Ignacio. *Problemática teórico-practica de la traducción subordinada de cómics (Análisis de un caso práctico: La colección de historietas de Astérix en francés y en español)*. Unpublished PhD dissertation. Universidad de Málaga: Facultad de Filosofía y Letras, May 2000.

Virno, Paolo. 'The Ambivalence of Disenchantment'. In *Radical Thought in Italy: A Potential Politics*. Ed. Michael Hardt and Paolo Virno. Minneapolis: University of Minnesota Press, 1996.

Von Savigny, Eike. *Wittgensteins 'Philosophische Untersuchungen': Ein Kommentar fur Leser*. Frankfurt a. M.: Klostermann, 1994.

Wagner, Richard. *Der Ring des Nibelungen: Die Walküre/The Nibelung's Ring: The Valkyrie*. Vocal score by Karl Klindworth; Tr. Frederick Jameson. Mainz: B. Schotts Söhne, 1904.

Wagner, Richard. *Gedichte*. Ed. Carl Friedrich Glasenapp. Berlin: G. Grote'sche Verlagsbuchhandlung, 1905.

Waisman, Sergio. *Borges and Translation: The Irreverence of the Periphery*. Lewisburg, PA: Bucknell University Press, 2005.

Weber, Max. *Economy and Society*. Ed. Guenther Roth and Claus Wittich. Berkeley:
University of California Press, 1978.

Weber, Samuel. 'Taking Exception to Decision: Walter Benjamin and Carl Schmitt'.
Diacritics 22: 3/4 (1992), 5–18.

Werber, Niels. 'Technologien der Macht'. *Jahrbuch der Deutschen Schillergesell-
schaft* 40 (1996), 210–43.

Wittgenstein, Ludwig. *The Blue and Brown Books*. New York: Harper and Row,
1958.

Wittgenstein, Ludwig. *Culture and Value*. Ed. G. H. von Wright. Chicago: University
of Chicago Press, 1980.

Wittgenstein, Ludwig. *Denkbewegungen : Tagebücher 1930–1932, 1936–1937
(MS 183)*. Herausgegeben von Ilse Somaville. Innsbruck: Haymon, 1997.

Wittgenstein, Ludwig. *Lectures on the Foundations of Mathematics: Cambridge
1939*. Ed. Cora Diamond. Chicago: University of Chicago, 1975.

Wittgenstein, Ludwig. *Philosophical Investigations*. Tr. G. E. M. Anscombe. London: Blackwell, 1953; 1997 (2nd ed.).

Wittgenstein, Ludwig. *Tractatus Logico-Philosophicus*. Tr. C. K. Ogden. London:
Kegan Paul, 1922.

Wittgenstein, Ludwig. *Tractatus Logico-Philosophicus*. Tr. D. F. Pears and B. F.
McGuinness. London: Routledge, 1961.

Wittgenstein, Ludwig. *The Wittgenstein Papers* [Papers, Photocopy of Manuscript
Notebooks] [Microform]. Cornell University (Reel 6).

Wittgenstein, Ludwig. *Wittgenstein und die Musik*. Ed. Martin Alber. Innsbruck:
Haymon-Verlag, 2000.

Wolfe, Cary. 'Flesh and Finitude: Thinking Animals in (Post)Humanist Philosophy'.
SubStance 37: 3 (2008), 8–36.

Zizek, Slavoj. *The Sublime Object of Ideology*. London: Verso, 1989.

Index

Note: Page references for figures are *italicized*.